Women Writers in Russian Modernism

Women Writers in Russian Modernism

AN ANTHOLOGY

Translated and edited by
TEMIRA PACHMUSS

University of Illinois Press
URBANA   CHICAGO   LONDON

Library of Congress Cataloging in Publication Data

Main entry under title:

Women writers in Russian modernism.

Includes bibliographical references and index.
1. Russian literature—20th century—Translations
into English. 2. English literature—Translations
from Russian. 3. Russian literature—Women authors.
4. Modernism (Literature) I. Pachmuss, Temira

PG3213.W6   891.7'3'0809287   78–8957
ISBN 0–252–00224–5
ISBN 0–252–00700–X pbk.

To GRETA GERELL

Contents

Preface 🖋

"You are a sculptor, Socrates, and have made statues of our governors faultless in beauty," said Glaucon to Socrates. "Yes," replied the latter, "and of our governesses, too; for you must not suppose that what I have been saying applies to men only and not to women." "There you are right," Glaucon agreed, "since we have made them to share in all things like the men."[1]

As early as the fifth century B.C., then, the great Greek philosopher insisted that women be allowed to play an equal role in society and be given the same recognition as men for their achievements. And yet Alexandra Kollontai, the ambassador from Russia, has complained in the twentieth century that poets, novelists, and scholars have passed by "the shining images of the nascent 'new woman' [. . .] offered by the reality of Russian life in silence." She continues: "They neither perceived nor heard them, nor did they comprehend them or distinguish between them."[2] Oblivious to this emerging self-awareness, men were not able, and did not wish, "to grasp this *novum* [the 'new woman'], to appropriate it and to stamp it upon [their] memory."[3]

Alexandra Kollontai's charges appear to be well founded. Despite the fact that the important women writers of the Russian avant-garde were enthusiastic in welcoming, and even contributing to, the aesthetic revolution at the turn of the century, their names and literary works have been largely neglected by contemporary scholars. The present volume seeks to correct this omission.

Some of these writers, among them Zinaida Hippius and Poliksena Solovyova, were only too painfully aware of the reluctance of the male-dominated literary world to recognize the literary achievements of Russian women; they often used the masculine endings of verbs and personal pronouns to disguise their true identities. To avoid emphasizing their sex, Hippius and Solovyova used the masculine forms corresponding to the term *chelovek* (a human being) in Russian. On more than one occasion Hippius insisted that she wished to write poetry not merely as a woman but as a human being, "kak *chelovek*, a ne tol'ko kak zhenshchina." She wanted to be a poet, without any extra-literary considerations impairing the critical evaluation of her work. She demanded further that a woman be, above all, a person. Only after asserting herself as a human being could she insist on her womanhood.

This book is a tribute to those Russian women writers who helped pave the way for the Silver Age in literature, and to those Russian intellectuals who actively sought to realize in their art a new personal, aesthetic, religious, and socio-political consciousness. Herein are samples of the poetry and prose of eight Russian women writers: Zinaida Hippius, Anastasiya Verbitskaya, Lidiya Zinovyeva-Annibal, Nadezhda Teffi, Mirra Lokhvitskaya, Poliksena Solovyova, Cherubina de Gabriak, and Adelaida Gertsyk. The volume contains a number of poems, short stories, and one play, all of which testify to the diversity of the literary and aesthetic rebellion which characterized the late nineteenth and early twentieth centuries in Russia. Since Zinaida Hippius' reputation as one of the most sophisticated and original poets in the history of Russian literature has been firmly established by modern-day scholars (even though her work was largely underestimated by her contemporaries),[4] only a few of her remarkable poems and stories have been included in this book. All of them reveal the poet's unique personal and metaphysical perception of the world and her particular emphasis on the importance of the individual and the significance of intuitive and spiritual revelation.[5] Lidiya Zinovyeva-Annibal and Nadezhda Teffi also distinguished themselves as poets. However, only their short stories appear in the present volume, for their fiction is endowed with special importance for the study of Russian belles-lettres of the period, with its undercurrents of ethical, religious, aesthetic, and socio-political thought. Although the reader may judge the content of some of these works to be antiquated in the light of contemporary tastes, he or she will be all the richer for having become acquainted with the literary endeavors of these feminine representatives of Russian letters. Their works belong to the history of Modernism no less than its more celebrated or sensational masterpieces.

In presenting only the above-mentioned writers within the larger context of Russian—and European—Modernism, I am fully aware of the limitations of my book. This complex movement of Russian literature and culture requires a more comprehensive anthology and a more detailed study. The period is in great need of scholarly attention, and I propose to accomplish at least a part of this task, since at least 80 percent of the material presented here is unknown to most students of Russian literature. It may very well be the reader's first introduction to the poetry of Poliksena Solovyova, Cherubina de Gabriak, and Adelaida Gertsyk, as well as to some of the best writings of Anastasiya Verbitskaya and Lidiya Zinovyeva-Annibal, all of whom played significant roles in the Modernist ferment in Russia. Unfortunately, in Soviet scholarly and critical evaluations this colorful, multifaceted, and Promethean movement is denigrated, belittled, and contemptuously referred to as that of Decadence, with all the "harmful influences" such a term implies. The works of these writers are even now proscribed in their native land, and their names are virtually unknown to Soviet readers.

This collection, however, is not only for students of Russian literature or for those who know little or nothing about the aforementioned writers. It is also intended for readers who wish to enlarge their understanding and vision of the European avant-garde, but who lack essential facts about Russian *art nouveau*. With this in mind, I have included some biographical, critical, and bibliographical data concerning figures whose works had a decisive influence on the direction of *le style moderne* in Russia. Although these early writers are less well known, they are no less deserving of attention than Valery Bryusov, Andrey Bely, and Aleksander Blok, figures ordinarily associated with Modernism in Russia around 1900. Since the expression "Decadence" is often used incorrectly and the whole movement is described in negative terms as a bourgeois malaise of aestheticism, eroticism, and "decadent philosophizing," it has been useful to first clarify and then redefine the term.

The works included in this volume were selected on the basis of the following considerations. First, they can help the uninitiated reader to understand various aspects of these writers' *Weltanschauungen* by revealing their most basic attitudes; second, they illustrate the writers' aesthetics and artistic craftsmanship; third, these works, which stand among the most curious of Modernist literary documents, epitomize and clarify the fundamentals of Decadence in Russia durings its initial stage. The fourth, and most important, consideration is their relevance to present-day dilemmas and ideas. A more detailed exposition of this movement may be found in my recent study, *Zinaida Hippius: An Intellectual Profile*. The introduction that follows, therefore, has been limited to a brief discussion of the complex views peculiar to these representatives of early Russian Modernism.

Unfortunately, because of space limitations, the play *Mirage* had to be drastically abridged, and only a few representative poems of each writer could be included in Russian. The original Russian versions of poems were selected on the basis of how well they illustrate the unique characteristics of each poet—in some cases, striking imagery; in others, sound instrumentation, individualistic use of colors, innovative meters—that is, those fragile aspects of the creative endeavor of poetry which are most easily (and often unavoidably) distorted or lost in translation. These poems are provided in the original for readers who may desire to make a closer textual analysis of the artist's poetic universe.

Responsibility for the English translations rests with me. They merely attempt to convey the meaning of the texts and not their poetic qualities, such as lyricism, sonority, and rhythms, together with the sound, weight, and stress of words in relation to one another. I believe that if anything is to be sacrificed in translation, it should be form rather than content. To the usual difficulties one encounters in translating from Russian into English (for example, the problem of compensating for the emotional and semantic richness of the Russian language due to its abundance of diminutives) may be added that impalpable quality, as it were, of some of the poems. Often the English versions fail to convey fully the idea or feeling behind words and images, especially those of color, fragrance, and emotion. It proved extremely difficult to render the poetic and intangible properties of the verses. Some lines had to be glossed; others, unfortunately, have acquired a melodramatic character; still others have become somewhat distorted due to a shift in emphasis resulting from translation. Sometimes words and expressions alien to the original have been added of necessity.

The translation of prose, and particularly of the Russian substandard language (in Verbitskaya's play, for example), has also presented certain difficulties. Russian slang expressions, fractured or disjointed sentences, and *Verfremdung* effects, such as those used by Verbitskaya and Nadezhda Teffi, can be reproduced only with great difficulty, if at all, by foreign equivalents.

The italics used in the texts follow those found in the original sources. The transliteration of Russian names follows standard rules, with few exceptions to allow for more commonly accepted spellings.

I wish to thank the Library, the Russian and East European Center, and the Graduate Research Board, all at the University of Illinois, for various grants given in the support of research, for the final preparation of the manuscript, and for the acquisition of the necessary source material. Finally, my heartfelt thanks go to W. W. Weidlé, Heinrich A. Stammler, Yu. P. Ivask, Louis Iribarne, L. H. Miller, Edward Napier, Ira Goetz, and B. Machne von Baumgarten for assistance in a variety of ways.

Naturally, I assume full responsibility for all actual information and interpretations of ideas.

University of Illinois
Urbana-Champaign

Temira Pachmuss

NOTES

1. Plato, *The Republic*, Books VI and VII, No. 10, Set Four (Chicago: Great Book Foundation, n.d.), pp. 77–78.

2. Alexandra Kollontai, *The Autobiography of a Sexually Emancipated Communist Woman*, edited, with an afterword by Irving Fetscher; translated by Salvator Attanasio (New York: Herder and Herder, 1971), p. 51.

3. *Ibid.*, p. 52.

4. Read, *e.g.*, Oleg Maslenikov, "The Spectre of Nothingness: The Privative Elements in the Poetry of Zinaida Hippius," *The Slavic and East European Journal*, n.s. IV (1966), 299–311, and "Disruption of Canonical Verse Norms in the Poetry of Zinaida Hippius," *Studies in Slavic Linguistics and Poetics in Honor of*

Boris O. Unbegaun (New York: New York University Press, 1968), pp. 89–96; Temira Pachmuss, *Zinaida Hippius: An Intellectual Profile* (Carbondale: Southern Illinois University Press, 1971), and Z. N. *Hippius: Collected Poetical Works, Vol. I: 1899–1918; Vol. II: 1918–1945* (Munich: Wilhelm Fink Verlag, 1972); Olga Matich, *The Religious Poetry of Zinaida Gippius* (Munich: Wilhelm Fink Verlag, 1972); Nina Awsienko, "Symbols-Ideas in Hippius' Poetry" (Ph.D. dissertation, University of Illinois, 1973); William E. Napier, "The Love Ethic of Zinaida Hippius" (Ph.D. dissertation, University of Illinois, 1974).

5. A volume of Zinaida Hippius' short stories entitled *Selected Works of Zinaida Hippius,* translated and edited by Temira Pachmuss (Urbana: University of Illinois Press, 1972), and a volume of Hippius' diaries entitled *Between Paris and St. Petersburg: Selected Diaries of Zinaida Hippius,* translated and edited by Temira Pachmuss (Urbana: University of Illinois Press, 1975), may serve as further examples of the poet's experiments in prose. Hippius' poetry is contained in Z. N. *Hippius: Collected Poetical Works (First Comprehensive Edition),* compiled, annotated, and with an introduction by Temira Pachmuss (Munich: Wilhelm Fink Verlag, 1972). Volume I deals with poetry written between 1899 and 1918; Volume II, between 1918 and 1945.

Introduction 🖋

By 1900, Realism in Russian literature was no longer in vogue and was being repeatedly challenged by the younger generation of writers. In accordance with the precepts of Belinsky and others, literature's goal was to re-create reality ("life as it is"), to explore problems of social significance, and to embody the didactic aims of the nineteenth-century radical intelligentsia. Literature was expected to instruct the reader and to familiarize him with important social and political questions, while Belinsky and his disciples appropriated for themselves the final judgment over literature and literary taste. At the end of the century, an aesthetic revolution took place against the prevailing norms and against the dogmatic treatment made fashionable by Belinsky, Chernyshevsky, Dobrolyubov, Pisarev, and their adherents. By this time the Realist school of writing was considered outmoded by the new Russian writers. They felt it had become intolerably poor in technique and artistic imagination, especially with the appearance of such minor writers as E. N. Chirikov, N. D. Teleshov, I. F. Nazhivin, S. I. Gusev-Orenburgsky, A. S. Serafimovich, and S. G. Petrov (literary pseudonym "Skitalets"), all of whom later joined Gor'ky's "Knowledge" group. The ethical and political bias of the latter was summarized by Nekrasov's line: "You may not be a poet, but you must be a citizen."

A few timid voices protested the civic ideas of the preceding generation as early as the 1880's, when the articles of two prominent writers, I. I. Yasinsky (1850–1931) and N. M. Vilenkin-Minsky, appeared in the Kiev newspaper *Zarya* (Dawn). Minsky openly advocated idealism and developed mystico-ethical theories

1

that combined the ideas of Nietzsche and the Oriental concept of Nirvana. Both he and Yasinsky inveighed against the absence of any aesthetic sensitivity in the critical writings of the period and deplored the outmoded approach of all contemporary critics. In the 1890's these challenging and protesting judgments became more vociferous. The movement was stimulated by D. S. Merezhkovsky's essay on "Reasons for the Decline of Russian Literature and Its New Trends" (1892–93), and by Peter Pertsov's discussion of the philosophical foundations of Modernism in *Molodaya poeziya* (The Young Poetry; St. Petersburg: B. M. Vol'f, 1895). Another influential man of letters and the editor of *Severny vestnik* (The Northern Herald, 1885–98), A. L. Volynsky-Flekser, defended idealistic philosophy and rejected "materialistic methods of criticism." This sudden call for idealistic aspirations, artistic craftsmanship, and poetic imagination was a natural rebellion against that spiritual void and dreary emptiness which characterized the literary output of the 1880's, with its stubborn adherence to the principles and prevailing outlook of the 1860's. Younger Russian writers were thus able to develop their "new ideas" and to lay the foundation for the blossoming of the Russian Silver Age.

The aesthetic movement referred to in the histories of Russian literature as Decadence or Modernism was part and parcel of the European renaissance at the turn of the century. In Europe, the awareness that a new era was approaching fostered hope for a renewal of the arts. There was a strong desire to overcome the traditions of the past and the older generation's fixed and stagnant attitudes. Typical of this new frame of mind was a statement made by the Norwegian artist Asta Hansteen: "We are standing at the end of a century; we are at the conclusion of an historical period. . . . Mankind is in a state of sickness, now roused to feverish excitement, now inert, weary, and discouraged [. . .] Something is dying, something has long been dead."[1] Notions such as *Weltschmerz, fin-de-siècle*, Decadence, and *nostalgie de la boue* were widely discussed in the 1890's throughout Western Europe. The strange mood of languor and decay was closely related to the Aesthetic Movement in England, and to Symbolism in France and Belgium. All of these literary currents—which in Russia quickly acquired a Neo-Romantic and mystical aspect—were in conscious opposition to Positivism, Realism, and Naturalism. A common property of these trends, which differed greatly in their national characteristics, was an extreme sophistication in literary art and a taste for the exotic. These groups aspired to create "new" movements, ideas, norms, and journals. The expressions New Humor, New Realism, New Drama, New Theatre, New Art, New Woman were bandied about in Belgium, France, England, and Germany. Various original concepts based on classical philosophies were formulated, such as New Paganism, New Hedonism, Neo-Christianity, a "new religious consciousness," and New Voluptuousness, as exemplified in *The Portrait of Dorian Gray* (1891) and as defined in one of Zinaida Hippius' diaries, *Contes d'amour*.[2] A new vision of woman appeared in Aubrey Beardsley's illustrations for *Morte d'Arthur* (1892) and *Salomé* (1893). Sensual, erotically aroused, morbid, and almost demonic, they represented the unique forms and motifs of *art nouveau.* Munch's women, too, were endowed with an ambivalent nature of piety and seductiveness which made them appear as Madonna and temptress at one and the same time. The feminine ideal and the worship of the refined, beautiful, and sophisticated should be viewed against the background of the aesthetic and exotic leanings characteristic of the age.[3] Underlying this movement was an insatiable desire for the new, stimulated by artists' no less intense yearning to free themselves of all the old, outmoded, and uninspiring ideas of the century then drawing to a close.

This new movement had a strong impact in Russia, where its partisans were cultured, extremely well read, and Westernizers in their outlook. Having undertaken the daring task of opposing the supremacy of the radical critics, as well as a revision of their critical canon, the early Russian Decadents were very susceptible to foreign influences. They were responsible for bringing about great changes in poetry, fiction, criticism, painting, sculpture, music, the theatre, ballet, and so forth. Searching for artistic freedom, the young Russian writers in St. Petersburg and Moscow wished to create a new literature which would be capable of expressing their unique moods and attitudes; they strove to formulate fresh philosophical generalizations. They were also intent on proving that their reaction was not a purely Russian phenomenon, but was linked to the idealistic and aesthetic renaissance that had been taking place in Western art and literature. They were eager to identify themselves with cultural trends developing in Europe. In their outlook and culture they were indeed very European, and one of their early tasks, their self-imposed duty, was the advocacy of Western culture and literature in Russia. They wanted "to reunite Russia with the realm of European culture she had lost."[4] Nevertheless, their first obligation was the creation of new poetic and aesthetic norms in their native land.

It was to be expected that this generation of the Modernist or Decadent writers, reacting adversely to the intellectual and artistic dogmatism of the 1860's and 1870's, would promote their "new ideas" and non-civic attitudes with impatience and rashness. They restated the doctrine of "art for art's sake," which had been relentlessly suppressed by the civic-minded critics of the 1860's. They not only stressed the aesthetic, the pleasurable, and (frequently) the perverted in their works of art, but, in the European fashion, they also manifested an ever-intensifying distaste for Realism.

The main contribution of the Decadent writers around 1900 was the formulation of their own aesthetic credo. The aesthetes of St. Petersburg and Moscow looked to Europe for stimulation, for new inspiration and new models. More specifically, they regarded impressionism in art, the aestheticism of Ruskin and Oscar Wilde, the music of Wagner, the works of Nietzsche (with his advocacy of extreme individuality), and the poems of Mallarmé, Baudelaire, Verlaine, and Rimbaud as the models for their creative thought. The *Sturm und Drang* movement, German Romanticism, Maeterlinck, Ibsen, and Hamsun likewise had strong repercussions in Russia. Especially attractive to these early writers was the Paris *fin-de-siècle*, with its "unusual" and morbid atmosphere accessible only to the select few. The Russian Decadents, very responsive to the main trends of the European *Zeitgeist*, favored refined artistic forms and the apotheosis of Beauty; in poetry, the musical and the intuitive were of a greater importance to them than the logical and the rational. They made allusions and intimations at the expense of narration, rejected old themes and rhythms, and manifested a clear predilection for problems of technique and style, diction, rhythm, neologisms, effective alliterations and assonances, and the creation of mysterious meanings. The new, "liberated" content of Modernist verse found more appropriate forms of expression, new metrical systems, new arrangements of tone and color—a new poetic language. Russian Decadent art acquired all the splendor of a fairytale-like autumn. It exercised a powerful influence on the subsequent development of Russian art and literature, for the early Decadents were anxious to broaden the personal poetic experience, to remove literary taboos, and to fathom the dark recesses of man and the world around him. By so doing, they succeeded in revitalizing Russian verse—which at the end of the nineteenth century had been reduced to the level of rather bleak, rhythmically arranged prose—and restored the standards of craftsmanship by creating new similes, bold images and metaphors, sophisticated rhymes, and "sound orchestration," sometimes even at the risk of obscuring meaning. In an attempt to free poetry from various social and political purposes, they insisted that the artist should not depict life by merely presenting surface reality or mirroring "life as it is."

In prose, instead of portraying characters through lengthy discussions of their social milieu, motivations, and interrelationships, the Modernist writers limited themselves to presenting basic psychological and intellectual dimensions. There is no stable, definable, socially determined man, they claimed; they replaced such a view of man with the concept of a deeper, "individual being" of the sort found in the works of Zinaida Hippius, Nadezhda Teffi, and Lidiya Zinovyeva-Annibal. Rather than define their protagonists exhaustively, in a static manner, these authors presented them in the process of maturation, involved in a search for the sources of authentic existence; hence their predilection for portraying the psychology of children in the process of becoming and seeking. Their refined prose concerned itself with visions, dreams, unusual situations, and exotic or morbid sensations.

The movement in Russia may be likened to Western European Decadence not only in certain mannerisms of form, but also in its haughty individualism and aristocratic aloofness. The Modernists' individualistic attitude frequently bordered on narcissism, since they often talked exclusively about themselves in their works, discussing the intimate details of their own inner worlds. Individualism reached the Russian Decadents primarily through the works of Nietzsche; their immoralism, often bordering on amoralism, originated in the works of Rimbaud. D. S. Merezhkovsky,

Zinaida Hippius, Valery Bryusov, and Fyodor Sologub, like the French Decadent poets, at times revealed an indifference toward ethical issues, refusing to choose between good and evil. Other Russian Modernists, such as Zinovyeva-Annibal or Mikhail Artsybashev, found their inspiration in eroticism. They treated this theme in all its variations; in the words of Renato Poggioli, "from the role of an innocent, pagan-like sensuality to that of perversion and even morbidity."[5] According to Poggioli, "The Eros of Decadence is also an Eros of exhaustion and fatigue [. . .] The poetry of erotic mysticism was an offshoot of both Christian dogmas and Eastern heresies."[6] The Decadents' predilection for certain "extreme" subjects—sex, disease, calamity, and death—was one manifestation of their protest against the asceticism of the previous age. Vasily Rozanov made the following important statement concerning eroticism in Modernist writing: "The god as old as Mother Nature, driven once and for all from the civic poetry of the 1850's–1870's, re-entered into the sphere that had always belonged to him."[7] These were, then, the diverse sources of Russian Modernism.

There were two periods of *art nouveau* in Russia. First came the aesthetes, or Decadents, who in the 1890's revolted against traditional concepts and reevaluated them in the light of their own artistic criteria. With strong romantic inclinations, these aesthetes turned toward Western culture; nevertheless, the metaphysical, religious, and (subsequently) socio-political proclivities which had been lying dormant within them gradually gained the upper hand. At this time, aware of the pitfalls of "art for art's sake," which (like any formula) limits the scope of art, several Russian Modernist writers began to advocate a more profound conception of the objective of art, together with a religious affirmation of life. Thus the second period of Modernism began about 1901, when Hippius and Merezhkovsky opened their St. Petersburg salon to the contributors of the journal *Mir iskusstva* (The World of Art, 1898–1904) for religious discussions. At this point the Decadent movement evolved into Symbolism. Its representatives longed for a new religious consciousness, for a "new, *inner* Church."[8] Highly individualized views and philosophical systems were developed, many of them embracing earlier metaphysical and religious concepts. Nietzsche's Dionysus and Stirner's lonely, proud superman found their expression in the philosophy of Vyacheslav Ivanov; Fyodor Sologub's simultaneous glorification of God and Satan was a reflection of Manichaeism; Aleksander Blok and Andrey Bely paid tribute to Vladimir Solovyov's Saint Sophia in their poetry. A pseudo-sacred religion of sex, transcending the boundaries of nature and uniting man to God, was reasserted in the musings of Vasily Rozanov, while the Third Testament of the Holy Ghost–Motherhood reappeared in the ecstatic dreams of D. S. Merezhkovsky and his wife, Zinaida Hippius.[9] The literary aesthetes and early Decadents—individualists and rebels against the utilitarian ethic and radicalism of the preceding age—became attracted to mysticism and "reformed Christianity." The source of this religious renaissance may be found in the Slavophilic concept of Russia's religious mission in the Western world, which had been given artistic formulation by Dostoevsky and was elaborated upon by many Russian poets of the period. As they turned to the Slavophiles and Russia's national tradition, Western European Decadence lost its hold on the Russian artistic imagination, and the literary movement of Symbolism was transformed into a metaphysical and mystical philosophy. It became an expression of a longing for artistic and individual freedom, a new *Weltanschauung*. Writers now insisted on a bond between religion and literature; they changed the artist's vision of reality. The new poet viewed his creation as a vehicle for revealing spiritual reality to the uninitiated and for imbuing the reader with mystical intuition and metaphysical insight. He wished to go beyond mere art and literature. He desired to create a new metaphysical and social awareness, a new man, a new society, a new religion, a new (ecumenical) church, a new Russia, and even a new Europe. Metaphysical thought and mysticism were prominent in the works of such figures as Zinaida Hippius. With her idea of ecumenity, active love, prophetic theurgy, and idealistic aspirations, along with the urge to disseminate her religious and philosophical ideas through her poetry and prose, she is but one example of the Symbolists' earnest desire to restore mankind to a true, real, and mysterious life.

In order to make its mark on Russian culture, the new generation needed a journal through which to promulgate their aesthetic and mystical views, and in which to exercise artistic freedom. This vehicle was found in the monthly periodical *The Northern Herald* when its editorship passed to A. L. Volynsky-Flekser in 1889. Flekser opened the pages of the journal to Dmitry Merezhkovsky, Zinaida Hippius, Fyodor Sologub, and Nikolay Minsky, allowing them to elaborate upon their "new ideas" in a manner charged with the most passionate idealistic transports of the spirit. These expressions of religious experience appeared side by side with findings based on empirical knowledge. When *The Northern Herald* ceased publication, *The World of Art*, a strongly French-oriented journal, raised the banner in defense of the new idealism in art. The Merezhkovskys' journal *Novy Put'* (The New Direction, 1903–5) provided a forum for the "God-seekers." In Moscow, *Vesy* (The Scales, 1904–9), having taken the *Mercure de France* as its model, published the works of both Russian and foreign contributors, among them Marx Voloshin, René Ghil, Maurice Maeterlinck, Rémy de Gourmont, Jean Moréas, Emile Verhaeren, and Giovanni Papini. *Apollon* (Apollo, 1907–17) advocated the newly emerging Parnassian poetry and, between 1910 and 1913, published the literary manifestoes of the Acmeists.

Due to the many facets of Modernism, the movement embraced trends and groups which seem to have had very little in common. The literary groups, as well as the individual representatives of Modernism, were characterized by a diversity of allegiances, even though they all had an essentially common origin: their opposition to any utilitarian function in literature. The great variety of works written at the turn of the century illustrate the Modernists' attempt to achieve balance and harmony, to attain faith and hope, to reach a modicum of compromise, and at times even to evade the difficulties of the issues raised in the search for new values. The Modernist writers turned to Pushkin, Gogol', Tolstoy, Dostoevsky, Tyutchev, and Fet in order to rediscover their ethics and aesthetics. Forgotten masters of the eighteenth century were revived as well. The Decadent writers during the first decade of the twentieth century all remained true to the romantic tradition of Lermontov, Tyutchev, Fet, and Polonsky. The Modernists, moreover, were united by their tragic premonition of the coming cataclysm.

The term "Modernism," then, is very complex. It is like the reflection of diverse symmetrical patterns in the mirrors of a kaleidoscope—heathenism and Neo-Christianity; a state beyond good and evil and mystical searchings; apolitical attitudes and active political preoccupations; pornography and the nobility of the lonely, pensive, melancholic spirit; utter hopelessness and the sensation of triumph; cosmopolitanism and nationalism; aristocratic alienation from the crowd and a "prophetic" tendency combined with a desire to "teach," as well as many other characteristic antinomies, find their expression within it. It produced many writers, each with a specific *Weltanschauung*, poetic universe, and literary technique. The "new" Nietzschean character, for example, appeared in the works of Zinaida Hippius, *Chortova kukla* (The Devil's Doll, 1911) and *Roman-Tsarevich* (1914), and in Anastasiya Verbitskaya's gloomy and pretentious heroes. Hippius exhibited interest in expressing both male and female views on the relationship between the sexes and the need for defining new roles for man and woman within (and outside) this interrelationship. She was equally adept at portraying the claustrophobia of women within old, outmoded views of male-female relations, and at expressing the confusion of men in these changing times.

Through Verbitskaya's works it becomes obvious that some writers in the movement did, in fact, have opinions and problems which led them to concentrate on issues particularly relevant to women. She was especially interested in a new image for woman and her new association with man. In marriage, said Verbitskaya, woman is either dominated by man or dominates him; there can be no harmony or unity within the prevalent definition of marriage. This view of matrimony and woman's possible alternative role in society was radical for that time. Along with her beautiful, graceful, and enigmatic heroines, Verbitskaya's protagonists explored the entanglements of sex, free love, and a "heightened mode of living." She was followed by E. A. Nagrodskaya (1866–1939), with her then tremendously popular novel *Gnev Dionisa* (The Wrath of Dionysus, 1910), and Vladimir Vinnichenko (1880–1951), who, in *Chestnost' s soboy* (Self Honesty, 1911), combined risqué scenes with defiant pronouncements concerning the liberation of the senses and the right of the individual to indulge in physical pleasure.

Although Verbitskaya did not claim to have a profound understanding of social problems or a thorough knowledge of Russian political life, she wished to draw the psychological contour of her protagonists against the social and political background of the day.

In correspondence with the Decadent moods of the period, she presented people trying to transcend the vulgarity and triviality of life. Verbitskaya's place in Russian Modernist literature is also dependent on her expressing those spontaneous upheavals in Russian cultural life which occurred around 1900. In her short stories, novels, and plays she poses questions which were important for Russian youth of the period: What is truth? What does the future hold? What should man do now for the future of humanity? Responding sympathetically to her concerns, Verbitskaya's audience read her books with great interest and enthusiasm. If we were to apply Vasily Rozanov's statement to Verbitskaya's works, it might be said that they, too, "came forth not as the expounder of others' ideas and aspirations, but as the guide and mentor for a new kind of 'taste.'"[10]

Lidiya Zinovyeva-Annibal was entirely submerged in the atmosphere of the *Zeitgeist*. She endeavored to create a completely new theatre of symbolic mystery-plays. In her works, valid psychological observations alternate with scenes of a sensual and erotic nature. Like several writers of the period, she heralded a new concept of love designed to enable woman to transcend the vulgarity and emptiness of her immediate surroundings. Together with other Modernist writers, Zinovyeva-Annibal was preoccupied with the individual's private world of Beauty and Harmony. Moreover, she was engrossed in the psychology of the emerging, "liberated" woman and in the portrayal of such a woman's fulfilled life outside of relationships with men.

The emotionally heightened style, impressionistic, colorful imagery, and erotic themes in Nadezhda Teffi's poetry, especially in *Sem' ogney* (Seven Fires, 1910), likewise make her an integral part of Modernism. She, too, divided the universe into a multitude of polar opposites, of which the polarity of the "dead" empirical world versus a higher, spiritual reality was the most fundamental. Behind the humor in her prose and poetry looms a deep sensation of hopelessness and sadness: humanity, in her opinion, can never attain the world of spiritual reality. Teffi's short stories strongly resemble those of Chekhov, and to some extent those of V. M. Garshin (1855–88); their elegiac tone, humanitarian attitudes, and impressionistic technique reflect the characteristics of the period. "Impressionism not only preceded Russian symbolism," claims

Vladimir Markov in his illuminating study on Russian Futurism, "but also accompanied it and became one of its facets, almost an ingredient."[11] Bryusov also viewed Russian literature in 1906 as a sequence of "Symbolism, Impressionism, and Decadence," in that order.

In her short stories and one-act plays, Teffi gave a negative view of marriage and suggested, as did Verbitskaya, that happiness for a woman cannot be achieved through union with a man. Probing deeply into the psychology of woman, particularly of the aging and lonely city-dweller, Teffi portrayed with sad humor the bewilderment and alienation of woman in the modern world. Since there is no activity open for her in contemporary society, she is forced to look for personal fufillment in matrimony. This proves a failure, however, especially because in such personal relationships the man makes a smaller emotional investment than the woman. On the whole, Teffi seems to be interested mainly in the social position and psychology of woman. She presents the emotional entanglements between men and women almost invariably through the eyes of her heroines.

Mirra Lokhvitskaya's poetry, like that of K. M. Fofanov (1862–1911), is Modernist in its romantic strain. It is highly lyrical and is characterized by a purely aesthetic but superficial mysticism, by eroticism, musical melodiousness, a tendency toward repetition, and by the absence of a strong will on the part of her persona. As with the poems of Fofanov, Lokhvitskaya's verse anticipated the future musical, "chamber" style of Igor Severyanin's *poezy*. Throughout his life, Severyanin worshiped the dominant mood, theme, and structure of Lokhvitskaya's and Fofanov's poetry. According to Markov, Severyanin "commemorated in verse the anniversaries of their deaths almost every year, and once even declared that he considered Lokhvitskaya superior to Dante, Byron and Pushkin."[12] It was only natural that declarations of the Ego-Futurists proclaimed A. A. Fet (1820–92), Lokhvitskaya, and Fofanov as their precursors—representatives of Russian Impressionism.[13]

Lokhvitskaya displayed Modernistic tendencies in her fondness for bright colors and in the picturesque imagery which her poetry exhibits as an escape from the commonplace and trivial in everyday life. She delighted in weaving stylized echoes of Oriental poetry into her own works, as did Konstantin Lipskerov (1889–1954) and Marietta Shaginyan (b. 1888). The inspiration for the biblical sonnets of Georgy Shengeli (b. 1894) and the Sapphic stanzas of Sofiya Parnok (1885–1933) may be found in her poetry. Lokhvitskaya's sensuality, so typical of Decadent poetry, was indicative of her search for the extreme, extravagant, and feverish. She was a Modernist also in her exploration of the mentality of woman seized by passion and love, so ardently expressed in her verse. Man appears in her poetry merely as a recipient or stimulus of woman's sensual nature. Lokhvitskaya also portrayed the "new" woman who was not afraid to reveal her innermost feelings and erotic desires.

Poliksena Solovyova glorified nature, solitude, *Weltschmerz*, and death in her beautiful filigreed verse. In her persona's closed, detached solipsism she saw an escape from the shallowness and boredom of life. Since her persona is completely passive, Solovyova's poetry may be viewed as one of contemplation. In her aesthetics, art is a means of salvation, of raising the soul from the temporal to the eternal. The poet enjoyed the seclusion of her own private world of dreams, the refined perception of beauty, and elusive moods. Her realm of reverie, beauty, harmony, and "correspondences" to "fragrances, flowers, and sounds" served as her abode on earth. Her "allegiance" to Modernism also found expression in her yearning for an extreme degree of refinement, beauty, and delicacy, and in her belief in the forthcoming dawn of a new spiritual life for man. Solovyova's verse conjures up visions of a poetic universe suffused with all the sublime colors of the rainbow. Frequently, however, in harmony with her decadent moods, she used paler shades to portray the four seasons of the year, the passage of time, the transience of human beings and of everything earthly. Solovyova's poetry is a song of evening, of late autumn with nature dying; it is a hymn of death. Hers was a cult of tranquil negation, a rhythmical flow of splendor, calm, evil, and malaise. The lasting appeal of Poliksena Solovyova's song lies in its perfect craftsmanship and verbal magic. It should be noted that Solovyova, like Teffi, chose a literary pseudonym (Allegro) which disguised her sex, so that no extra-literary criteria could be applied in evaluating her work. As her friend Zinaida Hippius observed somewhat later, "People wouldn't say, 'This is a good piece of poetry, considering that the author is a woman!'"

The impressionistic quality of Cherubina de Gabriak's verse is achieved by a remarkable and swiftly alternating sequence of colorful and memorable images. She, too, tended toward the extreme in art by using magnificent colors and expressive imagery in her attempt to transcend the tedium and insignificance of everyday life. De Gabriak's gaze was always directed toward the sky, the sun, and the stars, hinting at mysteries of cosmic proportions. Her persona attempts to unveil them in order to understand their symbolic meaning. Together with other Decadent poets, de Gabriak wished to establish a link between Beauty and the "essence of things," as mirrored in a work of art. Like other avant-garde women writers of her day, she was preoccupied with specifically female feelings and desires, as well as with breaking away from the stereotyped view of woman (virtuous and dutiful toward her husband and family) that had generally dominated nineteenth-century Russian literature. De Gabriak unabashedly revealed the erotic curiosity and passion of contemporary woman.

The poetry of Adelaida Gertsyk, the last Modernist writer selected for the present anthology, is based on "sound instrumentation." Her verse depends on alliterations, assonances, and the "fleeting" nature of verbs and nouns, thus creating a strong evocative effect. She has skillfully availed herself of Slavicisms and old Russian song rhythms, aspiring to an "artistic folklore" somewhat similar to the sectarian melodies of Aleksander Dobrolyubov (1876–1944?) and the poetry of Lyubov Stolitsa (1844–1934), Pimen Karpov (1884– ?), and Marina Tsvetaeva (1892–1941). Her religious poems resemble those of Zinaida Hippius, being at once personal *méditations religieuses*, prayers, and hymns to God.

Taken as a whole, the works of Zinaida Hippius, Mirra Lokhvitskaya, Anastasiya Verbitskaya, Poliksena Solovyova, Lidiya Zinovyeva-Annibal, Cherubina de Gabriak, Nadezhda Teffi, and Adelaida Gertsyk were part of nascent Modernism's expression of its new mystical, religious, ethical, and philosophical perceptions, the expression of a *Weltanschauung* that protested and denied the social and civic obligations of the preceding generation in favor of complete freedom for the artist's spiritual and aesthetic aspirations. This attitude included a denial or obliteration of any outmoded views of man or woman and the nature of their roles. The Russian Silver Age was greatly enriched by the clarion call for craftsmanship, the aesthetic appreciation of art, and the unimpeded artistic self-expression of these women writers.

Some of these authors' visions may appear distorted and even ludicrous to the modern reader. The religious thought which was typical of the Russian intelligentsia at the turn of the century has little validity today, though its impulse—the ardent quest for a higher meaning beyond the banal and quotidian—is certainly contemporary. Indeed, the very essence of their movement, which involved the earnest search for an inner transfiguration and the expression of man's unique individuality and spiritual worth, is not unfamiliar to contemporary youth. The literary aspirations of these avant-garde writers to transcend the accepted notions concerning the role and function of woman in society and the family, and to share an equal place with man, is much in vogue in today's world.

Only one prophecy of these Modernist writers has come to pass: the catastrophe which they felt was imminent, and which manifested itself in October, 1917, as the Bolshevik *coup d'état*. Their hopes for an immediate religious, metaphysical, and cultural renewal of their native land proved to be mere illusion. Nevertheless, however difficult it may be to reconcile such ideas with the contemporary world, the modern reader should not remain unacquainted with the spiritual maximalism and metaphysical philosophy of these latter-day Russian writers, who searched, as did Diogenes, for the ultimate truth. The works of the Russian Modernists not only demonstrate the diverse attitudes of Russian intellectuals at the beginning of the century, but also reveal the immense aesthetic renaissance of the age. The Modernists were indeed the harbingers of the Silver Age in Russian literature.

NOTES

1. Asta Hansteen, "Tidens Tegn" (Features of the Time), *Nyt Tidskrift* (Oslo, 1894), p. 675.

2. See *Between Paris and St. Petersburg: Selected Diaries of Zinaida Hippius*, translated and edited by Temira Pachmuss (Urbana: University of Illinois Press, 1975), pp. 60–100.

3. For more details concerning literary Modernism, see Stephen Spender, *The Struggle of the Modern* (Berkeley and Los Angeles: University of California Press, 1963); Harry Levin, "What Was Modernism?" in *Refractions: Essays in Comparative Literature* (New York: Oxford University Press, 1966); Irving Howe, *Literary Modernism* (New York: Fawcett World Library, 1967).

4. D. Svyatopolk-Mirsky, "V. Ya. Bryusov," *Sovremennye zapiski*, XXII (1924), 416.

5. Renato Poggioli, *The Poets of Russia: 1890–1930* (Cambridge: Harvard University Press, 1960), p. 86.

6. *Ibid.*

7. V. V. Rozanov, "On Symbolists and Decadents," *Russian Literature Triquarterly*, No. 8 (Winter, 1974), 282. Read further about Rozanov in Heinrich Stammler, *Wassilij Rozanow: Ausgewählte Schriften* (herausgegeben, übertragen, eingeleitet und annotiert von Heinrich Stammler; München/Hamburg: Ellermann, 1963); *Vasilij Rozanov: Izbrannoe* (herausgegeben von Eugenia Zhiglevich und Heinrich Stammler, mit dem einführenden Aufsatz von Heinrich Stammler, "Wesensmerkmale und Stil des proteischen Menschen"; München: Neimanis, 1970); "Wassilij Rozanov (mit Uebertragungen aus seinen Essays und Aphorismen)," *Merkur*, 140 (München, 1959); "Apocalyptic Speculations in the Works of V. V. Rozanov and D. H. Lawrence," *Welt der Slaven*, IV, 1 (Wiesbaden, 1959); "Conservatism and Dissent: V. V. Rozanov's Political Philosophy," *Russian Review*, XXXII, 3 (1973); "Apocalypse: V. V. Rozanov and D. H. Lawrence," *Canadian Slavonic Papers*, XVI (1974).

8. N. A. Berdyaev, *Samopoznanie* (Paris: YMCA-Press, 1949); N. Zernov, *The Russian Religious Renaissance of the Twentieth Century* (New York: Harper & Row, 1963).

9. Read further on the subject, C. Harold Bedford, *The Seeker: D. S. Merezhkovskiy* (Lawrence: University Press of Kansas, 1975). Read also Heinrich Stammler, "Julius Apostata Redivivus. Dmitrij Merežkovskij: Predecessors and Successors," *Welt der Slaven*, XI, 1–2 (1966), "D. S. Merežkovskij—1865–1965: A Reappraisal," *ibid.*, XII, 2 (1967), and "Russian Metapolitics: Merezhkovsky's Religious Understanding of the Historical Process," *California Slavic Studies*, IX (1976), 123–138.

10. Rozanov, "On Symbolists and Decadents," p. 294.

11. Vladimir Markov, *Russian Futurism: A History* (Berkeley and Los Angeles: University of California Press, 1968), p. 4.

12. *Ibid.*, p. 32.

13. Cf. the chapter "Ego-Futurism: A History," *ibid.*

Zinaida Hippius

✓ 1869–1945

Zinaida Nikolaevna Hippius was an influential experimenter among early Modernist writers during the two decades preceding the October Revolution. Active in promoting new art forms and a view of Symbolism permeated with religious philosophy in Russian poetry, she also distinguished herself as a prolific poet, fiction writer, playwright, essayist, and critic. Her activities in the religious and philosophical societies in St. Petersburg and her fashionable literary *soirées* added to her fame in Russian literary circles. In Renato Poggioli's estimation, Hippius was "the uncrowned queen of the literary life"[1] in St. Petersburg. "Clever and beautiful, she acted not only as the Sybil but also as the Sylphide of the philosophical and religious circle that formed around her husband [D. S. Merezhkovsky, a pioneer in Russian Symbolism at the turn of the century] and herself."[2] Only a few readers in the West are acquainted with the works of Hippius or are aware of her "long and glorious past," to use D. S. Mirsky's statement concerning the enduring place she has earned in the history of Russian Modernism.

For Hippius, literature was a profound spiritual experience. The central theme of her creative work is the spirit and its efforts to attain the ultimate restoration of a harmonious relationship between love and eternity, life and death, and the real and the miraculous.[3] In her eyes, literature was a means of embodying for humanity the unity of the transcendental and the phenomenal. "We are using art," Hippius stated in 1908, "to provide an evolution of the world toward the ultimate goal of mankind,"[4] namely, the attainment of love, harmony, and the absolute spiritual freedom of the individual. Art is that beginning which gives birth to beauty, refinement, morality, and religious thought. Challenging the social and ideological approach to creative art, Hippius insisted on paying more respect to universal culture and to the mystery of aesthetic beauty and harmony. More consideration should be given to the eternal properties of art—the love of God, Christian ethics, poetry of feeling, and elevated thought. The immediate objective of art was, in her view, the reorganization of life: "The aim of art is to improve reality, to move it forward, to assist in the transformation of reality. This is the eternal goal of art."[5] It is false to separate art from life, for the "artist is able to show a *new* reality; he is able to create *new* objects and *new* conditions [. . .] He is justified in his creative work only when his artistic will can lead the reader to the truth, i.e., to the improvement of reality."[6] Hippius had in mind spiritual reality, since material reality was not of interest to her.

Symbols and the intensification and deepening of the reader's aesthetic perception were of major significance in Hippius' eyes. She held that the artist, the critic, and the reader should develop to the utmost their capacity for religious reflection and mystical thought, because she was convinced that the mysteries of the universe could not be resolved by technology and science. Philosophical and religious matters were the basis of Hippius' *Weltanschauung;* like other Russian Symbolist writers, she separated the empirical world from a spiritual world of mysterious significance and immanence. Her poetry and prose reflect an antipositivistic, dualistic view of a world divided into the realm of physical phenomena and a higher reality, eternal, indivisible, and intangible. Hippius' own law in art was formulated in an aphorism: "Art should materialize only the spiritual." Art reveals the divine spirit; in art the divine logos assumes a human image; the purpose of art is "to transform the Word (the principle) into the Flesh (the content of human activity)."[7] Sharing Andrey Bely's aesthetics— "The Word Is the Flesh"[8]—the poet wished to promote the moral and spiritual amelioration of human beings. These tenets constituted the essence of Hippius' metaphysical outlook throughout her life. Although her aesthetic philosophy was clearly indebted to

such thinkers as Plato, Zoroaster, Mani, Goethe, Vladimir Solovyov, Dostoevsky, and Henri Bergson, to name only a few, the
poet nonetheless transformed and developed her ideas to suit her
own metaphysical and religious system of thought, with its own
inviolable code of internal laws.

Like Goethe, she postulated that *Alles Vergängliche ist nur ein
Gleichnis,* and in her poetry she portrayed the world as a chaotic
interplay of spirit and matter. She conceived of poetry as a path to
the knowledge of ultimate mysteries and as an intuitive access to
pretersensual reality. Poetry, she insisted, should originate in the
artist's spiritual and religious ecstasy. Hippius' poems present her
metaphysical and profound experiences in imagery that is strik-
ingly, uncannily concrete. Her poetic universe appears as a hor-
rifying vision, a Manichaen world in which evil often gains the
upper hand over good and the Devil overpowers God. Colors,
sounds, images, and moods blend in the eerie spectre of Hippius'
universe, a physical and emotional void which instills mystery and
dread. These moods, however, are always counterbalanced by
idealistic strivings and an ardent faith in God and His mercy.
Zinaida Hippius' poetry is gripping in its seriousness, sincerity,
and poetic finish. It is based on music made tangible through a
stream of images and ideas. On the level of syntax, "poetry as
music" means the repetition of words or sentences as an echo or
refrain, the use of parallel structures and rhyme schemes. In essence, Hippius' poems are spiritual psalms, reminiscent of pious
hymns or chants such as the "Gloria in Excelsis." They are dreams
about a kingdom of new people endowed with new souls and a
new religious mentality—a kingdom which can never be attained,
yet for which man must always strive. Her craftsmanship and the
restrained beauty of her images set the poet apart from her
contemporaries.

Hippius began her artistic career as a poet of aestheticism and
of aristocratic aloofness from the coarse and obstreperous crowd.
She voiced a longing for an ideal vision of the universe, for "that
which is not of this world." Her moods of melancholy, solitude,
alienation from her fellow man, and a yearning for the thaumatur-
gic became especially intense at the turn of the century. At this
time, however, the tenor of her work suddenly changed—she became conscious of her personal will, determination, strength of

ZINAIDA HIPPIUS

intellect, and individual calling. Now she was absorbed in religious and socio-political matters. Continuing to protest the positivism, materialism, primitive straightforwardness, and utilitarianism of the nineteenth-century radicals, she advocated an apocalyptic Christianity which believed in the Second Coming. A salient feature of Zinaida Hippius' poetic temperament was her determination to serve humanity. She wished to participate in the creation of the new man, whose spirit would be enlightened and dignified and whose flesh would be transfigured and ennobled.

Hippius' voluminous prose is also remarkable and deserves close attention by students of contemporary literature. Her early narratives resemble medieval novellettes in their mysticism, verbal refinement, artistic imagination, craftsmanship, and occasional sophistry and wry humor. Sergey Makovsky, a Russian *émigré* writer and cultural historian, stated that Hippius is effective as an "author of striking and elegant short stories that are permeated with wit and poignant feeling, and which at times are based on complex psychological problems." He added: "And what beautiful language, always psychologically true, always remarkable in its veracity of colloquial intonations!"[9] Another influential critic of the day, Anastasiya Chebotarevskaya, whose critical evaluation of Hippius captured the essence of the success of her prose, observed that the writer's

stories are imbued with a very pungent *topicality:* practically all of the short stories broach one or another aspect of post-revolutionary sentiment. The themes [. . .] however replete with scalding contemporaneity, touching upon motifs of suicide, war, terrorism, etc., are nevertheless always intimately linked with the talented author's overall *Weltanschauung* — with her ideas of *God* as the religio-philosophical beginning of All, of *rebelliousness* as the inception of creation, and of *inquiry* as the foundation of the meaningful truth of life [. . .] *Dialogue,* in which Z. Hippius is extraordinarily successful, serves as a strong weapon in her prose [. . .] everywhere may be heard those very authentic, genuine, "singularly found" words for a given attribute, for which such a master of the word as Flaubert advised belletrists to search. Therefore, the language in a majority of Z. Hippius' short stories is such a beautiful, authentically Russian literary language that, admiring its ingenious expressions (especially in dialogues), one may only wonder: "Where in the world did the author manage to hear all this?"[10]

Hippius was fond of treating psychological problems, both her own and those of her characters, by way of introspective analysis and by presenting entangled feelings of guilt, self-depreciation, and spiritual crises, particularly those of young people. Her preoccupation with the "burning questions of the day" and her technical polish and sophistication made her a fashionable and important writer in pre-revolutionary belles-lettres. It is indeed unfortunate that Hippius' short stories, so deserving of detailed analysis and evaluation, have escaped the attention of contemporary literary scholars. Her works are significant for a deeper insight into the art of Russian Modernism.

The first two volumes of Hippius' stories, *Novye lyudi: rasskazy* (People of Today: Short Stories, 1896) and *Zerkala: vtoraya kniga rasskazov* (Mirrors: A Second Book of Short Stories, 1898), imply a rejection of conventional ethical concepts and norms of behavior. Hippius' heroes seek new philosophies of life and are engrossed in debates on harmony, the beauty of the world, God, and love. The feverish atmosphere in some of these narratives is reminiscent of Dostoevsky's novels. The descriptive method shows a certain similarity to that of the Belgian poet Georges Rodenbach, with his emphasis on "everything that is secluded, deserted, and silent."[11] Hippius' protagonists advocate the Nietzschean philosophy of egoism and the pursuit of personal happiness at the expense of social considerations. She was also very successful in the portrayal of child psychology, as in "'Mest'" (Revenge, *People of Today*), for example. Hippius likewise understood and portrayed the "progressive-minded" Russian students who rejected old values and norms, believing (as did Turgenev's Bazarov) only in science and technology. Like Turgenev, Hippius never thought that science and technology could explain the psychological complexities inherent in human nature and the metaphysical principles underlying the universe.

Hippius' interest in psychology is manifest in the stories "Rodina" (Home Sweet Home), in *Mirrors: A Second Book of Short Stories,* and "'Dver'" (The Door), in *Lunnye muravyi: shestaya kniga rasskazov* (The Moon Ants: A Sixth Book of Short Stories, 1912). She could understand quite well the mentality of servants and those semi-educated Russians who affected the flowing style of the upper class in their speech. She could also accurately read the psychology of the mob, which does not reason but acts blindly, attributing the blame for its atrocious behavior to the "one in authority."

Religious divination, reflections on beauty and harmony, social concepts, and the preaching of Neo-Christianity and ecumenity (*sobornost'*) are concepts intrinsic in the fourth book of Hippius' stories, *Aly mech: rasskazy* (The Scarlet Sword: Short Stories, 1906). Andrey Bely described *The Scarlet Sword* as "intimate sighs about the Ecumenical Truth."[12] He then added: "The Easter chime, clear and inviting, resounds pensively in the author's quiet speeches. Artfully and adroitly, she reveals the deathly essence of the platitudes expressed in those views about a Christianity which is crowned with cathedrals falling to pieces."[13] He concluded his accolade: "Z. N. Hippius is the most intelligent of our contemporary figures of belles-lettres. Her refined and capricious intellect permeates the background of her entire art."[14] The critic E. Koltonovskaya admired "both the author's and her heroes' serious search for the meaning of life, for its new forms, for new moral laws, and for a new beauty."[15] She was likewise impressed with Hippius' virtuosity in the realm of language, with her ability to present complex psychological states, to sketch compelling pictures of nature, and to characterize her heroes by their individualized speech patterns.

In *The Scarlet Sword,* we find Hippius' rejection of Pisarev's and Chernyshevsky's treatment of social ideas in art, and her insistence on the mystery of aesthetic beauty and harmony. Her polemics concerning the Russian radical critics' "newest" ideas on the "profits" and "usefulness" of literature, and their negation of the soul, are presented in "Vne vremeni—stary etyud" (Outside of Time—An Old Etude). Hippius' musings on religious matters and the "new religious consciousness," which she endeavored to create, find expression in "Sumasshedshaya" (The Mad Woman). Vera, the heroine, is opposed to the "enlightened," purely rational attitude of her husband toward man in general. Feeling at ease (like Hippius herself) only with those people who are eager to create the "new religious awareness" that would include God and a profound search for the meaning of life, Vera frequents the gatherings of various sectarians—seekers of God. She hopes to find such new people, who would "arrange their lives in the name of God," among them. Hippius' preoccupation with psychological entanglements, married life, parenthood, love, understanding, and the place of woman in society also finds its artistic expression in the story.

The psychology of Vera recalls the growing awareness of Ibsen's Nora in *A Doll's House* (1879). Vera, like Nora, comes to understand the stifling quality of the role she is expected to play all her life. Hippius' story has perhaps more universal significance, however. Unlike Ibsen, who was particularly concerned with the sociological question of woman's emerging consciousness, Hippius is speaking of the human spirit in general, seeking to break free of mediocrity and narrowmindedness in order to develop its full potential.

The stories written by Hippius in this period reflect the affirmative elements of her religious philosophy. Her characters strive for an "enlightened love" of God, the elevation of the flesh, and the ability to achieve understanding and harmony among people. Mystical clairvoyance, spiritual contemplation, and an awareness of the beauty and mystery contained in nature play an important role in the stories in *The Scarlet Sword*. Here Hippius upheld her belief that Heaven, earth, and man sustain one another, and that together they form one integral unity.

Chernoe po belomu (In Black and White, 1908), the fifth book of stories, has a symbolic title, as do all of her volumes. It expresses the poet's abandonment of attempts to reveal the existence of the magical, all-embracing Word which can resolve all conflicts, upheavals, and blows befalling humanity. Wishing to dwell on more mundane and contemporary matters, Hippius no longer writes in symbols, hints, and allusions, but "in black and white." Here the reader finds direct references to the themes which were important in Russian belles-lettres at the time. For example, Hippius dwells on the treatment of death in Tolstoy's "Smert' Ivana Ilyicha" (The Death of Ivan Ilyich, 1886), and on the critical portrayal of the basic indifference and complacency of people toward love, spiritual friendship, and death—a view which she shared with Chekhov. Professor Akhtyrov's life has been completely egocentric. Like Ivan Ilyich, he has considered his existence to be the center of the universe. His self-centered attitude has been the trap in which he has remained all his life. As in Chekhov's stories and in "The Death of Ivan Ilyich," where the family, friends, and colleagues of the deceased man soon forgot him, Akhtyrov first fears and then forgets the death of his only son. Even though Hippius clearly abstains from endowing her characters with a striving for a love of God, the book nonetheless reasserts her faith in the sublime.

In *The Moon Ants* psychological and religious considerations, and the themes of spiritual metamorphosis and uplifting ideals, are again in the foreground. Hippius' indebtedness to Dostoevsky is evident in "On—bely" (He Is White), a memorable story of great significance to the poet herself. Like the short stories "Ivan Ivanovich i chert" (Ivan Ivanovich and the Devil; *In Black and White*) and "Oni pokhozhi" (They Are Alike), "He Is White" makes use of an ancient myth which pictures the Devil as an enchanter, although here Hippius also emphasizes the celestial elements of his nature. In most of Hippius' works the Devil symbolizes temptation. Sometimes she relates him to eroticism, and often to *poshlost'*, in the tradition of Gogol' and Dostoevsky. Her engrossment with the Devil is, however, chiefly of a religious nature,[16] although her Devil theme may also be viewed as the expression of her personal surrender to the desire for separation from other people, inertia, and occasional spiritual prostration.

The structural scheme of Hippius' stories is sound. Intrigue is introduced at the beginning of the narrative; the reader is immediately immersed in the atmosphere, and themes and moods unfurl with acumen. Humor, psychological divulgences, and dramatic events are artfully interwoven. The heroes and their idiosyncratic modes of thinking and speaking are drawn in sharp relief. The characters thus created produce a clear impression and can be easily distinguished from one another. Humor is not infrequently used in Hippius' narratives. Tension between the comic and the tragic is created in many of her stories, as in "Home Sweet Home," for example. Her use of a style which combines both literary and colloquial, even substandard, expressions is also very effective. Many scenes and dialogues testify to her exquisite sense of humor and sophisticated craftsmanship. Likewise impressive are her descriptions of nature, which are full of symbolic import and suggestiveness, as in "The Wild Bear" (*The Third Book of Stories*, 1902). Here nature appears, especially in its nocturnal aspects, as in some of Turgenev's stories; in "Bezhin lug" (Bezhin Meadow, 1857), for instance, and in Tyutchev's poetry, it is a hostile mysterious force.

Hippius succeeded in creating an atmosphere which sustained the development of her ideas and the unfolding of her plots. All of her stories reveal the originality of the poet's artistic universe. Her emphasis on aesthetic, religious, and philosophical aspects in literary works helped set the stage for a new twentieth-century literary movement, Russian Symbolism. Hippius never relinquished the premises she formulated at the turn of the century: art is real when it guides the reader toward the spiritual and stimulates his search for God. Like Dostoevsky, she saw the tragedy of human existence in man's loneliness, his inability to love, his aloofness from the spiritual, and his lack of faith.

Zinaida Hippius' philosophy retains its validity even in the light of modern existentialism, for her works are surprisingly relevant in today's cultural climate. The American scholar Vasa D. Mihailovich claims that she "might be more relevant today, especially to the searching and troubled young generation, than at any other time save that of the period when she was at the zenith of her influence—in the decade before the Revolution." The central themes of her short stories (the search for God, a preoccupation with problems of good and evil, the treatment of love, passion, marriage, and a sense of responsibility toward oneself and one's fellow man) are very relevant today. The philosophy underlying Zinaida Hippius' art still has the power to stimulate the reader with the Christian ideals of eternity, absolute reality, all-embracing love, and the view of nature as a reflection of the spiritual realm.

NOTES

1. Renato Poggioli, *The Poets of Russia: 1890–1930* (Harvard University Press, 1960), p. 111.
2. *Ibid.*, p. 112.
3. For more details, read Temira Pachmuss, *Zinaida Hippius: An Intellectual Profile* (Southern Illinois University Press, 1971).
4. Z. Hippius, "Iz dnevnika zhurnalista," *Russkaya mysl'*, No. 2 (1909), 157.
5. Anton Krayny (Z. Hippius), "Propisi," *Novy dom*, No. 1 (1926), 20.
6. Z. Hippius, "Iskusstvo i lyubov'," *Opyty*, No. 2 (1953), 116.
7. Andrey Bely, *Simvolizm: kniga statey* (Moscow: Musaget, 1910), p. 94.
8. *Ibid.*, p. 95.
9. Sergey Makovsky, *Na Parnase Serebryanogo veka* (Munich: TsOPE, 1961), p. 98.

10. An. Chebotarevskaya, "Z. N. Hippius, *Lunnye muravyi: shestaya kniga rasskazov.* Al'tsion," *Novaya zhizn'*, No. 5 (1912), 269.

11. *Gallereya russkikh pisateley* (Moscow: Skirmunt, 1901), p. 515.

12. Andrey Bely, *Arabeski* (Moscow: Musaget, 1911), p. 437.

13. *Ibid.*, p. 439.

14. *Ibid.*, p. 445.

15. *Obrazovanie*, No. 9 (1906).

16. For more details, read Pachmuss, *Zinaida Hippius: An Intellectual Profile.*

AUTUMN

Longer, darker
Are the cold nights,
But the days keep getting shorter,
And the sky—lighter.
The distant thistle
Grows more sparse and dry,
And the wind in the sedge,
Where the shore is high,
Is more drawling and hollow.
The water cools,
The dam is silenced,
And the heavy ooze
Settles to the bottom.
With vacant eyes
Autumn boldly
Gazes through the trunks
Of pensive pines,
Of golden birches,
Straight, with fragile leaves—
And, like the Fates,
Weaves and entwines
The strand of a gray web
Along the clusters of rowan trees,
And soothingly beckons
Into the depths of the dreamy park . . .
There dusk abides, and sweetness,
Everything heeds Autumn,
And a peaceful joy
Embraces my soul.
I welcome death
With delirious delight,
I've no need, no need
For immortality's tortures!
The final shadows
Of final visions,
Of living exhaustions
Float, slip away—
Incorporeal—they melt—

Before eternal rest . . .
Let me doze 'neath the earth
Without visions,
Resigned to peace,
In endless slumber . . .

1893

ОСЕНЬ

Длиннее, чернее
Холодные ночи,
А дни все короче
И небо светлее.
Терновник далекий
И реже и суше,
И ветер в осоке,
Где берег высокий,
Протяжней и глуше.
Вода остывает,
Замолкла плотина,
И тяжкая тина
Ко дну оседает.
Бестрепетно Осень
Пустыми очами
Глядит меж стволами
Задумчивых сосен,
Прямых, тонколистых
Берез золотистых,—
И нити, как Парка,
Седой паутины
Свивает и тянет
По гроздьям рябины,
И ласково манит
В глубь сонного парка ...
Там сумрак, там сладость,
Все Осени внемлет,
И тихая радость
Мне душу объемлет.
Приветствую смерть я

С безумной отрадой,
И муки бессмертья,
Не надо! Не надо!
Скользят, улетают—
Бесплотные—тают
Последние тени
Последних видений,
Живых утомлений—
Пред отдыхом вечным ...
Пускай без видений,
Покорный покою,
Усну под землею
Я сном бесконечным ...

THE LIGHT

Groans,
Groans,
Exhausted, fathomless,
The prolonged tolling
Of funeral bells,
Groans,
Groans . . .
    Complaints,
    Complaints against the Father . . .
    Burning, piercing pity,
    A yearning for the end,
    Complaints,
    Complaints . . .
The knot grows tighter, tighter,
The path—steeper, steeper,
All around—narrower, narrower, narrower,
Gloomier—the clouds,
Terror obliterates my soul,
The knot strangles,
The knot grows tighter, tighter, tighter . . .
    Lord, O Lord—no!
    The prophetic heart keeps faith!

My God, no!
We remain under Thy wings.
Terror. And groans. And darkness . . . but above these
Thy unflinching Light.

1915

СВЕТ

Стоны,
Стоны,
Истомные, бездонные,
Долгие звоны
Похоронные,
Стоны,
Стоны ...
    Жалобы,
    Жалобы на Отца ...
    Жалость язвящая, жаркая,
    Жажда конца,
    Жалобы,
    Жалобы ...
Узел туже, туже,
Путь все круче, круче,
Все уже, уже, уже,
Угрюмей тучи,
Ужас душу рушит,
Узел душит,
Узел туже, туже, туже ...
    Господи, Господи—нет!
    Вещее сердце верит!
    Боже мой, нет!
    Мы под крылами Твоими.
    Ужас. И стоны. И тьма ... а над ними
    Твой немеркнущий Свет.

HOMEWARD

They babbled
  fairy tales to me
    about the earth:
      "Man lives there. And love."

But, in truth—
  there's only evil,
    Disguises. Masks.
      Lies and filth. Lies and blood.

When they suggested
  I be born—
    No one told me the world was like this.

How
  was I
    to disagree?
      Now, all I want is—home! To go home!

1938

ДОМОЙ

Мне
  о земле—
    болтали сказки:
      «Есть человек. Есть любовь.»

А есть—
  лишь злость,
    Личины. Маски.
      Ложь и грязь. Ложь и кровь.

Когда предлагали
  мне родиться—
    Не говорили, что мир такой.

Как же
  я мог
    не согласиться?
      Ну, а теперь—домой! домой!

THE WORD?

They would pass by, and again depart,
They could not deceive me . . .
There is a certain, single word
Which encompasses the entire essence.

The others—are dried feather-grass.
The others—are all flotsam,
Gray dust.

A girl walked across the street,
An auto screamed a word to her . . .
And then, the crowd stood over her,
But the girl is gone—there's only dust.

Don't you agree that people
Have such odd ears and eyes?
Don't you agree that everywhere
Lines and sounds are so obscure?
The whole world is here,
Yet its essence is lost to us . . .
But the animals know the word,
The mute animals:
A Pekinese,
Naked and coarse-skinned,
Trembling on a May evening
At the doorstep of some club,
Watches cautiously—
And is silent for thirteen years,
As the cat is silent
In the bakery on Muette.

Animals can't speak
People can't comprehend,
And the world grows gray, like dust,
Falling into uselessness . . .

1923

СЛОВО?

Проходили они, уходили снова,
Не могли меня обмануть …
Есть какое-то одно слово,
В котором вся суть.

Другие — сухой ковыль.
Другие — все муть,
Серая пыль.

Шла девочка через улицу,
Закричал ей слово автомобиль …
И вот, толпа над ней сутулится,
А девочки нет — есть пыль.

Неправда ли, какие странные
Уши и глаза у людей?
Неправда ли, какие туманные
Линии и звуки везде?
А мир весь здесь,
Для нас он — потеря …
Но слово знают звери,
Молчаливые звери:
Собачка китайская,
Голая, с кожей грубой,
В дверях какого-то клуба,
Дрожит вечером майским,
Смотрит сторожко —
Молчит тринадцать лет,
Как молчит и кошка
В булочной на Muette.

Звери сказать не умеют,
Люди не знают,
И мир как пыль сереет,
Пропадом пропадает …

FROST

How this bitter cold's exhausted me,
This frost in my heart.
If only I could weep to thaw my heart,
But there are no tears . . .

1942

МОРОЗ

Как эта стужа меня измаяла,
Этот сердечный мороз.
Мне бы заплакать, чтоб сердце оттаяло,
Да нет слез ...

A WHITE GARMENT

*To him who triumphs I shall give
white garments.* — BOOK OF REVELATION

He tempers me—with His remoteness,
I accept the test.
I accept with resignation
His love—His silence.

And the more mute my love,
The more unattainable, constant it becomes,
And the more beautiful is my anticipation,
The future union—more indissoluble.

I know nothing of time and calendars;
I remain in His hand—I am His creation . . .
But to triumph—as He has triumphed—
I desire the ultimate trial.

So I surrender my daring soul
To the Creator of my torment.
The Lord has said: "I shall send a white garment
To him who triumphs."

1902

WORDS OF LOVE

Love, love . . . Oh, not even love itself—
I loved love's words undaunted.
In them I sensed a different existence,
Elusive and unfathomable . . .

Words live only while the soul is alive.
They are amusing—they are unusual.
I loved, and still love love's words,
Pervaded with their prophetic mystery.

December, 1912;
St. Petersburg

NO!

She will not perish—I tell you!
She will not perish, Russia.
They will ripen—believe me!
Her golden fields.

And we shall not perish—believe me!
But what's our salvation to us:
Russia will be saved—I tell you!
Her resurrection is at hand.

February, 1918

PERHAPS

How this strange world troubles me!
The longer I live, the less I understand.
There are no answers. Always there is only: perhaps.
But the most honest and direct is: I don't know.

My pensive agitation has no answer.
Why, then, do my days increase it?

What is its origin? From where?

               Somewhere—

I don't know where—the answers exist . . . perhaps?

                      1938

THE KEY

I was given a cherished key,
   And I guarded it.
It jingled imperceptibly . . .

   The final hour has expired.
I step onto a steep bridge.
   The river's ooze seethes.
And the waves batter dimly
   Against the gloomy granite,
Indistinctly and constantly,
   They mutter about their own affairs,
Rising under the bridge
   In a rusty foam.
A freezing wind sweeps
   Broadly in its whistling flight . . .

I cast my now useless key
   Into the seething waters.
It disappeared, slicing the waves,
   And settled somewhere on the bottom . . .

Forgive my pining,
   Do not think of me.

                      1921

THE MAD WOMAN

I

Along the way, Ivan Vasilyevich found plenty to talk about. It was astonishing to me, since those two or three times I had seen him before—I think, at the priest's and at the mayor's—he had been silent, stiff, and seemed to be a sullen and unsociable man. In the small, remote district town where I came to spend about a month, he had been serving as the district police officer for something like ten years. I remember that, when I found this out, I immediately thought his sullenness was completely natural. The little town was worse than any village: empty, dusty streets, slanting rows of overgrown, soft grass on the market square, gloomy huts surrounded by half-sandy, half-swampy fields, not one garden, not one forest to be seen. The little town immediately struck me as being horrible, but we often judge by our own yardstick and refuse to believe that something which seems awful to us could possibly be otherwise in reality, or at least for some.

We were travelling by post—I, to visit a friend on a distant estate; Ivan Vasilyevich, on business to the district town. We left at the same time, and since we were going the same way to the first station, Ivan Vasilyevich invited me to ride in his carriage.

"From Makarikha you will be able to travel faster, since the road there is a bit better," said Ivan Vasilyevich. "But here, before we reach Makarikha, you will probably be a bit bored. The distance is great—twenty-six *versts*, and the road passes through a forest. You probably already know what a lot of forest roads we have."

The road, for a number of *versts*, actually did pass through a forest. There were potholes, puddles from the fallen rain, thickly interlaced roots, and some other sort of things—not exactly stumps, nor rotten pickets, either. The forest road was indeed very interesting. We travelled on at a slow, constant pace. From the branches which bent toward us from both sides of the forest, thick and dark, there came a smell of freshness, dampness, and the strong, sharp fragrance of fir trees. The scent of apples seemed to float in the air. The sun had not quite disappeared, and the sky, suffused with its last light, was quietly turning from blue to gold. The solitary troika, with its bells dully ringing, cautiously drove on—one moment the driver would be engrossed in his thoughts, and the next, be dozing.

I looked to the side, close by, at Ivan Vasilyevich, at his white cap; now his face seemed to me to be absolutely free of moroseness, and only very serious—one sometimes sees such simple solemnity. From under his cap his face appeared dark. He could have been about fifty, or perhaps younger.

He was strong, heavy-set, and somewhat stiff. When he looked at me, I saw the same serious, immobile simplicity in his brown eyes. He had an unusual wrinkle on his cheek: a long, deep furrow which extended from his eye down to the very middle of his face. It was as sharp as if someone had purposely marked him on his cheek. I noticed that he never smiled, even when he talked cheerfully, as if these wrinkles didn't allow him to smile. In general, however, the face of Ivan Vasilyevich was very ordinary. I have difficulty recalling him now, either because I had seen him too many times, or had seen men who resembled him.

He didn't begin speaking at once. He would, however, answer my questions simply and willingly. Then suddenly he asked me:

"Have you heard of my misfortune?"

"You have . . . a sick wife, don't you?"

"Yes . . . She is in the hospital in the provincial capital. The second year has gone by."

"The second year? What have the doctors said? Is there hope?"

"How can I say? Mental illnesses belong to an area . . . that science knows little about. I can't get any definite answer. I know nothing."

He uttered these last words with such a strange expression that I raised my head.

"How is it that you know nothing? The type of illness is certainly known?"

"No . . . Neither the type of illness nor the cause is known. Even . . . of course, I admit this to you in a moment of weakness . . . but I don't hide it, such moments do occur . . . It seems to me that she's not mentally ill at all, and never has been."

"What! Then why did you commit her to an insane asylum?"

"I didn't commit her . . . You must excuse me. I made a slip of the tongue; these are only momentary thoughts of mine. She is no stranger to me, you know. I know nothing about medicine. The doctors know better than I."

Although I saw that Ivan Vasilyevich himself desired to speak with me, to ask him any further questions was completely inappropriate, and I fell silent, waiting to hear what he would say.

He took off his cap, ran his hand through his short hair, and, having slightly raised his heavy eyelids, glanced at me and all around. The road, as before, went through the woods. Night was falling and the twilight was such a quiet, fragrant, golden color!

"By now I've become accustomed to my sorrow," continued Ivan Vasilyevich. "Little by little one grows used to everything. Before, how hard it was to say anything more about it. How can you explain to someone else what you yourself don't really understand? It would seem to be quite simple—and yet, in reality, it's not so simple at all. However," he added in all seriousness, and with an almost indifferent simplicity, "most likely it's true; after all, she's not a stranger to me . . ."

I glanced at him, at the strange wrinkles on his cheeks, at his kind eyes, and I asked him to tell me from the beginning how this "misfortune" had occurred. Here is what he told me.

II

"My wife, Vera Ivanovna, is now a bit over thirty. However, she looks much older—thin, pale, her face dominated by dark brows. She married me when she was sixteen and a half; if only you could have seen how she was in bloom! Simply a beauty! She was, I must tell you, of a noble family; that is, her mother was an impoverished princess, an orphan who had married a minor official in our district town. I didn't know her. At the time that I met Vera Ivanovna, her father had long been married a second time to a woman from a very simple family; they had many children, and Vera looked after them. In spite of this, she graduated from high school. They were poor; Vera had no dowry, but it didn't matter to me—I already had a position as an assistant in another district. I thought, somehow we would make a living. I liked Vera very much.

"As for myself, you see, I entered Kazan' University; I had dreamed of another road, but I didn't finish my education. I was involved in an incident—you know, in his youth a man is hot-blooded and unreasonable, and our time was so peculiar . . . it wasn't a serious incident, yet I was expelled from the university. I can firmly say"—here Ivan Vasilyevich glanced at me almost severely—"that I have remained true to my strong convictions. Just as I was then—I am now. Only my reasonableness, tenacity, and experience have increased. My sole belief is in humanity—love of man, and strong, vital help to him who needs light and bread. Don't consider this a boast, because I'm not speaking of what I have done, but only of what I always believed in. My sister and I were also the children of a minor civil servant in Kazan'. When our parents died, my sister became a village schoolteacher, and I entered the service of the district government. For a long time I tormented myself over my entering the civil service, but then I understood how much good I could accomplish there. For three years my sister wouldn't associate with me, but then she, too, understood it. It was pretty hard at the beginning, and even now, at times, it isn't easy; however, what a comparison one could make! Things change from year to year. Thirty or forty years ago a man such as myself, with my convictions, wouldn't have been tolerated for even one day, yet now I am held in the highest regard at the governor's. Yes, the principles of humanity and enlightenment are beginning to triumph. Everything is moving in that direction."

"Is that so?" I involuntarily challenged him.

"Yes, sir, it is. Haven't you noticed it yourself? You will see that it's true, if you speak with someone of higher rank. The wind is blowing in that direction. Mankind is developing, and though progress is slow, culture, science, and knowledge are performing great wonders."

"That means you believe that men are on a straight path to universal happiness?" Again I didn't restrain myself and interrupted him.

He raised his brows in surprise.

"How can it be otherwise? The straight path, perhaps, isn't smooth, and patience is still required . . . but all will develop of its own accord, and its own will. Think of it like this: education spreads, superstitions are extinguished one after another; the intellect is developing, and with it a reasonable gratification of needs, and a respect for another's individuality in the name of the ideal of mankind."

I saw that this conversation could lead us far afield, and so I didn't voice my objections. Ivan Vasilyevich returned to our former discussion.

"And so, I married Verochka. Remembering back to that time, I can see that even then there was something not entirely normal about her. There were no hysterics, nothing of that sort, but, as the doctors say, an aggravated sensitivity. I think that it was so even then. I loved her, I tell you truthfully, with all my soul. But she, to put it simply, was ecstatic all the time. She would continuously tell me how much she loved me — so much so that later she would even be angry with herself.

"'I cannot express my love. I would like to, but I am unable to. Help me, if you have any pity for me.'

"I would calm her down.

"'This,' I would tell her, 'Verusha, is your romanticism. I know that you love me, and I am happy. What more could you want?' There was no reason to be surprised at her romanticism: after all, she wasn't quite seventeen years old, whereas I was no longer an innocent youth.

"However, she became angry at me more and more often. Then once she suddenly said:

"'You amuse yourself with me as though you were playing with a doll. I know nothing about you. Tell me, what do you think about?'

"This reproach wounded me, since, after all, I am a just man. What could I do? She was such a young thing, and so pretty, and I was so in love with her. During this period after the wedding . . . I, of course, came to my senses, and begged her pardon.

"'Just wait a bit, everything will come in time.'

"Then she pleaded: 'Give me some sort of work. I'm bored.'

"I was glad to do this. I saw that in time she would be a real woman — and not only a woman, but a human being as well. But now she was such a child. And so again I said:

"'Wait a while, everything will work out. Take care of the household, of the apartment. Speak with good people, try to understand them. I will order some new books for you from St. Petersburg, and you read the old ones that I already have. You really should read them, too.'

"This was all right with her, and she agreed. I travelled; she attended to the house. The little town in which we lived was even worse than my present one. The location, however, was somewhat more pleasant; it was surrounded by a stream and some woods. I managed to find a nice apartment—a new little house with three rooms—like a doll's house. I introduced Vera to the wife of the archbishop and the wife of a member of the court; you know how it is, the usual country society. They're very kind people. They were worse then, less educated, but now one might say that even in our town we have a marvelous society, all quite educated, and not apathetic.

"And so, sir, that's how we lived. We lived there one year, two, three. Vera became completely accustomed to our new life. She read many books, we subscribed to the newspapers, and I, by then, you know, discussed with her everything that was in my soul just as I would with a dear friend. I talked about my work, my doubts; I shared everything with her. She would reason everything out properly, and she established ties with our society. Moreover, she had friends among the townspeople. Even throughout the neighboring villages she struck up acquaintances. People would visit, and she would speak with quite a number of them. I didn't interfere. It was a good thing, as I'm not such a good friend of the nobility. There was such ignorance in our villages that, if Vera spoke with the townspeople, only good could have come of it.

"Then an official from St. Petersburg arrived in our town. Such a pleasant man, you know, quite young. We took to him, and he dined with us on two occasions. Verochka would tell him how she visited various villages, and things like that, and he would praise her and talk about enlightenment and about the ignorance of the people. I listened and was happy. But then, in my most joyous moment, I realized for the first time that something wasn't quite right with Vera. She had been talking animatedly, and then suddenly became quiet and pensive.

"'What's wrong with you?' I asked.

"Our guest looked at us.

"She raised her eyes to him and said harshly: 'Yes, we're not very good. We live basely and occupy ourselves with base pursuits.'

"Can you imagine how that startled us! I simply couldn't come to my senses. I couldn't even understand what she was talking about. The official was a most honorable man. And indeed she knew me quite well, I thought.

"I couldn't find the right thing to reply, while the official, although he retained his composure, turned red and, smiling, politely asked: 'Why are you so harsh, Vera Ivanovna? What don't you like?'

"It was summer and we sat drinking tea. She got up from her chair, walked up to the window, looked out at the street, sighed, and said indifferently: 'No, it's nothing, forgive me . . . I am speaking in general terms. What we do is not base, only boring.'

"'Are you bored? But . . .'

"'No, I am not bored, but these affairs, mine and yours, are boring. You continue to think about the happiness of mankind, and perhaps about reading physics books. But imagine—what if everything were already achieved, and everyone, even Mit'ka— the drunkard from Ukhabny—were living, right now, as we do. What if they knew everything that we know. So what?'

"I jumped up.

"'Vera. What are you saying?'

"She continued: 'Well, so there's happiness. Only it's a boring happiness. Wouldn't you agree that it's a boring one?'

"The official gave her a great deal of sensible advice, developed some broad ideas—a charming, eloquent person! She didn't answer, as if she agreed.

"Afterward I rebuked her severely. She didn't even say one word to me; it was as if I weren't even talking to her. I reproached her with her old romanticism. She smiled ironically and then left. For three days I was angry at her—then it passed, and we again lived as we had before."

Ivan Vasilyevich sighed and fell silent as if remembering something—then he began talking again.

III

"Everything was as it had been before—yet it was somehow different. Vera was very depressed and silent. And if I, as before, upon returning from a trip, would begin to tell her about something (many curious things do happen when travelling), she would not respond. If I walked through the room, she would remain silent, sullenly following me with her eyes.

"'What's the matter with you, Vera?'

"'Nothing. Talk. I am looking at you. All of you are very interesting people.'

"What a nuisance! If only she would have explained what was bothering her. No, she would only sit in her corner and watch me constantly, and in that sullen way follow me. At times I would be beside myself:

"'Why do you watch me like this? Do you want to write a novel or something? Then write. It's an occupation, after all.'

"'Why shouldn't I watch you? You're an interesting type.'

"She would say this, smile ironically, and walk out.

"In spite of everything, I pitied her. Perhaps she really was bored? So young, no children, and I was constantly travelling. How could she be happy with the company of the archbishop's wife and the wife of the local government official? Of course, I dreamed of seeing Vera a real woman, a person working as I did, as much as possible for her younger fellow men, her uneducated brothers; I conceived of her as a helpmate . . . But she was young yet. Youthful years would pass and she would freely take to that task. After all, do we not have many truly sacred jobs for women in our remote provinces? To teach and to nurse—these two words mean so much.

"However, I saw that Vera was bored with me. I'm not a beast; we didn't live according to the Domostroy. Whatever a person wishes for himself, he has the right to have. That's the way I talked to Vera. She seemed to be happy. Well, that's fine, I thought.

"I let her go to visit with her family in the district capital. From there she wrote, 'I am going to Moscow for a month with my aunt.' Let her visit the theatre, I thought. She spent approximately three months in Moscow, and in February she returned. It happened that exactly at that time an army regiment was transferred to our town. It became gay—terribly so. In the spring there were picnics, horseback riding, rides in the carriage; the commander of the regiment gave evening parties, where even the priests' young wives danced—there were two of them living in the town then.

"My Vera became very busy and gay. She told me hardly anything about Moscow.

"'Was it pleasant there?'

"'Yes.'

"'Well, are you satisfied now?'

43

"'I? How?'

"I was having difficulty explaining myself.

"'What do you mean, how? In general . . . with life, you know . . .'

"'With whose life? With my own?'

"Her answers were somehow simply out of place. I continued, nevertheless: 'If you don't want me to understand—it's not really necessary.'

"Here she embraced me tenderly: 'Don't be angry; I'm happy. Only don't ask me about anything again.'

"I confess that these words struck me as both offensive and insulting. Not ask! Who was it that cared for her, that arranged it so her life could be free, happy, gay—arranged it, perhaps, without approving of it, though with hopes for the future? And suddenly this 'Don't ask'! What kind of secrets had she acquired?

"Vera, at that time, read hardly a single book. Well, she was a lady, like any other, only somehow more active. She would gallop on horseback daringly and tirelessly, dance until dawn in the club. A certain officer (he was from a good family and handsome) was courting her ardently. She would laugh, and together they would either lag behind the others or go in front of them—and then, well, they began to be noticed. You know, giving cause for gossip leads people into sin. And they did indulge in gossip.

"So, once when we returned home, I hinted to her about the gossip. What was this? She puffed up indignantly, her eyes became evil.

"'What, are you jealous or something?'

"And, not waiting for my reply, she took the candle and left.

"I thought to myself: What will come of this? You know, in the depth of my soul I felt very nasty and somehow numb. For the first time I couldn't sleep that night. However, I overcame that nonsense, and all went well.

"Vera at once became more restrained with that officer Stoletov, but she was gloomier than a dark cloud. I, however, calmed down. 'Everything,' I thought, 'will be all right. Life will take care of itself.'

"One time, you know, Vera and I were returning from visiting a member of the local courthouse—he had had a rather small party and we were returning home late. The streets were deserted; it was already autumn, although still warm. From time to time black clouds would pile one upon another, now covering the moon, now uncovering it and becoming brighter again. To tell you the truth, I was tired out. I had just returned from a business trip to the district capital that day, and then—that party. I don't play cards, so most of the time I dozed. On the way home I was quiet; Vera was also silent. When we were already in front of the house, I said to her:

"'You know, Verochka, my transfer most likely will go through. That little town is better than ours, it's closer to the capital . . .'

"I didn't manage to finish what I was saying, when suddenly she let go of my hand and began to sob. I was simply astounded. Right in the street, and, you know, she cried very rarely; I wasn't accustomed to it. We had discussed my new appointment long before, and there was nothing unexpected about it for her. As for myself, to tell you the truth, I had wanted it for a long time. The new job was almost the same as the other, only more responsible, which meant I could accomplish more good in it. I had already grown accustomed to my job, and had even come to love it.

"Vera was weeping torrents.

"'What's the matter with you?' I said, even becoming angry. 'Please tell me.'

"Through the sobbing I suddenly heard: 'If you only knew how unhappy I am. There's nothing I can tell you! Oh, I'm so unhappy!'

"You know, I was shocked! Of course, I thought, she had fallen in love with Stoletov! That was indeed a nice thing for me! Here I was worrying myself about gossip, whereas it was a far more serious problem, and one I hadn't even thought about.

"You know, I loved her deeply. And a loving husband, no matter what convictions he may hold, feels in the first moments after such a disclosure nothing but pain and anger. One must wait for that first moment to pass. Luckily, I have the ability to remain silent; and then later reason, will, and respect for another's personality awaken within me.

"We proceeded silently, isolated from each other; the moon showed through the clouds. Vera had by now stopped sobbing and was barely weeping. I felt very depressed; however, I thought for a minute and said:

"'Vera! I am a human being and you are a human being. Let's talk like two people. You are not my slave, remember. If you have come to love someone seriously, then tell me. Can it be that you don't know me? I love you—but above everything else I value personal human freedom. I will agree to a divorce.'

"We had already reached the porch of our house. Vera entered first. She knocked on the door, and then turned toward me; I saw how her eyes sparkled with surprise from under her black lace kerchief. She didn't have time to reply, for the door opened at that moment and the candle light illumined us. Silently, we ascended the stairs. I was displeased both with the candle light and with Vera's silence. She undressed without a word and then went into the bedroom. When I entered, she was sitting in a white gown, sad and quiet, at her dressing table.

"However difficult it was, I wanted to begin our conversation once more, but she anticipated me:

"'Here is what I will tell you, my dear friend, Ivan Vasilyevich.' (It was the first time she had addressed me this way.) 'You consider me to be more stupid than I am. I know you well, and I know your convictions also; think, if I had fallen in love with Stoletov—what would I have to be unhappy about? You would have given me a divorce; well, you would have grieved for a little while, but soon you would have calmed down, because you would have acted according to your convictions. But the fact is, I haven't fallen in love with anyone, I am not going to leave you, and I have no place to go.'

"She said all this without looking up. I was terribly happy, I even held out my arms to her.

"'Vera!' I cried to her. 'Vera, my dear! Please, forgive me! What were you crying for? What are you unhappy about?'

"She neither looked up nor moved.

"'You won't understand this, Ivan Vasilyevich. I am suffocating; it's disgusting.'

"'You are not cheerful? And here you went to Moscow . . .'

"She sprang up. I looked, and again there were tears in her eyes.

"'Not happy! And do you think that this gaiety is important to me? It is like vile, dirty vodka! And not even vodka, but just dirty water. For, after all, one can become drunk with vodka. It's even more suffocating than being with you . . . Yes, being with you is suffocating. Everywhere—this offensive closeness and filth.'

"I frowned a bit.

"'What exactly do you want, Vera? What is it that you don't like? What is it—romanticism, philosophy? You don't see the meaning of life, or what?'

"I got ready to reason with her in all seriousness. She was my wife, and it was my responsibility to support her in moments of doubt. In the past I had often come upon such restless minds. Many people are subject to the same experiences.'

"But the things that she began to tell me I couldn't understand at all. She kept repeating 'It's suffocating; it's suffocating.' At last she became bitter:

"'Why is it that no one loves you? Why? You're a good man and are kind to people, but when you meet a real person, he can't love you. No one can love any of you "humanists," you people who think only about "utility" and about your own nobility of thought. They feel that you are leading them into an abyss. If everyone were like you, you would all fail!'

"'Vera, come to your senses! Why are you being so unjust? When have I ever thought about myself? My faith in mankind . . .'

"'Might just as well be in an empty rubber boot.'

"I looked at her simply with horror.

"'Now you've told the truth, everything is going your way. Go ahead and enjoy it! There are others like you, with your faith in rational public welfare, in enlightenment through physics books—all of you are born like that, all of you are born with pride. Or there are the silent ones—the officers with their Moscow gaiety . . . well then, lead on, lead them all on under the cover of your great nobility! Sew God's earth into the skin of a dead ram! And you will succeed in doing it; only for a long time afterward you will all be cursed!'

"I had never seen her in such a frenzy. I no longer argued, but only tried to calm her down. I even begged her forgiveness and assured her that I understood her, although most decidedly I understood neither what was wrong with her nor where her fierce words had come from. We talked through the night. But I was by now hardly listening to her. She just repeated what she had already said—that I, in fact, believed that all was going for the better, whereas she could see that it was all turning out for the worse. In short, whatever I would say, she would state the opposite . . .

"'You, that is, the humanists,' (Imagine what a word she had invented!) 'are slowly stifling the human soul by pressing against it with the weight of your bodies. But the body needs a living soul. You have forgotten that small detail!'

"I wanted to voice my objections, when she added: 'But the soul doesn't live only by reading physics books.'

"Then I gave up. She either was trying to be original or was ill. I didn't contradict her and she seemed to calm down. She even became affectionate toward me. It was as though we were completely reconciled.

"And then the following happened: she caught a bad cold shortly after our conversation that night, and her leg began hurting her. It got worse and worse. I took her to various doctors, but there were no positive results. Then I received my appointment here in this town, and I moved her to this place while she was still ill. She became very quiet and submissive. In the summer I sent her with some of her acquaintances for a *koumiss* cure. She was ill for two years, if not longer. She suffered terribly; she had cramps in her leg and could hardly walk. The third year I took her to Moscow. There they cauterized her leg. What she went through! But after that she started to recover and to walk, with only a slight limp."

IV

"I know," continued Ivan Vasilyevich after a brief silence, "that you're going to ask me if Verochka was religious. No, she wasn't; nothing of that sort was evident in her. One couldn't reproach her with being particularly religious. Of course, she occasionally went to church, there were long church services, she received communion as was customary (we were very open in our manner of life), but to fast, to pray hypocritically or something like that—no, never! There was never anything of that sort.

"It's rather difficult, you know, for us to be carried away with the clergy. We live with the priests in a secular fashion; we are acquainted with their families, trying to be friendly to them in every possible way. On the other hand, to tell you the truth, our priests and their wives constitute the least educated section of the urban population. It seems that they're not quite equal to us—everybody feels it, they themselves most of all. This fact, of course, does them credit. You understand, I'm not speaking of their idleness—

you can judge for yourself—but of the average level of intellectual development. It's natural that academicians among the clergy, if they live in the realm of pure learning, usually become monks. If there is an intelligent man (even if he is a priest), one who understands morality and the moral significance of religion in its true historical meaning—he won't go to the village; his place is somewhere in St. Petersburg. The village doesn't interest him, although it's there that he would be most useful. We in the village get priests of our own level; and for the most part they come for bread. He will acquire a bit of learning in the town seminary, our own brother peasant, and he's ready. He will gradually learn to pasture the flock. Well versed in dogmatism and in what he's learned by rote, he will explain, if necessary, to the peasant woman, which icon of the Mother of God—of Vladimir or Kazan'—walked through the air, or to which of them the priest must offer a service for someone's lost eyesight—this he can do; what else is necessary? They understand each other, the priest and the peasants, because before the seminary they used to catch crayfish together. Such a priest doesn't philosophize, and since he is strong in his faith, he doesn't engage in heresy. Not long ago, even in our province an utterly simple little peasant was appointed priest—in his own village. It's true, he didn't have a strip of land and, although he studied in a district school, he never managed to complete his education. So he scraped together a living somehow; he was an agent for the Singer sewing machine company, and he was always travelling through the district. He became friendly with our priests and, imitating them, he engaged in a little missionary work. Certainly you know our schismatic region. There are so many schismatics here! Our priests liked him, and so they helped him out. Now he's a priest in the village, and he's doing quite well.

"In the city, of course, the priests are somewhat more educated and polished, but all the same, you know, they're of that same type. This is, of course, good for their position. It's quieter. I look at it this way: All this is normal and necessary for the future when the natural course of events will itself establish our cause.

"Here I've been speaking to you about our district. We have schismatics, and Stundists, and Molokans, and other various sects —multitudes of them; however, now there are fewer of them. Why? Do you suppose from missionary work? Not a bit of it. Which of them would our missionaries convert, and to what? Maybe some leave because of business or something of that sort, but this decrease is actually taking place according to the natural flow of events. The wind is beginning to blow from another direction. Before, they were spied upon, vigorously persecuted, and treated with caution, and this made them bristle with resistance, meaning 'We'll fight you! You will remember us!' But today—no one even cares to glance at them. I, for example, visit the district when something or other has happened. I don't even try to understand their beliefs! I ask for the sake of form: 'Are you Molokans? Old Believers? Good. Stundists? That's good, too. Just pay a small fine, and continue your religious activities if you wish.' They see, the Old Believers especially, that no one is interested in them, so all of a sudden they cool down; their belligerence evaporates. They become more attentive toward their work—and even send their children to the church school! The young boy grows up a bit; he looks around and sees that an ecclessiastical man has more time at his disposal, his position is more secure and more profitable; some of these boys may even get to the seminary. So, time takes its own course quietly and peacefully.

"Some of the sectarians, I tell you, interested me. They said, 'We are neither Molokans nor Stundists, nor Baptists.' 'Who are you then? Dukhobors?' 'No.' 'Who, then?' 'We,' they said, 'are "seekers." We,' they continued, 'are something quite different.' I, however, didn't care to look deeper. I replied that there is no such sect, and therefore I would report them as Molokans—it makes no difference whatever to me. 'But if you want to be more exact,' I said, 'go to the priest, perhaps he will be able to describe your attitudes better.' I really don't know if they ever went.

"By the way, as people—the sectarians are all right; they are even quieter and more educated than the clerics, only their reading matter is foolish. They've become all mixed up. The Dukhobors as well as the Tolstoyans are, in my opinion, abnormal, because they've appeared prematurely.

"But excuse me, I have digressed from my story. This digression wasn't irrelevant, though, since my Verochka, as she recovered a bit and we became settled in our town, gradually became interested in these beliefs. Once she even drove out with me to the village of Bezzemel'noe, just for the ride. She had a chat with the townspeople and even asked some of them to visit her. I said nothing. Even long before this she had been interested in people.

"'You, Vera, rather than merely listening to them, should read something or other to them, tell them something.'

"'What could I tell them? What could I teach them? I myself know nothing.'

"'Well, my dear, there is always something to teach the peasants.'

"She smiled.

"'You never talk to them, so don't judge what they know or don't know. Anyway, let them stay untouched by your "knowledge." They don't stifle me. Whereas you, well, you are convinced that one must live in the name of man, and yet there is this stuffiness in your life. You can't limit your life to only mankind.'

"I saw that she had begun to get irritated with me again. I had had, for a long time, but one thought concerning her. If Verochka, I thought, had had a child, none of this would have happened. But how could we adopt a child all of a sudden? However, here chance came to my aid. Vera herself got the same notion.

"Her stepsister in the provincial capital had died. She had been married to some sort of a clerk; her husband was still young. They had about five children and were living in poverty. The youngest, Andryusha, was only ten months old, and he was a sickly child as well.

"Vera returned from the town in a serious mood. Then she asked me:

"'Ivan Vasilyevich, let us take Andryusha. Let's adopt him. It doesn't matter that he's sickly. I'll nurse him back to health.'

"I was the happiest of men; however, I purposely didn't agree right away so that she wouldn't think that I only wanted to give her a toy to play with.

"She went to fetch the child. It went all right with us, although Andryusha would often fall ill. It seemed as if Verochka had spent all of her life romping with children, she loved him so much. I began to take to the child as well. We adopted him.

"Although Vera was occupied with Andryusha, her character changed little. Whenever we would converse, she would not abandon her own thoughts, all of them being contrary to mine. (She made friends with the sectarians and talked to them; however, it was still with a certain moderation.)

"Soon afterward there was a further addition to our family. My sister arrived. Although we hadn't seen each other for many years, I loved and respected her and had long before tried to persuade her to come live with us. She was older than I and, when I first started working, she was already teaching in the village. For three years following that, she didn't write to me, yet we remained close because we understood each other. She didn't come to see me while she was physically well. She was so energetic—while living in the village she learned about surgery and that sort of thing. That's the way she was. But that year she fell ill; she wasn't young anymore, and, well, she agreed to rest, to give up her post, and to stay with me. If there is sufficient strength, a man will always find some work to do.

"I also thought that Klavdia would be of some help to Verochka.

"Klavdia was older and more experienced, and a person very worthy of respect because of the excellent work she performed.

"However, I immediately noticed that she and Vera didn't take to each other. Perhaps it was because they were very different. Klavdin'ka was an elderly person, similar physically to me—large boned, although not fat, big, her face energetic, her lips compressed. Verochka, although she had grown pale and thin, was still very beautiful. She was not very tall, or fashionably dressed, but always attired carefully and somehow accurately. In every detail of appearance they differed; for example, Vera's brows were very thick, dark, and slanted. My sister was fair, and her brows were hardly even noticeable.

"And as far as character is concerned, there, too, they bore little resemblance. Verochka was easily irritated, and she would often scream, but Klavdia's tone of voice was so unemotional and restrained; it was like the beating of a hammer. I never noticed any malice in Klavdia, though there was some peevishness, a trait which must be excused in old maids. But what a marvelous person! Such energy, such forcefulness in her activities, such honesty! It was very unpleasant for me that it wasn't working out well between her and Verochka. But, it's nothing, I thought; it will turn out all right.

"Vera took care of our child; Klavdia did the housework, and she also frequented the hospital (she was acquainted with the district doctor). Klavdia didn't take care of Andryusha, though, as he was still too small.

"Even then Vera was negative toward both of us, and she would often become annoyed with Klavdia. Klavdia evidently felt sorry for me. She considered Vera hysterical, unbalanced, and immature, and one time she even told me that she noticed signs of abnormality in her. This was unpleasant for me; I loved both of them, but what could I do?"

V

"Everything, you know, followed in its own course. I was satisfied with my work, and my superiors were likewise satisfied with me—I worked as hard as I could. Even a little wheel, if it spins properly, is indispensable in the gigantic mechanism of the entire world. Hitches occur, of course, little knots, but they don't disturb the general direction; they can't impede the flow of history.

"One unpleasant incident did occur. During the cholera epidemic an additional surgeon was sent to us from the town. He was, you know, a man of the common people, from the town bourgeoisie, still young—but how surprisingly quickly everything is assimilated nowadays, if a man comes in contact with modern enlightenment! He was still somewhat crude, but of course he had only just pushed his way into the world of educated people. Only very recently had he understood what science is and begun to feel that he, an educated man, was surrounded by such ignorance. I very much liked this Kasyan Demyanych's confidence about everything. I even invited him to stay with us for a while, since there was no room at the hospital. In our town proper there wasn't one case of cholera. We had built a temporary barracks, though, and someone from the district city was lying ill there. He convalesced, and after that there were no more cases of cholera. Kasyan Demyanych, however, still lived with us, went to the barracks and to the hospital; and in his free time he took an interest in the town. Before this, he had never been away from the large provincial center.

"He got along very well with Klavdia. She would sit and talk with him for a long time, obviously taking good note of his words; Klavdin'ka was very well-read. I sometimes entered into their conversations, and at those times we would discuss a great many things.

"Only Vera was always quiet. She would be silent, and then smile ironically. I wouldn't interfere with her, for I was afraid of what she might say. Although I disapproved, she didn't avoid the peasants; yet she looked askance at Kasyan Demyanych. Whereas I felt we had to be glad that such types came; we had to forgive a lot and not turn up our noses.

"There was an important summer holiday—the dean of the cathedral was conducting the service. Vera and I had just returned from the service (we had to go there, you know, we were in the public eye; this was, in a way, an established custom), and Klavdia was waiting for us with tea in the dining room. We sat down. Kasyan Demyanych wasn't there, and he hadn't been in church. Klavdia said: 'Today Kasyan Demyanych wanted to avail himself of the occasion to speak to the people . . . You know, about measures to prevent cholera. Indeed, we lack even the most primitive notions of hygiene.'

"She didn't manage to finish what she was saying, when the door opened and in flew the town constable.

"'Your honor, a disturbance! On the square they're beating the doctor!'

"'What are you saying!' Such a thing had never happened in my district. I grabbed my uniform and cap and ran out. Where was the doctor's assistant? They informed me that he had run to the square, too.

"You have perhaps heard that, during the cholera epidemics, barracks were destroyed in some places, and even doctors were beaten up. What was to be done? Indeed, there is still a great deal of ignorance and darkness in Russia! Russia has until now been resisting the real light. Yet we must be grateful that the light has at last begun to shine. We know where it is. In our town, however, the population was of a different sort; furthermore, we had no cases of cholera, so I thought that nothing would happen. What sort of riot could take place?

"And I was right—there was no riot. We immediately arranged the trial and the punishment. We managed to calm their passions, and before half an hour had passed Kasyan Demyanych was sitting in our dining room, while Klavdia treated him to tea.

"They had succeeded, however, in giving him a huge black eye, so that his face, naturally, had acquired a terribly evil, gloomy, and fierce expression. Such barbarity can drive one to hatred; I understand this.

"Klavdin'ka sympathetically inquired: 'How did it happen? Were they drunk? What did you say to them?'

"'What did I say? Nothing in particular. I talked about cleanliness and about the role of disinfectant in times of cholera. They were able to understand.'

"'Then how did it happen?' I asked. 'Is it true that Evtikhy Ivanov was the first to strike you?'

"'The devil take him, how am I supposed to know . . . what a violent peasant. You see, I spoke to them about disinfectant, then I described to them the situation in a cholera hospital, and they listened. Only some old woman squeaked: "We should hold a service to the Mother of God!" I answered that during a cholera epidemic it is dangerous to hold church services, since they would allow the infection to spread through the crowd. They began to hoot; however, nothing happened, and I continued. Again someone shouted: "Save us, Lord!" This, to tell you the truth, irritated me considerably, and I said: "It would be better for you to be thinking about disinfectant, do you understand?" "How could we not understand," they shouted, "you believe in disinfectants rather than in God." At this point I became very angry and they began to shout: "Beat him, brothers, what kind of a doctor is he who has been sent to lure us into believing in disinfectants . . ." I began to yell myself, and then they started to hit me.'

"I was never so vexed and indignant; yet, I couldn't suppress a smile. 'A disinfectant faith! What a thing they've concocted!'

"My Verochka burst out into loud laughter. Klavdia looked at her: 'I am amazed at your laughter and thoughtlessness. Kasyan Demyanych is young and sincere, and he has suffered for his youthful, honest zeal . . .'

"'Yes,' I said. 'You don't know our people. It is still impossible to talk to them that way. You just can't come out and insult some of their superstitions. You have to sidestep a lot, carefully leading them forward, without prematurely taking away from them something that they themselves, in time, will discard.'

"'Ah yes, yes,' suddenly Vera began to speak emotionally and stood up. 'I recognize you, Ivan Vasilyevich, in these words. You lie, dissemble, and avoid these people whom you designate the "ignorant folk." Take this away, and then this, and so on. And in this way you hope to rob them entirely!'

"'Vera! Vera!' I tried to reason with her.

"'What do you mean "Vera!" I am speaking the truth. Somewhere or other you have dreamed up some kind of petty human happiness, and you self-righteously proceed by any means to shove it down the throat of the entire world! You have decided for yourselves and for others as well what everyone needs, what's right for everyone. And how has it happened that the most narrow-souled have been able to cut down the broadest? How has it happened that life, obedient to these narrow-souled ones, has arranged itself as if to please them?'

"Klavdia couldn't contain herself: 'It's your sectarians with their broad souls, apparently, who thrashed Kasyan Demyanych . . .'

"'There is nothing to get angry about,' Vera answered calmly. 'You are all so disgusting to me, with your self-satisfied, successful stupidity, that I would have left you long ago, if only . . . unfortunately, there weren't people like you, and the same situations, everywhere. Man for man, man in the name of man . . . How much scope and breadth there are in these words!'

"She burst out laughing. Klavdia, although obviously restraining herself, nevertheless hissed: 'I see that you want to jump higher than your own head.'

"'Man is created in such a way, Klavdia Vasiliyevna, that he is able to live only as long as he knows or believes that there is something higher than he. Those who have lost this necessity are dead people. Not only you and your dear brother, but perhaps one half of the world now, and even Kasyan Demyanych, are such people. The young are like shiny, red apples, but there are worms in them.'

"No one contradicted her.

"'I want to find such people,' she continued, 'who will look into life—not into death . . . Such people who will arrange their lives not for their own sake, but in the name of the One Who is higher than they.'

"Klavdia again spoke to her, and so affectionately: 'What are you waiting for then? Go on, look for them . . . Read the *Chetya-Minei.* They may even sprinkle you with holy water to free you from the evil eye.'

"Vera just glared and walked away. At the door she said:

"'I'm not going anywhere. You will bite right through everyone's veins . . . And there are millions of you approaching from everywhere. I perished long ago, but I am not sorry for myself. I am only sorry for our child.'

"Three of us remained in the room. I heard Klavdia saying to the doctor in a low voice: 'You know, she's not normal.'

"The doctor only nodded his head. Klavdia then said more loudly: 'How sorry I am for my brother! But now I am also worried about the future of their unfortunate boy.'

"It was then, for the first time, that I began to think about Andryusha."

VI

"Well, now, there's not much left; we're approaching the end of my story. Fortunately, we'll soon be leaving the forest. And from the forest to Makarikha it's only about half a *verst,* not more. How quickly it becomes dark! The sun hasn't set so very long ago, and already its afterglow can't be seen. If you're not bored with my story, I'll finish it, otherwise there won't be any time—we'll soon be arriving."

I earnestly entreated him to finish, and Ivan Vasilyevich pulled his hat down more tightly and continued his story.

"It was an extremely difficult time for me. It was hard to live with Vera. She was becoming pale and withered, and I didn't know how to help her. I tried not to say anything against her without reason, but in spite of this her irritability didn't lessen. Every trifle caused an outburst and those eternal accusations. For all of us— even for herself—life in our house was unbearable. Whereas before she had been so unassuming, now she had become almost cynical. It wasn't that she spoke rudely, just awfully unpleasantly, positively cynically. She quarrelled once, for example, with Klavdia; I listened quietly. Then she finished with her and turned to me.

"'You, Vanya,' she said, 'are a little better, since at least there is no malice in you. Do you know what you resemble? Imagine soup being served, not for dinner, but alone and when no one is hungry. Very full bowls are served on a plain table without a cloth. It's a light, bright yellow broth with big circular globs of grease, which move slowly because the broth is barely lukewarm. And not one drop of salt has been added to it; it is absolutely bland. One has to eat this soup with a little teaspoon. That's what you all are like. As for those of you who are malicious as well, it's as if someone came up and spat into the soup.'

"It was so unpleasant to listen to her that I actually got up and walked out.

"The only consolation in the house was our Andryusha. Vera would change completely when she was with him (and she spent more and more time with him). She was so good natured, and even sang songs to him. I, too, became terribly attached to the child. I dreamed of how he would grow up with me, how I would teach him, how he would enter the university . . . It's terrible, you know, the way children fill you with a thirst for life! Whatever you might say—that is real immortality!

"'Well sir, he was growing up; he would get sick occasionally, but then he would recover. He followed Vera everywhere she went. Numerous times Klavdia hinted to me, wasn't it harmful for an impressionable child to be constantly in the company of Vera, who was so nervous?

"'He can already understand. You should hear what she's teaching him! Superstitions worse than any old nanny. And three days ago when those peasants came to you for some reason or other, Vera Ivanovna invited them into her room, and they had mystical conversations about the *Chetya-Minei,* and the child was there. Really, brother, such an education isn't rational. You are an unpardonable weakling.'

"Well, I wasn't guilty of any weakness. I'm a decent and humane man, that's true; I'm very patient, but if something goes against my beliefs, I do have character. I'm saying this without boasting, and you, I think, have already arrived at your own opinion of me. Klavdia, as women do, anticipated the events, and besides she didn't love Vera, whereas Vera was still dear to me. I remained silent, although I involuntarily began to worry. And, as I said, I became terribly attached to Andryusha.

"Once during Lent we were sitting in the parlor after tea. Klavdia was reading a book; Vera came in, having just put Andryusha to bed. She took something from the table and said to me rather casually: 'Tomorrow I plan to go to mass with Andryusha. I am taking him to receive communion.'

"'Communion? No, my dear, that's absolutely unnecessary.'

"She approached calmly, sat down next to me, and frowned sternly.

"'Why? I, on the contrary, believe that it is essential for the child.'

"'Your reasoning is wrong. Remember, we even discussed this together once. First of all, Andryusha's health is important to me, not to speak of the crowding and the stuffiness in the church. Just think, they bring so many unknown children there, yet there is only one spoon . . .'

"Vera frowned even more severely.

"'Splendid! And what else?'

"'And then also, I think that so long as he cannot consciously accept or reject these rituals, they must not be thrust upon him. They must not even be discussed with him at this time, because that would be, if you like, unscrupulous coercion. When he grows up, his reason will tell him what is to be done. Then, he will have his own will.'

"Vera didn't say a word. She just silently stared at me.

"'You have let the nurse go, and this is fine. I beg you,' I added firmly, 'not to discuss anything of this kind with the child. If necessary, be content just to give him the most simple and brief explanation.'

"I must confess that, knowing her whimsical thoughts and lack of restraint, I expected a fit of anger from her, but she continued to stare at me and suddenly said, with an ironical smile:

"'I understand you. Only one thing is not clear to me: why do you yourself go to church and receive communion? Does that mean that your reason tells you that it's necessary?'

"I was already angry; however, I restrained myself.

"'You do understand, Vera, that for me it's a matter of conscience. Every adult who happens to be in a church may, in his soul, pray in whatever manner he desires. Only he must not offend his neighbor with the demand that he convert to his religion. Finally, one must understand and pay attention to the fact that there is a period of childhood in the life of mankind . . .'

"'Splendid,' Vera interrupted. 'I am not concerned with you. However, you said "childhood." If what you have said is true for children (let it stand according to your words!), then why do you hinder them from going to church—the real children who need this nourishment in order to grow? Is that not coercion? If we have something, even if it's very little—the tiniest thing—why shouldn't we give it to the child? Place a spark in him—and it may flare up. As for the compulsory ignorance to which you would doom my son . . .'

"'He's mine, too. Vera, don't keep harping on it, and please don't try to catch me with your feminine tricks. It will also be futile to attempt to dissuade me in any way. You understand my words very well, so now let's please end this unpleasant conversation.'

"Perhaps I was cruel. Here Klavdia interfered again:

"'Why do you worry, Vera Ivanovna? The boy will enter a high school, and he will learn everything in due time. Indeed, to stimulate his oversensitive impressionability, to influence his fantasy while he is still so nervous—this would be to prepare him for a less than enviable future. I am convinced that my brother will put an end to it.'

"I had never before seen Vera in such a state! She jumped up, very pale, almost terrifying. She wanted to speak—but she was panting.

"'You . . . you . . . it is not enough that you have ruined me . . . In addition, you want to ruin my child as well . . . To deprive him of everything which is dear in one's childhood . . . Of that which enables a man to remain spiritually alive throughout his life . . . You will gnaw through his veins in no time . . . Oh, you godless, godless people!'

"I firmly took her by the hand.

"'Calm down, Vera. Come to your senses,' I said almost severely. 'Everything has its limits.'

"She pulled her hand away, turned to me, and spoke quickly, almost imploringly:

"'Tell me, Vanya, it was a joke, wasn't it? You obviously don't understand it yourself—but you do believe me a little, don't you? You do believe that I wish Andryusha no evil? You won't decide what I should tell him and what I shouldn't? Certainly you know me—have I ever been a bigot? Or dishonest? Or hypocritical? Vanya, Vanya, do forgive me if I was concerned with myself, if I was angry with you . . . what do I matter? It's Andryusha I'm worried about now. Leave him to me, Vanya!'

"I cannot tell you how I pitied her. But I was concerned about the child, seeing her in such a frenzy, and I understood that I could not, had no right, to yield anything to her just at that moment.

"'My convictions, Vera, are unshakable. Remember that Andryusha is also my son. I have no human right to abandon him to the will of such a whimsical and abnormal woman as you . . . no matter how much I love you. Do you hear me?'

"This time she didn't even pull her hand away. She only raised her eyes to me and then fell silent. I began to think that all had resolved itself and that she had come to her senses somewhat. But, no, she gave a kind of rigid laugh and quickly left the room.

"The next day she didn't take Andryusha to the church. A few days later, however, Klavdia told me that she still insisted on her desire, and that morning I had to stop them on the threshold almost by force. Such a mode of life developed in our family that I can't even describe it; besides, that would take a long time and would be very painful. Finally, hideous scenes began taking place, even in front of the child. I was forced to tell Vera that I would send Andryusha away if she didn't calm down. Klavdia, after a great deal of trouble, obtained permission to open something like a kindergarten or a small school in our town; she had even found a suitable location. Later on I really planned to send Andryusha there, but for the time being I wanted only to scare Vera. For indeed, it was impossible to continue living like that. We were all exhausted, and Andryusha wept every day.

"Vera listened to me calmly.

"'Yes,' she said, 'it is time to put an end to it. It is impossible to live this way. I am tired.'

"She slowly walked to the bedroom and lay down. From that day on we didn't hear a word from her. Andryusha would call her—she seemed not to hear him.

"'Vera,' I would say to her, 'Do go to him.'

"'Why? I myself can see that I am harmful to him.'

"There was no longer any clamor in the house, but the atmosphere, instead of being better for that, was even worse. The child was weeping, walking around pale and ill.

"'Mama is dying. Mama needs some medicine.'

"Later, it seemed that by force of habit everything had settled down—but what a life it was! Vera would be in bed until dark, as if constantly thinking about something. Although there was little reason for hope, I nevertheless hoped that she would change her mind. If not, then what next—I didn't know myself. All of us were exhausted. Klavdia's complexion had become jaundiced; Andryusha tossed in his bed every night, and his disposition began to deteriorate. The atmosphere in our house, you know, was just as if there were a corpse there.

"One evening Klavdia and I were sitting in the drawing room with only one candle, in silence. We would spend hours like that. Suddenly the door squeaked. It was Vera.

"I was surprised. I looked at her—and remained silent.

"She sat beside me, at the table. How she had changed! She had aged ten years and her expression was unpleasant.

"'Are you well, Verochka?' I inquired. I involuntarily posed the question, seeing her in this condition.

"'Not very well.'

"Klavdia cut in: 'You should undergo treatment, Vera Ivanovna. Perhaps you ought to go for a *koumiss* cure in the summer.'

"I am convinced that she meant well. But Vera, all of a sudden, replied in her old way: 'Be quiet, you!'

"Klavdia, in order to avoid a quarrel, lowered her eyes to her needle work and only grumbled through her teeth: 'Mad woman!'

"I had hoped that Vera hadn't heard it—but she had and, as if suddenly rejoicing, she began to talk quickly and excitedly: 'Yes, yes, I am mad . . . that is, I am not really mad, but my nerves are shattered . . . Isn't it so, Vanya?'

"'Vera, do calm down.'

"'I am calm now, but I am ill. I feel that I am ill. I cannot control myself. I would like to undergo some treatment. I have come to inform you of that.'

"'What, do you wish me to send at once for Fyodor Ivanovich?'

"'No, what's the matter with you! I would like to go to a specialist in the provincial capital. Yes, to Lazarevsky . . .'

"'To Lazarevsky? But isn't his specialty . . . nervous disorders?'

"'Yes, he is a psychiatrist. He has his own hospital. He has other patients. I want to join them.'

"'Vera, what's wrong with you?'

"Suddenly she frightened me.

"'I am ill, really. Take me there tomorrow, Ivan Vasilyevich. I would like to rest, to undergo a treatment.'

"You know, I laughed at this, although I didn't feel at all like laughing.

"'Do you really want to be committed to a mental institution?'

"I was joking, but she looked at me so seriously and imploringly and said in a low voice: 'I beg you, Vanya, do take me to the doctor. If I go and stay there for a while—I will feel more at ease. Obviously, I must go away somewhere, but where?'

"And what do you think? In that quiet tone she persuaded me to take her on the following day to the provincial capital. Of course, I didn't doubt for one second that they wouldn't keep her in the clinic, since she was completely healthy. I thought that we would have a nice drive, and that the doctors would prescribe some regimen or other for her. I was even glad. She took leave of Andryusha indifferently, as if she were dead. The farewell was very short, but, nevertheless, I was amazed. She didn't even say good-bye to Klavdia, which was unpleasant for my sister.

"Vera remained silent throughout the journey, no matter how much I tried to entertain her. When we arrived, it was already night; she was tired. We stopped in a hotel, and the following day I took her to the hospital. Not just one, but three doctors examined her. They questioned her; she was silent. She was so stubborn in her silence that even I was surprised. However little it had been, she had spoken with me in the morning. They began to question me—but what could I tell them? I told them only that she had complained of a nervous disorder. Then they began to examine her. She started to scream, but didn't say a word.

"One of the doctors took me into another room and asked me again if there had been fits. What kind of fits? No, there weren't any, I answered.

"'Why, then, did you bring her here?'

"'I have brought her because she herself wanted it.'

"Again they began to ask me various questions. You know, I'm not an eloquent man in the first place, but then I became simply tongue-tied. As soon as I would begin to speak, I would see that I was babbling some kind of nonsense, that I was unable to explain what kind of illness it was, its cause, how it had begun, or even its manifestations. After all, I couldn't tell them all about our daily life as I'm telling you now! Moreover, from their scientific point of view, that would have been perhaps unsatisfactory.

"They called me back into the first room. Vera was standing by the window, without her hat and with her back to me. The doctor who had been with her said to me in an extremely gentle voice:

"'Vera Ivanovna has agreed to live here and undergo some treatment. Isn't that so?'

"Vera answered, without turning: 'Yes, I will stay here.'

"I stood with my mouth agape, but they immediately took me away.

"'Don't irritate the patient,' they said. 'Everything has gone so well.'

"I hastened to ask them questions—they told me a muddle of things, namely, that this was obvious, that that was definite, and that she was sensitive; they even spoke about fits . . . I simply lost my head and became completely confused. I asked them when she would recover. But they again began telling me various things— that her pupils had dilated and that something else was abnormal . . . For the time being, they continued, nothing could be determined; they would be able to say more later, and an improvement could come either quickly or more slowly.

"I simply can't remember how I managed to make arrangements for a room for her and all the rest of it. I must admit that all of this was a great surprise to me. The doctors thought that I was merely grief stricken. Of course, how could they guess that, while taking her to the psychiatric hospital, I had never expected that they would keep her there? They were very sympathetic toward me and gave me some hope. They even congratulated me on the fact that everything had proceeded so well. They were very polite.

"I wanted to say good-bye to her, but they didn't allow it.

"Yes, sir, that's how I left her there. As I was going home from the provincial capital, I regained my senses a little, came to myself. Of course, I'm not a doctor, and Vera had been so close to me all the time—it was difficult for me to see how her illness had originated and how it had been developing. But the eye of the specialist sees all the symptoms at once. The treatment, even a certain regimen, would bring nothing but good to a shattered, sick organism . . ."

Ivan Vasilyevich fell silent for a moment. I looked at him and asked: "Well, do you see her often?"

"I? How should I answer your question? I go there often—sometimes as much as twice a month. But since that day I have actually seen her only once, shortly after I had taken her to the hospital. She came out to a private reception room to see me. (The doctors are such nice people! And the hospital is beautiful and clean!) She came out, emaciated, small, limping as usual, dressed in a gray robe, her hair cut short. She was very pale except for her black eyebrows. Her gaze—and here even I noticed it—was abnormal. She was looking straight at me, yet as if she didn't see me at all.

"She sat down and folded her hands.

"'Vera,' I said to her, 'do you want to go home?'

"She answered quietly and in a low voice: 'No, Ivan Vasilyevich, I will not go. I am all right here.'

"'What's good about this place? You'll feel better at home. Let's go.'

"I was thinking: 'If the doctors allow me to take her home, I will try to take her. What will happen then?'

"She said once more: 'No, I will not go home. It is more peaceful here.'

"I even became angry.

"'With the insane people?'

"To that she answered: 'Isn't it all the same? It's more peaceful for me to be with them. Don't disturb me or yourself, and don't come to see me. I won't recover soon. They won't let me go home—and why should you want me home? It's true that you have to pay for me here . . . But at home I would also cost you something.'

65

"'Vera,' I retorted, 'you don't even ask about Andryusha!'

"She stood up.

"'What is there to say about that? Good-bye, Ivan Vasilyevich. Don't disturb me. Indeed, I feel fine here.'

"She left. I wanted to see the doctor, but he wasn't in. I asked the nurses about her, but they would only say: 'She is all right and quiet.'

"Imagine, from that time onward she didn't want to see me even once. She would send me a message through the nurse, saying that I shouldn't worry her and that she felt fine and at peace with herself. The doctors also said the same: 'Don't trouble her if she doesn't want to see you.' I asked them if there was any improvement. Sometimes they would answer that there was some improvement; sometimes they would say that there had been an improvement, but that at present she had taken a turn for the worse. Once I asked them to let me see her through the glass door. There were several inconspicuous patients there. Vera was quietly sitting in an armchair with her hands folded on her lap. Her profile had become very sharp and her complexion was yellow, as if she were dead. Illness never adorns anyone.

"I haven't seen her since. I go there often, but I never dare to ask for a meeting with her. You know, one gets used to any grief. And already Andryusha recalls her only rarely. Although he is sickly, he is nevertheless growing up, becoming a melancholy child. I don't speak with him about Vera; I don't speak with anybody about her—only with you have I indulged in chatting . . . Of course, there are some moments when one recalls everything as it once was, and one begins to think . . ."

Suddenly he turned to me. In the approaching darkness I could hardly see his wide, pale face and his blinking eyes.

"One begins to think, and then many things again become incomprehensible. I have told you everything from the very beginning; I have tried to portray Verochka for you . . . Also the circumstances of life under which her illness developed. Perhaps it will be easier for you, an impartial listener, to form a true opinion . . . The judgment of a stranger has great value. Please tell me, how does it all appear to you? . . . What would you say? For, indeed, there are some symptoms . . . that is, is she not a mad woman?"

I looked once more at Ivan Vasilyevich's troubled and pitiful face, and I understood that he again had encountered those moments of "weakness and doubt" which he had mentioned at the outset of his story. He was expecting some words from me. I thought about how human words are sometimes needed, but how in reality their truth is unnecessary and even harmful, and I said:

"Well . . . the specialists will find out . . . Even you yourself had noticed signs of insanity in her. Anything is possible . . ."

We drove out of the forest. The hooves of the horses echoed down the even road; the bells trembled and began to ring; it grew light all around us. There remained half a *verst* to the station.

AN ORDINARY EVENT

The day passed approximately as did all other days, and Professor Akhtyrov, although very tired, hoped to continue his work in the evening after dinner, when he had rested for half an hour. He was still working on "Discussions Concerning Biology," preparing it for its third edition.

Professor Akhtyrov was a zoologist. He lectured at the main university and at the women's university, enjoying an enviable, well-earned reputation. No longer young but calm and imposing, with a thick, black beard and very pleasant, kind eyes, always confident and positive, well read, he enjoyed among the youth the reputation of an extremely honest and sympathetic person. Moreover, he had his own "convictions." He had not even exerted any effort at all to win this reputation, for he really was honest, responsive, and firm in his beliefs.

Three years ago, during the period of unrest at the university, he had had to pay a particularly high price for his firm convictions. In his honor the male students would greet him with ovations; the female students presented him with an oration. Later, everything ended well.

Now the rumor was being circulated that Akhtyrov was to suffer again. Today, when he returned home from the university (where he had not lectured, but had merely conversed with his students, who had shouted so loudly), he found a deputation from the women's university. Female students, clad in black, were sitting in a semicircle in his living room. Upon his entering the room, one of them rose and read an address. Deeply moved, he replied verbosely. Then he asked the young ladies to sit down, and they began to converse in a simple, friendly fashion. They were charming and a little shy. As always, Akhtyrov spoke with authority, cheerfully and reasonably, very progressively, and it seemed to all of them that everything he said was true and absolutely clear. Therefore, both Akhtyrov and his students were very pleased with one another.

After their departure, Akhtyrov went to yet another meeting which also pleased him in many respects, and it was only after that meeting that he finally returned home shortly before dinner.

His apartment was small and devoid of all pretension; it was located in the Petersburg Side. His family had already gathered at the table in the clean, long dining room. Akhtyrov; his wife Vera Nikolaevna; their daughter Manichka, who was ten years old; and Vladya, quite a big boy, already a student of the fourth level in the high school. He did not look his thirteen years—he was tall, lean, frail, pale, and had a small but serious face.

Akhtyrov loved his children very much, yet he never pampered them. His attitude was simple, quiet, and reasonable.

He also loved Vera Nikolaevna very much. She was a sedate and charming woman. Her face was ordinary, yet rather pleasant and youthful.

Deep in his heart, by the way, he considered her narrow minded and uneducated, incapable of understanding much, as she had not been even a student of the women's university! She was merely a graduate from an institute for girls of the gentry! Akhtyrov hardly ever talked to her. Their silence, however, neither oppressed nor worried him in the least, and they had lived together for fifteen years in enviable harmony, true peace, and prosperity. Both of them were endowed with kind, good-natured characters.

Akhtyrov had to restrain Vera Nikolaevna's occasionally excessive, ardent feeling for her children; he would chide her condescendingly. But as the years passed, he became used to her attitude—it no longer bothered him.

"Are you tired?" Vera Nikolaevna asked her husband, sitting down to dinner. "How is everything—all right?"

"Yes. Please pass me a meat pie. Why is Vladya wrapped up in that shawl?"

"He isn't feeling well. I did not allow him to go to school today."

"Well, my dear, you jump to conclusions too quickly—not allowing him to go to school and wrapping him up in a shawl! Our children are very healthy. I don't remember them ever being seriously ill. You exaggerate each illness. One of the children would catch a cold, and you would immediately start running around with the mustard plaster."

"That was a case of influenza . . ."

"If one behaves rationally, then influenza is not dangerous. Vladya is pale; his organism, however, is healthy. How do you feel, Vladya?"

"Not bad, only I am cold. And I am not hungry."

"Then don't eat if you aren't hungry. There is nothing to worry about. By tomorrow you will be all right."

They finished their dinner in silence. Akhtyrov was considering his seventeenth "Discussion," which he planned to begin tonight after a short rest. He did not manage to rest, however. There was the bell, and two students entered. Akhtyrov had a rule: always, at all times, to receive his students. He went with them to his study.

For about an hour and a half one could hear from the study the soft yet firm sound of the professor's voice. The two students' voices could not be heard.

After they had gone Akhtyrov settled down to write, and he worked into the late hours. He worked well, though, and he was pleased with what he had written.

The next day Vera Nikolaevna informed him that Vladya was getting worse and that she had sent for a doctor. They had found out that week that Vladya had pleurisy; therefore, in addition to their family doctor, another one, a professor with whom Akhtyrov was on very friendly terms, was invited to treat Vladya.

After several consultations with the family doctor and detailed instructions to Vera Nikolaevna, the professor would usually go to Akhtyrov's study. If Akhtyrov was at home, the professor would advise him that Vladya's illness was serious and lingering. Then he would light up a cigar, and together they would discuss various social problems of the day, as the doctor was not just a narrow-minded specialist.

Akhtyrov had known for a long time that Vladya was seriously ill, that he would require serious treatment, and that patience was needed. Akhtyrov was displeased with all that; also he grieved because he felt sorry for his boy. Every day, whenever he happened to have some free time, he would enter the patient's room, ask his wife several questions, and sit down at Vladya's bedside.

The light in Vladya's room was dim; the room smelled of something warm, moist, and acrid. Vera Nikolaevna moved noiselessly, and the old nurse, Avdotyushka, puttered about.

Akhtyrov wanted to hire a nurse, but Vera Nikolaevna objected—Avdotyushka was still a very brisk, strong, old woman. Furthermore, it was she who had brought up Vera Nikolaevna and their two children. Vladya loved her, whereas a stranger might be irksome to him.

Sitting at Vladya's bedside, Akhtyrov could see a small, thin, birdlike face looking up from the pillows, its dim eyes contracted in pain. Vladya's face was so thin that it was covered with long wrinkles, like that of an old man.

Vladya moaned almost all the time. If he did say anything, it was always one and the same thing:

"Oh, mama, oh, oh, I am so, so tired . . . Oh, how tired. I am tired . . . My side is tired . . ."

Sometimes his eyes would clear up; then he would recognize his father and turn his head toward him a little:

"Daddy . . . you?"

He would try to smile, an effort which would deepen the wrinkles gathering around his mouth. Then his eyes would close again, and he would resume his faint moaning.

Akhtyrov would leave Vladya's bedroom with an unpleasant, painful, and annoying feeling. He was sick at heart with pity for his only son. If only they would give him some injections! But then he trusted the professor completely.

How long would it all last? Everything had been turned upsidedown at home; his wife was nervous and overtired, and Manichka seemed to have been lost in the shuffle, somehow.

Returning from his lectures, Akhtyrov would inquire every day: "Is he better today?"

And every day he heard: "He is the same."

Finally he even got used to this answer, just as he had become used to the dim light in Vladya's bedroom, to the boy's irregular breathing, and to his somewhat hoarse moaning.

Many other events were taking place at the same time—the unrest at the university continued, even though the lectures had resumed; therefore, Akhtyrov was especially busy. At this time he was also very preoccupied with his brochure concerning vitalism, which was to appear without fail by Easter. It was already February.

Akhtyrov's students would come to see him almost every day, and he always received them.

One day, on the way home, he met three of his students on his staircase. Together, they entered the apartment which Akhtyrov opened with his key, and he took his guests directly to the study.

These students had come to see Akhtyrov because of his last lecture about the theory of evolution, Darwinism. That lecture, with its extremely scientific nature, was received with animation and acclaim. The students hoped to obtain some additional information in a private discussion with the professor.

Immediately and very willingly, Akhtyrov began to discuss the subject. Actually, he merely reiterated what he had already said, yet his voice was so confident, rich, slow, and clear that it seemed to the students, as well as to Akhtyrov himself, that he was further augmenting and developing the thought which, with its entire scientific value and thus with a certain complexity, was at the same time unusually critical, vitally real, and progressive.

The students smoked, as did Akhtyrov. The blue, heavy smoke filled the room. Akhtyrov's slow, booming voice modulated rhythmically beneath this layer of smoke. The words and sentences especially emphasized by the professor sprang out and floated above the smoke still more clearly and firmly.

". . . the biogenetical law . . ." "The problem of adaptability and non-adaptability of distinct individuals . . ." "The change of functions . . ." "Teleology and causality as the principles of explanation
. . ."

The door of the study suddenly opened. Akhtyrov looked up through his glasses and through the smoke in the room, unpleasantly surprised, to see who had disturbed him. He could not immediately discern that it was his wife who had entered his study. She never entered his room when he had students with him.

She said loudly to Akhtyrov, without looking at the students: "Come here."

And she immediately left, having shut the door. Still more displeased and bewildered, Akhtyrov went to the door.

"Pardon me, gentlemen. I'll be back in a minute."

His wife was waiting for him just outside the door. Before Akhtyrov could ask her, "What do you want?" or "What's the meaning of this?" she spoke.

"Vladya is dying," she said in a calm and not particularly low voice. "Let's go to him."

"What?" Akhtyrov said with overwhelming consternation which darkened his mind. "What—Vladya?"

"He is dying," his wife repeated. "Come quickly."

She left him and went down the corridor.

Akhtyrov felt his knees begin to tremble with an inane, quick quivering from his bewilderment and an obtuse, indefinite fear. What did she say? He felt himself getting angry and wanting to laugh simultaneously. Of course, he knew that Vladya was seriously ill. Seriously, that is, dangerously. Dangerously . . . that is, in danger for his life. Akhtyrov had reiterated these words for himself earlier, and he had also heard them from the doctor. Not even once, however, had he thought about Vladya's death. And all of a sudden she had said, "He is dying." What was that? How could it be?

He re-entered his study, trembling with a blind, bewildering fear, but he controlled himself somewhat, having taken heart at the sight of the students' faces so familiar to him, at the blue stripes of the smoke so habitual to him—after all, everything was exactly as it had been five minutes earlier, when life was taking its normal and usual course. Nevertheless, he said, with a special, kind, apologetic, and even confused smile:

"Pardon me, gentlemen . . . I must interrupt our interesting discussion . . . My son . . . He is not well . . . Rather ill . . . I must go to him."

The students immediately rose and said good-bye, trying not to make any noise, out of sympathy for the professor. Akhtyrov's smile was still the same as he escorted them to the door, but his knees continued to tremble.

After the students had left, he went on tiptoe to Vladya's bedroom. He had no doubt that there was some misunderstanding, yet at the door he was again frightened . . . Not on account of Vladya—he was simply possessed by a terrible fear.

Gently he opened the door and entered the room. He expected to see a faint candle and perhaps several doctors at Vladya's bedside. But there was no one there, with the exception of his wife and Avdotyushka, and the lamp on the table was burning brightly; it didn't even have a lampshade.

The bed stood in the middle of the room, its head facing the wall. Something small, helpless, and dark was lying on the pillows, from which there came a modulating, slow death-rattle. His wife was standing at the foot of the bed, silently, motionlessly, doing nothing, but looking at the dark spot whence came the wheeze.

Akhtyrov went up to her and touched her sleeve.

She immediately turned to him and, when he began to whisper something, she led him to the furthest corner of the room.

"Is he worse then?" Akhtyrov whispered. "When? We must send for a doctor . . ."

His wife answered him in a very low voice, but not whispering: "The doctors were here. Vasil'tsev left just before you came in. He wanted to stay, but I asked him to leave. Why should he be here? We'll stay. Nothing can be done. It is the agony of death."

"What do you mean . . . agony?"

"He was very bad last night. There was very little hope. I wanted to tell you about it this morning . . . You left. Then, when the last rites were being administered, he regained consciousness . . ."

"The last rites?"

"Yes, and he was so happy. After the last rites the agony set in. Come close to him, don't be afraid, he is unconscious. He no longer suffers!"

She took his hand, the hand of this tall, confused, numbed man, and led him to the boy's bed. Akhtyrov obeyed her like a child, thinking nothing, only afraid again, and trembling. Vera Nikolaevna seemed quite a different person to him—grown up, all-knowing, and all-understanding, whereas he himself was small, helpless, and merely obedient.

At the bed, he could not master his blind terror and could not look at that thing which had before been Vladya, at that very spot precisely where this shocking and bewildering terror was taking place. Akhtyrov sat down on a chair and covered his eyes with his hand. There was the same death-rattle, only slower and calmer. Vera Nikolaevna was standing motionlessly, as quietly as if she were not present at all. From under his hand Akhtyrov could see the nurse Avdotyushka, who was kneeling and who at times, very silently, even without a sigh, crossed herself and bowed. Her large shadow bent rhythmically and straightened out again on the wall.

Then Akhtyrov felt Vera Nikolaevna bend over him and embrace his head with quiet but imperious affection.

"Don't cry, dear, don't," she whispered. "Don't. It's God's will. He is relieved of his pain now. Don't cry, dear."

Her words were so simple, and her voice was so quiet that Akhtyrov shrivelled again, as it were, under this voice, like a tormented child who understands nothing.

He was not aware of how much time had elapsed. He regained his consciousness when there was no longer any wheezing. Vera Nikolaevna went to the head of the bed and bent over it . . . Then she knelt and pressed her head against the blanket.

Avdotyushka, the nurse, said loudly: "Lord, takest thou . . ."

Akhtyrov did not hear the rest, he jumped up and, trying not to look at the bed even inadvertently, ran out.

In the dining room he suddenly caught sight of Manichka, pale, quiet, with large eyes.

She rushed to him.

"Daddy! Daddy! You . . ."

But he jumped aside from her, for she too seemed frightful to him; everyone seemed frightful to him. He walked away briskly, as if running away, to his study. There he lay down on the divan and covered his face with a cushion, bewildered like a frightened animal.

No one had ever died in Akhtyrov's family throughout his whole, long life. He could not remember his father, but his mother was still alive and lived in the provinces with her married sister. Akhtyrov had witnessed such an ordinary event as death only from a distance while attending various requiems and funerals. Perhaps in the depths of his soul he had a firm, completely unconscious conviction that nothing of that kind could ever happen to him or to a member of his family. It could only happen to others.

When his apartment filled with the unknown people, their whispers, the smell of incense, and when morning and night the priests offered requiem masses, Akhtyrov thought that it was not his own apartment, but somebody else's, and that he had to get away somewhere.

But he could not leave; he could not even show his fear. On the contrary, he felt that he had to do something, but what—he did not know.

During the requiem he stood with a candle in his hand, in the corner, trying all the time not to look there where lay the main cause of his trembling knees, frightening and bewildering.

Frightening . . . but why? If that was Vladya, then where was he now and what was he like now? Better not to look at him. Impossible to look at him.

Vera Nikolaevna, still the same, that is, all-knowing, mature, and silent, approached him several times, embraced him, weeping silently and deeply as if not noticing it herself. Then Akhtyrov watched as she, confidently, simply, and efficiently, went up to the table, changing something here and rearranging something there, and then stood close to it, motionless.

He even wept once, without, however, experiencing any grief. He was completely overwhelmed, bewildered, and afraid.

After the strangers had departed, only that frightening thing and a nun who read prayers in a low, masculine voice remained in the hall.

Vera Nikolaevna sat in the hall by herself for a long time; the nurse would come in, whisper something loudly, bow down, and cross herself in the corner of the room.

It was hot and smoky from the candles, and it was cloudy with the blue incense. It seemed to Akhtyrov that he too had to stay, and he did stay, sitting beside Vera Nikolaevna on the divan which had been pushed aside, and he again covered his eyes with his hand, as he now had been doing.

He also feared the nun, for she too was from the incomprehensible world which had suddenly burst into his life, changing everything in it. The words which the nun was reading were also from that incomprehensible world, unusual, strange, and very frightening, even though he could not understand them at all.

". . . Thou art my support and my stronghold, my God, in Whom I trust," the low voice droned, solemnly and monotonously. "It is He that rescues me from every treacherous snare, from every whisper of harm. Sheltered under His arms, under His wings nestling, thou art safe. . . . Nothing shalt thou have to fear from nightly terrors, from the arrow that flies by daylight, from the trouble that infests the darkness . . ." [Psalms 90:1–7]

Akhtyrov ceased listening. After all, it was impossible to listen for very long, because this droning of words seemed to become a single, menacing roar. The breathing of the candles was hot and fragrant in the blue mist, and it seemed at times, because of the trembling flame, that something was trembling, stirring under the heavy gold of the hearse-cloth. The shroud was covered with cut flowers which, slain by the incense, no longer exuded any fragrance.

The black nun turned the page. She coughed and resumed her reading in a voice still lower, more hollow, and even more frightening: ". . . Except the Lord build the house, they labor in vain that build it: except the Lord keep the city, the watchman waketh but in vain. It is vain for you that rise up early, and so late take rest, and eat the bread of toil: for so He giveth unto His beloved sleep. Lo, children are an heritage of the Lord: and the fruit of the womb is His reward . . ." [Psalms 127:1–3]

"Perhaps God really does exist . . ." Akhtyrov thought; that is, he did not really think, but simply said these words to himself, without any feeling, in an unaccustomed and cowardly manner. This idea, however, left him immediately and never returned again.

Vera Nikolaevna, who had been sitting quietly beside him, suddenly turned her narrow, tense face with its clear, swollen eyes toward him, embraced his shoulders as she often did, and whispered:

"Go to him, dear. Go there with me. Look how handsome our boy is! He is so happy now! Don't grieve so. Go to him, don't be afraid—he is happy."

He rose obediently and humbly after her, and she, still embracing him, led him up to Vladya. Akhtyrov resigned himself silently—she wanted him to look at Vladya, therefore he had to comply with her wish; it was impossible not to do so. And so he looked at Vladya.

The boy was lying there, so pleasant and light; he no longer had any wrinkles on his face, which was now so all-knowing. In this respect he resembled his mother, whose face now also appeared all-knowing—through its tormented, living features.

After having looked at the dead face, Akhtyrov was no less afraid, and it was still with fear, curiosity, bewilderment, and incomprehensibility that he peered at it. The most incomprehensible thing was the fact that it was indeed Vladya and that he was able to recognize him. Akhtyrov's fear, rather than passing away, now flowed into an excruciating feeling of pity toward his son, as well as

for himself who had lost his son. Akhtyrov no longer loved him—
who was there to be loved? Therefore, this biting pity was more
insufferable, and beside this pity which would not leave him stood
his senseless, completely dark, degrading fear.

Vera Nikolaevna caressed Vladya's hair tenderly, as if he were
alive, and she straightened his small, weak, not yet stiffened hands.
In her movements Akhtyrov again saw something simple, necessary, all-knowing. It was almost frightening in her, just as it was in
this clean, nice boy lying so silently, heavily, looking as though he
understood the significance of death.

Akhtyrov bent clumsily over the golden shroud which felt cold to
him and which scratched his nose—he bent over and began to
weep, fogging his glasses.

The nun continued to read: "Lord, my enlightenment and my
Saviour, before Whom I stand in awe. Lord, protector of my life,
from Whom I fear . . ."

But Akhtyrov no longer heard anything; he no longer remembered God—he only wept, shedding stinging, shameful tears,
fogging his glasses.

Vera Nikolaevna, again affectionately and with pity, embraced
his shoulders and led him out.

Then Vladya was buried. Many strangers, acquaintances, and
others came. At the funeral everything was simple, noisy. In the
apartment everything had been arranged as it was before, but a
strange, variegated smell, alien to the apartment, reminding him of
the fear and the impossibility of what had taken place, was percep-
tible for a long time after.

Akhtyrov did not receive any visitors; he went nowhere and did
not work. Timid and bewildered, he just kept looking at his wife,
who was doing the same things she had done before, namely,
taking care of dinner and Manichka's coat. Only her voice was
lower.

Fortunately, the lectures at the university were over—Akhtyrov
could stay at home.

By now he was already ashamed of his childish behavior and
wished to go somewhere. He planned to take a trip to Kiev, to visit
his mother, but for some reason or other he was afraid to leave
his wife, Manichka, and their apartment alone. So he did not go
away.

Gradually, toward spring, he began to see some of his close acquaintances again. Once he happened to open his unfinished manuscript "Discussions Concerning Biology." He reread it and got carried away. His former clear, confident thoughts peeped out and gladdened him. That unnecessary, frightening, absurd, and alien world began to fade away.

It receded.

And then, well, then it sank completely into oblivion.

THE DOOR

Tishin, a third-year student, a small, dry little man with a pleasant, serious face, was considered intelligent. Indeed, he was intelligent, talented, and persistent. He loved science, without any pedantry, affectionately, faithfully. He had already thought of writing a book on the philosophy of history. "But it has to be alive, that's what's important! I will cover a wide range, unlike those dried-up scholars who outdo themselves with their own books; my book will be alive, reasonable, firm, and vibrant. Do you understand?" he insisted to his best friend Moshin.

To this, Moshin said, "Hmm," and screwed up his nose. Indeed, it was possible that this was just a daydream. But Tishin worked so ardently and seriously; he loved his work so sincerely that quite possibly it wasn't just a dream.

Those who were not interested in his dreams and never spoke with him about anything knew Tishin from a different point of view, and respected him as a good friend with "honorable" but "extreme" convictions. Something would barely get started at the university, and the two friends—Tishin, thin and dry, and Moshin, a tall, husky lad with black eyebrows (also very efficient and seriously studious)—were there right away. They always supported the most energetic, radical decisions, yelling themselves hoarse at their desks until they forgot themselves; and once Tishin paid for this and almost lost a year at school. A lot of important things turned out well, yet because of some nonsense he had to pay for it. Anyway, whenever he would get up on the desk and start to shout, important and unimportant seemed to be one and the same to him.

Tishin entered the long, resounding university corridor. All the way to the university he had been so busy with the new, unexpected idea which had just occurred to him, pertaining to the French Revolution, that he failed to see the horse trams running at him, and several times he tripped in the thawing puddles. It seemed to him that his new thought was important, and simple, and so clear and alive that it could immediately become essential and drastically change much, if not everything. Only a thought could overturn, destroy, and create anew. Tishin, by the way, was modest and insecure; he understood that perhaps he was mistaken and that his thought was possibly naïve, but that in any case it was necessary to work it out and suffer over it. Right now he wanted only to convey it to Moshin.

"Nevertheless, it's something," it occurred to him. "Well, second class, incomplete—let's grant it! But it should still have some value. Or am I so naïve? There are no gross scientific errors here, it's a fact."

In the corridor, where they had not yet lit the lamps, it was gloomy from the wet, yellow day which peered in through the large windows. Students were running along this corridor in the twilight; a din of modulating exclamations hung under the ceiling, and Tishin understood right away that something was happening, something was in the works. His chest swelled familiarly and pleasantly. He felt as if he had been lifted lightly and was soaring upward, and he went up to where the others were, walking quickly at first; then, without even noticing it himself, he started running.

From a distance, he saw that a crowd was gathering in one place, near the partially glass door of the auditorium. Tishin couldn't even remember which auditorium it was, so easily did all of his thoughts suddenly fly away.

The crowd became dense; it increased, darkened, thickened, and grew incensed and compact.

Tishin became one with it. He joined in the ranks, became inseparable from it, and was rooted in its center, so that the people crowded not only in front of him, but also behind him, breathing and shouting at the back of his neck.

"What is this? What's going on?" Tishin hollered, not to anyone in particular, catching at that time separate cries in the waves of rumbling voices.

". . . What is this? . . ."

". . . What for? . . ."

". . . It's locked . . ."

". . . They've locked it . . ."

". . . Gentlemen, gentlemen, do you hear?"

". . . They've locked it . . ."

". . . Devil knows what's going on!"

". . . Who's been locked up?"

". . . When were they locked up? Long ago?"

". . . Why did they lock them up?"

". . . Who? Very many?"
". . . Whoever it might be! It's a fact!"
". . . Gentlemen! Friends!"
". . . It's locked . . ."
". . . They've locked it . . ."
". . . Open it up . . ."
". . . It's all the same who! Outrage! Gentlemen! Now, fellows!"

Three steps away, Tishin saw the back of Moshin's neck, red and sweaty. Moshin, too, was yelling something and pushing the people in front of him, who were pressing against the huge door. From the distant rows and from the crowd which was again increasing, still other voices could be heard: "What? For what? Who?" But those closer up were all crying: "It's locked! They've locked it! Outrage!" and they kept on forcing their way forward. Tishin was yelling, too; the fiery, confused, happy, strong wave deluged him completely; it was as if he couldn't feel his own body, small and heavy—it felt as if it were huge, light, strong, almost winged. It was not thinking, not judging, not seeing—it was just strong.

He didn't know if he had just wanted to hear it or if they had actually shouted that they had to break down the door; he felt that he and all the others had decided to do so and that their decision was already being accomplished. The din of shouts was suddenly drowned in song—perhaps with words, perhaps without. Tishin also sang and with all his might pushed toward the door itself, and saw Moshin also forcing his way through, flailing his arms, pushing, and shouting in his bass voice, "Heave-ho! Heave-ho!"

The door shook, bent, and gave way; the glass, screeching piercingly, flew out and shattered.

The "individualists" ran on both sides. One had a pince-nez dangling on a cord, and it bounced around as he ran.

"Gentlemen, gentlemen! This is a misunderstanding, an unfortunate coincidence! The auditorium will be opened right away . . . Gentlemen . . ."

But the screeching voices were drowned in a new wave of song, clear and strong—perhaps with words, perhaps without . . .

The two friends were walking from the university along the riverbank; it had already grown dark, and greenish-yellow fires lit up the puddles.

"What is this?" said Tishin in a strange, weak voice. "Why the devil did we break the door down? Indeed, considering it reasonably, what the devil did we smash it down for?"

Moshin, having pushed his cap on the back of his head, tried not to take such big steps for his friend.

"Hm . . . Yes. Considering it reasonably, of course. There was no need whatsoever. However, my friend, one does not start thinking about something once it's been set in motion. That's precisely why it is in motion. What's it to you? We broke the door, and it wasn't the end of the world. And we will again."

"So we're going to break down all the doors? No, Moshin, tell me this. Here, for instance, we are talking together right now; we indeed understand what needs to be done, and why, and how. Or when I am alone . . . Just today, as a matter of fact, I was walking and I had one thought, not an abstract one, but alive, active, and I wanted to tell you about it; together we could have thought it out . . . But then this door, I became involved—and forgot everything. And now I barely remember, as if I lost my memory. I have to regain my consciousness. One becomes involved—and by God it's as if one is reborn."

Moshin remained silent. Then he smiled broadly.

"But you know what? Please don't be offended. I would say exactly the same about myself. We, my friend, are both gregarious people. Yes, indeed! When we're alone, by ourselves, we live and think independently, but once we join a crowd, right away we become part of it; whatever the crowd is, we are, too. We become an indivisible unity. Indeed, we aren't billy goats, you and I, nor are we leaders; we're simply the most ordinary sheep. But don't think I mean it in a negative sense—because we are also a force. The billy goat can do nothing alone, but a herd, if it makes a dash, can trample everything. You say that the door was nonsense. Are we really to blame? The leaders are guilty. Where are they? Why are they silent? Tell me, point out the door which we must break—and we'll break it. And furthermore: tell us what to build, just give us a spark, and we'll build it, we'll create it, we'll accomplish it, because we are the force. I don't know what this idea of yours was that you were talking about, maybe it was good and valid, but only if the real leader thought it out; whereas you and your idea are nothing, you can only attempt to break down the door! We'll break down many doors to come, as long as they, the leaders, remain silent. They've lumped all of us, the force, together, and all around us the doors have been locked; darkness, suffocation, silence—and yet we're supposed to blame ourselves for not having done the right thing? The teachers are to be blamed, not we. The vital force must be cherished! It must be cared for! As long as we are blind and silent, we are a herd! All of us! And only those who disapprove of our actions are to be blamed!"

Moshin even took his cap off in his excitement. His friend remained silent, quickening his step.

"Don't be offended that you're part of the herd," Moshin continued. "I don't know everything; perhaps someday even you will become a leader, but now our thoughts and concerns are distinct from one another. My friend, this shouldn't worry you! That's just for now! We, I say, are not guilty of this! We are not to be blamed. But that there is a sense of the herd, a human fire in us, that's what's great! We are the force, you can believe me!"

Tishin glanced at his friend.

"Yes," he said. "It seems to me that you're right. So what? We'll think what we can think and do what we're able . . . so long as they remain silent!"

Mirra Lokhvitskaya

🍃 1869–1905

Mirra Aleksandrovna Lokhvitskaya, the Russian Sappho, a poet much admired at the turn of the century by both critics and readers, was born in St. Petersburg. The elder daughter of A. V. Lokhvitsky, a renowned lawyer and professor of law in the northern capital, she was educated at home and later at the Moscow Alexandrian Institute, from which she graduated in 1888. She then married Evgeny Zhiber, a St. Petersburg architect. Her poems were published by such prominent journals as *Severny vestnik* (The Northern Messenger), *Sever* (The North), *Vsemirnaya illyustratsiya* (The World Illustration), *Nedelya* (The Week), and many others. The first volume of her verse appeared in 1895, and a year later she was awarded the Pushkin Prize for poetry. The second award was announced in 1904, after the appearance of the fifth volume of verse, but it was conferred after her death on August 27, 1905. In 1908, the posthumous publication of the volume *Pered zakatom* (Before the Sunset) by her family completed her work.

Literary journals printed Lokhvitskaya's verse eagerly. Vasily Nemirovich-Danchenko, a brother of Vladimir Nemirovich-Danchenko and himself a prolific writer, recalled in his reminiscences that even "the most absurd billy goats of the editorial world would mellow when receiving the short Sapphic hymns of Lokhvitskaya for publication."[1] "Into what a beautiful world could she transport those who knew how to listen to her poems!" he added. "They frequently carried Vladimir Solovyov and myself into a magic, poetic dream-land!"[2]

After the turn of the century, elements of mysticism and motifs of suffering entered Lokhvitskaya's verse. In fact, her poem "Krest" (The Cross) resembles Zinaida Hippius' metaphysical treatment of such abstract cosmic notions as time, eternity, and the cross as a symbol of suffering:

> I love the beauty of the sun
> And the Hellenic Muse's creations,
> But I worship the Cross,
> The Cross, as a symbol of suffering.
>
> What meaning has the discord between time and place?
> We'll all dissolve into infinity.
> And poised above us in the gloom of black eternity
> Alone—the mournful Cross.

> Люблю я солнца красоту
> И музы Еллинской создания,
> Но поклоняюсь я Кресту,
> Кресту, как символу страдания.
>
> Что значит рознь времен и мест?
> Мы все сольемся в бесконечности;
> Один во мраке черной вечности—
> Простерт над нами скорбный Крест.

Valery Bryusov once remarked that Goethe's words about the two souls which reside in man could be applied to Mirra Lokhvitskaya. Her "first soul," at the heart of Volume I of her verse, aspired to clarity, meekness, and purity. It was filled with love of and sympathy for people, and with a fear of evil. Her "second soul," at the basis of Volume II, expressed sensual passion, "heroic egoism," and disdain for the crowd. According to Bryusov, these "two souls" within the poet began to struggle with one another in her subsequent works; she became attracted by sin, and as a result the verses acquired a demonic tenor. On the artistic level, these songs of sin and passion are particularly striking. But, psychologically, the battle between the poet's two souls and her desperate search for salvation imparted to her subsequent volumes a profound and tragic tone. "The inner drama of Lokhvitskaya's soul, which is imprinted on her entire work, will always excite and at-

Mirra Lokhvitskaya

tract the reader,"³ Bryusov assured his audience. He praised the artistic perfection of her verse, her colors, and the melodiousness of her verse. With a refined poetic vocabulary and keen observation, she conveyed both her maidenly dreams and the charms of sorcery—themes reminiscent of the Middle Ages. Bryusov found that she was equally successful when speaking of her own tormenting desire to experience the sensations of passion. In many of her poems, Bryusov observed, Lokhvitskaya attained a classical perfection in artistic polish.

Lokhvitskaya's poetic talent is especially evident in Volumes II and V, which may be viewed as the artistic records of her more or less consistent moods and attitudes. Volume I is also noteworthy, because in it she manifests her departure from the old devices practiced by poets contemporary to Pushkin. She often used impressionistic images, as, for example, in her poems "Krasny tsvet" (The Red Color), "Spyashchaya" (The Sleeping One), "Gnomy" (The Gnomes), "Son" (The Dream), "Koldunya" (The Sorceress), "Noch' pered pytkoy" (The Night before Torture), "Otrava mira" (The Poison of the World), and "V vechnom strakhe" (In Eternal Fear). These poems are striking in their sensual evocation of fragrances and their imaginative ingenuity. The drama which forms their poetic center is based on a medieval witchcraft trial and is poignant in its intensity. As a critic from *Russkoe bogatstvo* (Russian Wealth), who reviewed Lokhvitskaya's first three volumes of poems, claimed, "Amidst the multitude of contemporary poets, who have lost their way in the misty maze of decadent rhetoric, Mirra Lokhvitskaya's poetry shines [. . .] like a beautiful nocturnal butterfly."⁴ Her poetry, spirited and melodious, aspires "to leave the humdrum of life for the sunlit realm of dream where there is only love, happiness, and the fullness of life [. . .] The kingdom of nature is the real temple in which are sung her best hymns, and in which are found her best consolations."⁵

Lokhvitskaya, in fact, found graceful and poetic words to express her love of men, children, nature, suffering, and loneliness. Her lyrics reveal the vitality of life, its elemental force, color, and the flame of passion. They resemble the poems of Bal'mont and Rostaine, though differing in their Oriental, and even biblical, inspiration.⁶ The idea and music of the Song of Songs underlie her entire work. The emphasis is on the divine nature of the human flesh, its mysterious perfection, the force of Eros which is ever present in the human blood, and its complete harmony with everything earthly—sun, air, grass, water, trees. Sensation is at the very core of Lokhvitskaya's poetic universe. Her poetry displays that craving for the realization of earthly existence which may be found in Salomé, Sulamith, Balkis, and Sappho, in the women of Sir Edward Coley Burne-Jones, Dante Gabriel Rossetti, and in Aubrey Vincent Beardsley. Even Bal'mont's poems appear less intense when compared with Lokhvitskaya's. The singularity of her poetic voice and vision is unparalleled in the history of Russian versification, for in her poetry the Hellenic cult of beauty is perfectly unified with the orgiastic outbursts of Oriental passions. The critic Nikolay Poyarkov maintained that "Mirra Lokhvitskaya's poetry frequently and characteristically reflects the sunlit and mysterious Orient, with its intoxicating types of incense, bright flowers, and narcotics; the Orient with its instantaneous passion and sensual love; the Orient of magnificent apparel and sparkling precious stones."[7] He referred to Mirra Lokhvitskaya and Zinaida Hippius in the following descriptive fashion: because of her refined intellect and metaphysical sophistication, Hippius was for him "the Queen of Sheba in the realm of Russian poetry"; Lokhvitskaya was a "modest Sulamith" who loved intensely and who was "infinitely diverse in the manifestations of her love."[8]

In her poetic technique, Lokhvitskaya excelled in the imitation of sounds—the dry and persistent clicking of castanets, or the humming of a bumblebee on a hot, sultry day. The sounds thus used cast a strange and magic spell, as in the poem "Kto—shchastye zhdet, kto—prosit slavy" (Some People Await Happiness, Some Ask for Glory). The poet is always in perfect control of rhythm, rhyme, and imagery. Remarkable also is her use of melancholic musical chords in the final stanza, especially in the last volume of her verse, which heightens its emotional intensity. For example:

> I search in vain. All is empty, all is dead.
> I call—only the wind sobs in answer.

> Ищу я напрасно. Всё пусто, всё мертво.
> Зову я—мне ветер рыдает в ответ.

"Svet vecherny" (The Evening Light), another poem in Volume V, is melodious and graceful; it appears to have been inspired by the holy martyr Athenogenes' canticle "Svete tikhy, svyatye glasy" (Gracious Light, Holy Voices). The poems "Srednie veka" (The Middle Ages) and "Navazhdenie" (Witchcraft) are indicative of Lokhvitskaya's mysterious and eerie poetic universe toward the end of her life. In general, dreams, reveries, and imagination were of special interest in her last poems. By this time she seemed to have only one ardent desire: to escape this world of suffering and disappointment. Her poetry of this period is reminiscent of Alexander Blok's later endeavor to find himself in the realm of passion, beyond all considerations of good and evil, heaven or hell. More than half of Volume V is taken by a drama in five acts and eight scenes, *In nomine Domini*. Its content is derived from the trial of 1610–11, known through the Inquisitor Michaelis' notes and published in the seventeenth century under the title *Histoire admirable de la possession et conversion d'une pénitente séduite par un magicien* (Lyon, 1014). The drama is a painful and tormenting nightmare, but its verse is graceful and free.

Of course, the critics of Lokhvitskaya's poetry included not only her admirers. Several censured her for dwelling on love, passion, nature, and on her poetic ego. F. Makovsky, an early Marxist critic, criticized her for lacking "social content" and for her "antisocial ideas."[9] Other critics disapproved of her allegedly pornographic allegories and poetic immodesties.[10] They described her as a typically Decadent poet whose work resembled the art of Bal'mont, Bryusov, Zinaida Hippius, and Fyodor Sologub. Significantly, the Decadent poets themselves did not recognize her as a kindred spirit, with the exception of Bal'mont, who sensed her spiritual affinity and dedicated several poems to her in his volume *Budem, kak solntse!* (Let Us Be Like the Sun!, 1903).

Lokhvitskaya's poetry is free from the "civic" motifs of Nekrasov and Nikitin, as well as from the *Weltschmerz* of Nadson, both of which were fashionable at that time. Some of her verse is indeed sensual and unabashedly erotic. This type of poetry was a great departure and source of perplexity for the Russian reader brought up in the "civic" tradition of Russian literature. The criticism of F. Makovsky and others, therefore, is not surprising. In her poetry Lokhvitskaya exercised the freedom of expression to which writers such as Verbitskaya and Zinovyeva-Annibal were calling attention—the freedom for women to express their individuality, to lay bare the passionate, erotic aspect of their emotions, to explore and portray elements of their nature which outmoded and stereotyped definitions of "female" and "femininity" had excluded. The so-called onesidedness of her poetic talent—"to sing of love and sensuality"—was alien to these criticasters. They denied her poetic inspiration, craftsmanship, originality, and the refinement of form, imagery, and thought. In Volume II of her verse (St. Petersburg, 1900) she gave this answer to her critics:

I do not know why they reproach me
For having too much fire in my poems,
For striving to meet the lively sunbeam
And refusing to heed the accusations of gloom.

For shining like a tsarina in my elegant verses,
With a diadem on my opulent hair,
For weaving myself a necklace of rhymes,
For singing of love, for singing of beauty.

I will not buy immortality with my death.
And as for songs, I love melodious ones.
And the insanity of my petty dreams
Will be voiced in my passionate, my feminine verse.

Я не знаю, зачем упрекают меня,
Что в созданьях моих слишком много огня,
Что стремлюсь я навстречу живому лучу
И наветам унынья внимать не хочу.

Что блещу я царицей в нарядных стихах,
С диадемой на пышных моих волосах,
Что из рифм я себе ожерелье плету,
Что пою я любовь, что пою красоту.

Но бессмертья я смертью своей не куплю.
И для песен я звонкие песни люблю.
И безумью ничтожных мечтаний моих
Не изменит мой жгучий, мой женственный стих.

Lokhvitskaya's preoccupation with sensuality, erotic passion, exotic flora, the mood of dreams and reveries, the cult of the ego, and the striving to escape the world of empirical reality—all these mannerisms and attitudes were typical of Decadent poetry in Russia. Her magical gardens, intoxicating fragrances, and sparkling stones and flowers formed a perfect setting for the passions and fantasies typical of Decadence. In Sam Cioran's words, Lokhvitskaya was "both hailed and disdained by her contemporaries as the Russian Sappho, poetess of Bacchic sensuality, singing of love's fiery passion, Queen of Dreams, Flowers, and Subterranean Worlds."[11]

In Lokhvitskaya's later work, however, the sensual emphasis is balanced with poems of a more abstract nature. Of course, her early death makes it difficult to ascertain the direction her artistic maturity might have taken. Unfortunately, the preponderant passionate and sensual world of her early poetry forms the basis for her artistic reputation and has, perhaps, led critics to underestimate the more intellectual aspect of her later work. Indeed, Lokhvitskaya was understood by her critics merely as a "singer of love and passion." But the later phase of her evolution as an artist contradicts their judgment, and shows a development away from excessive indulgence in love and striking imagery toward a more restrained expression of the spiritual, of sadness, and of solitude. Poems such as "Oh We—the Sorrowful" lack the verbal ornamentation of the earlier period. The imagery in "The Seraphim" is striking in the repulsiveness of its blood and gore and its expression of physical pain, all of which would have been unusual for Lokhvitskaya's early work.

The poems here are arranged chronologically to show the poet's artistic development. In her early poetry Lokhvitskaya explores erotic scenes and moods, uses erudite references, and probes emotions of female passion and sensuality. But gradually her poetry becomes more personal and abstract. There are fewer scenes with subterranean creatures and languishing queens; rather, she portrays domestic settings, the love between a man and a woman, the evocation of maternal love ("My Sky"), a mother's joy in her child, and descriptions of a woman's feelings in various personal situations. Later poems echo the poet's feelings of loss, loneliness, isolation, and sorrow. There is a desire for something otherworldly, but no longer is it expressed in a search for dazzling southern scenery, an attraction to the netherworld, and the exploration of particularly female sensitivity. Furthermore, in her later verse the poet no longer confines herself within a specifically female consciousness.

Mirra Lokhvitskaya was not only a representative poet of the feminine side of Decadence. Like other Symbolist poets, she believed in a higher reality; it found expression in her poetry as those ethereal, eternal gardens permeated with spiritual significance. The same ambiguity is inherent in the poetry of Zinaida Hippius and Alexander Blok: the spirit and the flesh, the divine and the demonic, the radiance of faith and the despair of disbelief, the bright sunrise and the gloomy sunset, the lofty, ethereal gardens and the despotic, dark impulse of human passion on earth.

NOTES

1. Vas. Iv. Nemirovich-Danchenko, *Na kladbishchakh: vospominaniya* (Revel: Bibliofil, 1921), p. 143.
2. *Ibid.*, p. 148.
3. Valery Bryusov, *Dalekie i blizkie* (Moscow: Skorpion, 1912), chapter entitled "Zhenshchiny—poety (Mirra Lokhvitskaya)." Also read Avrely [Bryusov], "M. A. Lokhvitskaya. *Stikhotvoreniya*. Tom IV. St. Petersburg, 1903," *Novy Put'*, No. 1 (1903).
4. P. F. Yakubovich, "M. A. Lokhvitskaya (Zhiber). *Stikhotvoreniya*. T. I, izd. vtoroye, St. Petersburg, 1900—T. II, izd. vtoroye, St. Petersburg, 1900—T. III, St. Petersburg, 1900," *Russkoye bogatstvo*, No. 8 (1900), 60.
5. *Ibid.*
6. Read more about the evaluation of Lokhvitskaya's poetry in "M. A. Lokhvitskaya (Zhiber). *Stikhotvoreniya: pered zakatom*. S prilozheniem neizdannykh stikhotvoreny iz prezhnikh let i portretom avtora. S predisloviem. St. Petersburg: K. P., 1908," *Vestnik Evropy*, No. 7 (1908); A. L. Volynsky, *Bor'ba za idealizm* (St. Petersburg: M. Merkushev, 1900), and N. Ya. Abramovich, *Literaturno-kriticheskie ocherki* (St. Petersburg: Pushkinskaya Skoropechatnya, 1909).
7. Nik. Poyarkov, *Poety nashikh dney* (Moscow: I. M. Kholchev & Co., 1907), p. 83.
8. *Ibid.*, p. 84.
9. For more details, read F. Makovsky, "Chto takoe russkoye dekadentstvo?" *Obrazovanie*, No. 9 (1905), 129.
10. E.g., P. F. Grinevich, *Ocherki russkoy poezii*, 2nd ed. (St. Petersburg: *Russkoe bogatstvo*, 1911), pp. 357–358.
11. Sam Cioran, "The Russian Sappho: Mirra Lokhvitskaya," *Russian Literature Triquarterly*, No. 9 (Spring, 1974), 334.

No, I've no need for the sun, nor the brilliant azure,
No desire for rustling leaves, nor singing birds;
All is inconstant, treacherous, and deceitful—
Leave the world—leave evil and suffering.
We'll live in the depths of an impenetrable cavern—
The entrance blocked behind us by a boulder,
And, in place of nuptial torches, multicolored fires
Of rubies, sapphires, and diamonds will flash in the gloom . . .
There earthly cares and storms will not touch
Our happiness—we'll guard it jealously,
In that night of our mute, subterranean kingdom—
We will be two, and love will bind us . . .
I will reveal to you the mystery . . . O, look deep into my eyes!
Do you know who I am? I—tsarina of the underworld! . . .
The zealous, old gnomes obey me alone—
It is they who have carved our cave in the cliff . . .

M. A. Lokhvitskaya (Zhiber)   1893
Stikhotvoreniya (Moscow: Skoropechatnya, 1896)   I, 73

THE QUEEN OF SHEBA

> *"Put me, like a seal, on your heart,*
> *Like a signet-ring on your hand, for*
> *love is as powerful as death."*
> —SOLOMON'S "SONG OF SONGS," 8, 6.

Bathing in the sun's gold rays,
In the warm azure of the firmament,
Twelve doves flew south
Far from Zion.

Pining, the queen had long awaited
Her plumed guests—
And into the golden-purple tent
Their lively flock drifted . . .

She went to meet them,
Descending from her shimmering throne,
Slender—like the palm of En-gedi,[1]
Fresh, like the rose of Jericho . . .[2]

Suddenly her beautiful face
Was bathed in a tender, burning blush,
And a snow-white dove
Alit upon her bare shoulder.

From its scarlet beak
She quickly took, with trembling hand,
A message . . . The swarm of slave girls
Fell silent and froze expectantly . . .

Just o'er her crowned head
A large fan barely rustled . . .
The queen, with downcast eyes,
Harkened to the royal message.
And each word of it,
It seemed, found echo
In her breast, where before
Self-will alone had dwelt:

"I kiss the delicate traces
Of my queen's lovely feet!
Her eyes, like two stars,
Glimmer through dark lashes . . .
What say I? . . . two stars?! . . .
Bright flashes of summer lightning are they!
And by them is my heart consumed,
Filled with the madness of love!

---

1. En-gedi—an ancient oasis on the western shore of the Dead Sea, famed for its vineyards. For more information, see Joshua 15:62; I. Sam. 24:1–4; Cant. 1:14; Ezek. 47:10; II. Chron. 20:2.

2. Rose of Jericho—a desert plant, *Anastatica hierochuntica.* It belongs to the mustard family and is native to Asia Minor, which includes the ancient city of Jericho that Joshua destroyed.

O, who can compare with her,
With my beloved! Her cheeks
Are like lilies, flowers of the field,
Drenched in the evening's glow . . .
What say I?!—the lily's bloom?!—
Scarlet roses are her cheeks!
And by them is my heart enraptured,
Filled with the madness of love!

How intoxicatingly subtle
The perfumes of her gown!
She captivates the eye, like the light of the moon,
The charm of a wondrous beauty . . .
What say I?!—The light of the moon?!—
Rather the brilliance of the southern sun!
And by it is my heart bedazzled,
Filled with the madness of love!"

II

The slave had finished . . . But far away
The Queen's dreams have drawn her,
There, to the promised land,
"Where milk and honey flow . . ."
Where an intoxicating well bubbles into a brook
And the juice of amber wines trickles,
Where the multibranched terebinth[3] grows,
And a canopy of plantains and olive trees . . .

Where palaces with their fairy tale glitter
Outshine the splendor of the southern lands,
Where myrrh, incense, and saffron
Stream fragrances from censers . . .
Seven steps . . . and a resplendent throne . . .
And, illuminated by most sublime glory,

---

3. Terebinth—an anacardiaceous tree, *Pistacia Terebinthia*, of the Mediterranean regions, yielding chian turpentine.

He—the fragrant blossom of the valleys,
"The narcissus of Sharon"—Solomon! . . .[4]
O moment, remembered by her even now,
When, under that powerful and vital gaze,
She, a seeming goddess,
Stood before him—
Before victory or disgrace,
Her involuntary fear concealed,
With a slyly lowered gaze,
With a subtle smile on her lips . . .

    —"What does Your Highness command
    In reply to the King of the East?"—
    Roused from her wondrous dream,
    Her lashes softly trembled . . .

More flushed than the rose of Jericho,
Still under the sweet dream's spell,
To Solomon's winged messengers
She spoke with a sigh:

    —"Not from the Queen—from his slave
    Tell your King
    That I worship him,
    And he gladdens my heart,
    That I marvel at his wisdom,
    His power, his wealth, his land . . .
    I love him! . . . And long to join him! . . .
    I am consumed by our love! . . ."

                   1894
                   I, 97

---

4. Reference to the rose of Sharon of the Bible (Cant. 2:1). The rose mentioned here is thought to be either a narcissus or the meadow saffron. In general, the rose of Sharon is the name of several plants, especially certain varieties of hibiscus and St. John's wort.

ЦАРИЦА САВСКАЯ

« Положи меня, как печать, на сердце твое,
как перстень, на руку твою, ибо
сильна, как смерть, любовь. »
Из « Песни Песней » Саломона 8, 6.

Купаясь в золоте лучей,
В лазури теплой небосклона,
Летят двенадцать голубей
На юг далекий из Сиона.

Гостей пернатых с давних пор
Ждала царица, изнывая,—
И в злато-пурпурный шатер
Их резвая вспорхнула стая …

На встречу им идет она,
Сойдя с блистающего трона,
Как Пальма Енгадди—стройна,
Свежа, как роза Ерихона …

На лике дивном горячо
Разлился вмиг румянец иежный,
И свеял голубь белоснежный
На обнаженное плечо.

Из клюва алого посланье
Поспешно, трепетной рукой,
Она взяла … Невольниц рой
Умолк и замер в ожиданье …

Лишь над венчанною главой
Чуть шелестело опахало …
Царица, взор потупя свой,
Посланью царскому внимала.

И слово каждое его,
Казалось, отклик находило
В груди, где прежде место было
Для самовластья одного:—

«Лобзаю легкие следы
Прекрасных ног моей царицы!
Ее глаза, как две звезды,
Горят сквозь темные ресницы ...
Что говорю я? ... две звезды?...
То молний яркие зарницы!
И сердце ими сожжено,
Любви безумием полно!

«О, кто сравниться может с ней,
С возлюбленной! Ее ланиты
Как лилии, цветы полей,
Зарей вечернею облиты ...
Что говорю я?—цвет лилей?—
Алее роз ее ланиты!
И сердце ими прельщено
Любви безумием полно!

«Как упоительно-нежны
Ее одежд благоуханья!
Пленяет взор, как свет луны,
Красы чудесной обаянье ...
Что говорю я?—свет луны?!—
То солнца южного сиянье!
И сердце им ослеплено,
Любви безумием полно!»

II

Окончил раб ... Но далеко
Царицу унесли мечтанья
Туда, в страну обетованья,
«Где льется мед и молоко ...»
Где бьет ключем сиккер душистый
И брыжжет сок янтарных вин,
Где теревинф возрос ветвистый
И сень платанов и маслин ...

Где блеском сказочным палаты
Затмили роскошь южных стран,
Где мирра, ладан и шафран
Струят с курильниц ароматы ...

Семь ступеней ... и пышный трон ...
И, славой вышней осиянный,
Он, — цвет долин благоуханный,
«Нарцисс сарронский» — Саломон!...
О миг, ей памятный до ныне,
Под взглядом властным и живым,
Когда, подобная богине,
Она предстала перед ним, —
Перед победой иль позором,
Тая борьбы невольный страх,
С опущенным лукаво взором,
С усмешкой тонкой на устах ...

      — «Что-ж передать прикажешь ты
      Царю востока от царицы?» —
      И тихо дрогнули ресницы,
      От чудной пробудясь мечты ...

Алее розы Ерихона,
Под грезой сладостного сна,
Послам крылатым Саломона
Со вздохом молвила она:

      — «Не от царицы, — от рабыни
      Скажите вашему царю,
      Что я его боготворю
      И осчастливлена им ныне!
      Что я дивлюсь его уму,
      Могуществу, богатству, краю ...
      Люблю его!.. и рвусь к нему!...
      И от любви изнемогаю.»

MY SKY

The sky and all the delights of the sky I see
In my child's sweet face—and I cannot tear my eyes away . . .
Innocent angel, by chance fallen to the earth,
How much happiness you've brought! Child, how dear you are
    to me!

The wind gusts and your curls flicker with gold,
They glisten 'round your dear tiny head like a halo,
You're just like a little cloud, drenched by the light of dawn,
Pure like the forest lily-of-the-valley—May's charming bloom!

With a gentle caress your deep blue eyes
Look into my soul and seem like the color of the sky,
Darkening for an instant before a spring storm . . .
I contemplate the sky in your gaze, child!

Where is that land of which our fairy tales murmur?
I'd carry you in my arms to that wondrous realm,
Silently, barefoot on sharp stones would I walk,
If only to spare you—the thorns of earth's path!

God! When You sent me a child, You opened the sky for me!
My mind was cleansed of vain, petty desires!
Into my breast You breathed new, mysterious powers!
In my burning heart You kindled—the flame of immortal love!

June 30, 1894
I, 103

THE FOUR HORSEMEN

(A Ballad)

I

Morning burst forth, burning crimson,
A golden dawn glimmered through the window . . .
—"Are you asleep, Maya, beloved daughter?
Come help me welcome a guest;
My guest outshines early spring,

His curls are spun from sunbeams,
His young laugh resounds with tenderness,
He brings gaiety and life!"—
   —"Let me doze in my charmed dream.
   Curly-haired youth, forget me!
   My reveries are filled with ecstasy . . .
   Let me finish my inspired dreams!"—

II

—"Come out! O Maya, beloved daughter,
Help me welcome another guest,
Dress in your finest array and your crown,
See, there breaks a glorious dawn!
My guest is quite famous and noble—
Look, his white steed approaches,
His azure cloak billows behind,
Magnificence and riches does he bring!"—
   —"Your guest is handsome—but his deceptive visage
   Hides so many infinite cares,
   So many cares of the petty—the earthly . . .
   Let me be lost in sweet dreams! . . ."

III

The purple sun has long since hidden;
Mysterious evening gazes through the window . . .
—"Come out, O Maya, beloved daughter,
Come help me close the shutters!
Someone sad, in mute silence,
Just now swiftly skirted the window;
Hesperus in his radiant brilliance
Shines his star above a clear brow . . ."
   —"In vain did you refuse this guest . . .
   Do you sense, the flowers have grown more fragrant?
   Fling open the shutters quickly, my mother,
   To drink in the fresh air is sweet to me!"—

IV

—"Sleep, my Maya, beloved daughter!
See, deep night already has descended;
Someone on a handsome black steed

Has softly approached and paused 'neath the window . . .
His wondrous face fills me with fear,
The moon plays in his locks,
His dark eyes so brilliantly burn,
His finery is shrouded in mourning crepe! . . ."
—"Arise, dearest, and open the doors—
It's my love who approaches,
I'll merge with him in a burning embrace,
And depart forever to the starry sky!"—

July 4, 1895
I, 127

DREAMS OF IMMORTALITY

There, on an island of the vast world,
I fell in love with a friend—beautiful,
Curly-haired, serenely joyful,
   Clear-visaged.
He floated in with the twilight of a wearisome day
And stayed with me till morning.

Misty shrouds fell
About his many-hued array,
His words were incoherent
And mysterious—his gaze strange.
Scarlet poppies, smoldering with a purple fire,
Formed a fragrant garland 'round his head.

He whispered inspired tales to me,
Evoked sultry visions:
Some innocent, some troubled,
   Some blessed.
Away into the forbidden distance, to the golden lands
My thoughts flew with him.

But, exhausted by life's daily
Pining from a nameless torture,
Once, in an anguished moment of parting,
In tears, I whispered to him:

—"O my friend, alone, without you, I am so sad,
Why can't you be with me forever?"

He said: "What can be forever?
Even centuries pass like moments.
On earth you will not find eternal
    Oblivion."
And into the rays of the dawning day, with a deep sigh,
He vanished, he abandoned me.

But in my hours of boring loneliness
I awaited this perfect bliss,
I, burning, summoned that unchanging,
That inseparable, faithful friend.
He appeared, and with the shadow of his quivering wings,
With that dark shadow he embraced me.

He gazed at me with a welcoming smile,
And my brow, overburdened with thoughts,
Overburdened with thoughts gloomy,
    Hopeless,
And my eyes, and my breast, wearied from yearning,
He touched with his healing hand.

I cast off this weary flesh,
I severed those useless chains,
Into those far-off spheres, beyond the stars,
    Renewd, enlightened,
He lifted me to the light of unbounded day,
  That he need never forsake me again.

M. A. Lokhvitskaya (Zhiber)   1896–98
Stikhotvoreniya (St. Petersburg: Suvorin, 1900)   II, 79

ГРЕЗЫ БЕССМЕРТИЯ

Там, на острове мира великого,
Полюбила я друга прекрасного,
Пышнокудрого, радостно-ясного,
    Светлоликого.
Прилетал он с закатом докучного дня
  И до утра гостил у меня.

Ниспадали покровы туманные
На одежды его многоцветные,
Были речи бессвязны ответные
И загадочны—взоры странные.
Алых маков, пылавших пурпурным огнем,
Был венок благовонный на нем.

Он мне сказки шептал вдохновенные,
Навевал мне видения знойные:
То безгрешные, то беспокойные,
        То блаженные.
В заповедную даль, в золотые края
С ним мечта улетала моя.

Но, от шума дневного усталая,
Изнывая от мук без названия,
Раз, в томительный миг расставания,
Вся в слезах, ему прошептала я:
—«О мой друг, без тебя мне так грустно одной,
Почему ты не вечно со мной?»

И сказал он: «Что может быть вечного?
И века промелькнут, как мгновения.
На земле не найдешь ты забвения
        Бесконечного.»
И со вздохом в лучах восходящего дня
Он исчез, он покинул меня.

Но в часы одиночества скучного
Я блаженства ждала совершенного,
Я, сгорая, ждала неизменного,
Друга верного, неразлучного.
И предстал он и тенью взволнованных крыл,
Черной тенью меня осенил.

И взглянул он с улыбкой приветною,
И чела, отягченного думою,
Отягченного думой угрюмою,
        Беспросветною,
И очей, и груди, истомленной тоской,
Он коснулся целящей рукой.

И я сбросила плоть утомленную,
Я вериги сняла бесполезные,
И в дальние сферы, надзвездные,
Обновленную, просветленную,
Он вознес меня к свету безбрежного дня,
Чтоб вовек не покинуть меня.

THE SERAPHIM

I

Gorged for a time with bloody slaughter,
Both servants and valorous hero are weary
And enter the dome of God's dwelling,
Where candles glimmer at the Master's feet,
And from the basilica's walls, with gentle smiles,
Gaze the blissful faces of the Seraphim.

II

The weary executioner has dozed for an instant.
The hung victim's frenzy grows.
A beaten body quivers on the rack,
No limit to these slow tortures is seen.
But there, above the earth, above this pitch darkness,
Soar the Seraphim with innocent smiles.

III

With a deep *"in pace,"* lacking strength and will,
A nun beats against the stones of a grave.
The echo of heavenly songs is heard
In that cold pit, with rats and mold.
But beyond—with the organ's roar, unseen in clouds of incense,
"Hosanna, Hosanna!" sing the Seraphim.

M. A. Lokhvitskaya (Zhiber)   1898–1900
Stikhotvoreniya (St. Petersburg: Suvorin, 1900)   III, 6

СЕРАФИМЫ

I

Резнею кровавой на время насытясь,
Устали и слуги, и доблестный витязь,
И входят под своды обители Божьей,
Где теплятся свечи Господних предножий,
И с кроткой улыбкой со стен базилики
Глядят серафимов блаженные лики.

II

Палач утомленный уснул на мгновенье.
Подвешенной жертвы растет исступленье.
На дыбе трепещет избитое тело,
Медлительным пыткам не видно предела.
А там, над землею, над тьмою кромешной,
Парят серафимы с улыбкой безгрешной.

III

В глубоком *"in pace,"* без воли и силы,
Монахиня бьется о камни могилы.
В холодную яму, где крысы и плесень,
Доносится отзвук божественных песен.
То—с гулом органа, в куреньях незримы,
«Осанна! Осанна!» поют серафимы.

OUR TIMES

What customs these are, what an age!
All lazily drag their burden,
Thinking of no one else.
Bored with their sleepy gatherings,
With everyday diversions,
With their affected gaiety.

We, entrenched in our humble desires,
Seek half-tints,
Hating dark and light.

No illusion of happiness beckons us,
Nor visions of celebration and power;
In our dreams, there's no such sight.

All has irretrievably vanished.
Where are those, then, who
Once shimmered with a golden aura?
Those, who strove toward the cherished goal,
Who shrank not from torture,
Nor groaned under the knout?

Where are those, ignorant of sorrows,
Who dissipated the years
In a wild, bacchanalian flash?
Where are you, people?—Gone, gone!
Everything's irretrievably passed,
Everything's extinguished without a trace.

And to the hypocrite's delight,
Life crawls along in a gray fog,
Deaf and dumb.
Faith sleeps. Knowledge is silent.
And over us boredom reigns,
The mother of shame and sin.

1898–1900
III, 15

I want to die young,
Neither loving nor grieving for anyone;
To burst like a golden falling star,
To shed my petals while still an unfaded flower.
I want those wearied by hostility
To find bliss twofold at my gravestone.
I want to die young.

Bury me to the side,
Away from the irritating and noisy road,
There, where the pussy willow inclines to the waves,
Where the overgrown bushes grow yellow.
So that the dreamy poppies may grow,
So that the wind may breathe the fragrances

Of the distant earth over me.
I want to die young.

I don't look at the path I've travelled,
At the madness of wasted years.
I can doze untroubled,
Once I've sung my final hymn.
Let the fire not completely fade;
Let there remain a memory of
What aroused the heart's thirst for life.
I want to die young.

1898–1900
III, 32

ENIS-EL-DJELLIS

In an ornamented tower huddled the harem
Of the lord of an eastern land;
There captives lived, not knowing why,
Languished, and awaited Spring.

The sun had inclined toward the pearly waves,
The air breathed wind and dreams.
An unknown knight on a white steed
Approached—and paused 'neath the window.

He watched as the birds, having touched the window,
Circled and drifted downward.
He saw—in the harem one lovelier than all,
The slave Enis-el-Djellis.

Her young lips were red,
Like the roses of southern lands.
More ethereal than the evening shadows
Seemed her seductive shape.

Her luxuriant braids coiled in the sun,
Like two golden streams.
And the knight cried out: "Enis-el-Djellis!
You'll be mine—or no one's."

Along the red clouds
The sun withdrew into its night chamber.
Glory to the names of those immortalized in love—
Theirs will be commended to the ages.

The tower has crumbled. On that dark cliff
There stands a silent cypress.
The slave Enis-el-Djellis
Dreams in the cold earth, murdered.

1898–1900
III, 64

A PRAYER FOR THOSE WHO ARE PERISHING

O, righteous God,
Hear my prayers
For the souls of those who are perishing
Without absolution;
For all those anguishing,
For all those suffering,
For those striving toward You,
For those ignorant of You!

I do not beg for obedience
And hope
For you, the humble,
Whose life—is silence.
For you, who are meek in spirit,
You, who are pure of heart,
The thorny paths
Are easy and joyful.

But for you, the rebellious,
Those who have sorely fallen away,
Who have confused ecstasy
With madness and evil,
For the torments of these chosen,

For the pain of their moment—
I beg awareness
And revelation!

M. A. Lokhvitskaya (Zhiber)   1900–1902
Stikhotvoreniya (St. Petersburg: Stasyulevich, 1900)   IV, 13

МОЛИТВА О ГИБНУЩИХ

О, Боже праведный,
Внемли моления
За души гибнущих
Без искупления,
За всех тоскующих,
За всех страдающих,
К Тебе стремящихся,
Тебя незнающих!

Не вам, смиренные,
Чья жизнь—молчание,
Молю покорности
И упования.
Вам, духом кроткие,
Вам, сердцем чистые,
Легки и радостны
Тропы тернистые.

Но вам, мятежные,
Глубоко павшие,
Восторг с безумием
И злом смешавшие,
За муки избранных,
За боль мгновения—
Молю познания
И откровения.

My sadness is always with me.
And even if I were a bird,
Even if two unfettered wings
Whirled me away to another place:
Into the land of the snows—where there's silence and shadows,
Or to the valleys of roses—in the midday heat—
    It is always with me.

My sadness is with me always.
In those hours, when, like a slave,
I bow before fate,
And in those, when pure, proud,
My immortal star from azure heights
Shines upon me—
    It is with me always.

IV, 28

O we—the sorrowful,
We—the damned,
Participants in good,
Defeated by evil,
In our dreams—exalted,
In our deeds—deceitful,
In our impulses—wild,
In our tears—pitiful!

Chosen by Fate,
Ignorant of happiness,
We wander—strange ones—
Amidst foul weather,
In love with a star,
By a star protected,
Unsatisfied,
Unsatisfying.

O we—the sorrowful,
We—the damned,
Participants in good,

Born in evil,
Have tasted the fruit
Of knowledge in sin,
Have forgotten our paradise
In the darkness of exile.

1900–1902
IV, 29

О мы—несчастные,
Мы—осужденные,
Добру причастные,
Злом побежденные,
В мечтах—великие,
В деяньях—ложные,
В порывах—дикие,
В слезах—ничтожные!

Судьбой избранные,
Чуждаясь счастия,
Мы бродим—странные—
Среди ненастия;
В звезду влюбленные,
Звездой хранимые,
Неутоленные,
Неутолимые.

О мы—несчастные,
Мы—осужденные,
Добру причастные,
Во зле рожденные,
Плода познания
В грехе вкусившие,
Во тьме изгнания
Свой рай забывшие!

BEFORE SUNSET

I love the faded blossoms
Of late-blooming violets and lilacs,
Half-hinted, half-tinted
By an entwining haze of beauty.
  The troubled soul is ill
  And embraced by the silent dusk;
  It is enraptured by approaching sleep
  And the peaceful charm of sunset.
What remains for the fire of hopes to illumine?
What can breathe with that bygone joy?
What will rouse
My sinking, half-closed lids?
  Nothing. No one. Desires are gone.
  The lightning has flashed mutely.
  I gaze with a smile of exhaustion
  At life, and the vanity of vanities.
The celestial path is hidden in a mist.
Grief subsides, wounds grow mute.
Blessed, blessed is Nirvana's rest—
To doze . . . to disappear . . . to drown.

Poems: Before Sunset
1903? (published 1908)

Anastasiya Verbitskaya

🍃 1861–1928

Anastasiya Alekseevna Verbitskaya's first publications appeared in the Russian newspaper *Russky kuryer* (The Russian
Courier), where she was in charge of its political section from 1883
to 1885. Later she appeared as a prose writer and playwright in
various journals, including *Mir Bozhy* (God's World), *Russkoye
bogatstvo* (Russian Wealth), *Zhizn'* (Life), *Russkaya mysl'* (Russian
Thought), *Nachalo* (The Beginning), *Obrazovanie* (Education),
Pravda (The Truth), and in the newspapers *Russkie vedomosti*
(The Russian Gazette), *Severny kuryer* (The Northern Courier),
and some others. Her works written before 1908 centered around
the question of the contemporary family and the interrelationship
between man and woman. To these belong her novellas "Razlad"
(The Discord, 1887) and "Po-novomu" (In a New Fashion, 1902),
the novels *Vavochka* (1898) and *Osvobodilas'* (She Liberated Herself, 1899), the short stories "Prestuplenie Marii Ivanovny"
(Mariya Ivanovna's Crime, 1899) and "Sny zhizni" (Dreams of Life,
1899), the drama *Chya vina?* (Whose Fault? 1904), and many
others. These works protest the false morals of Russian society and
the position of women in it, as well as challenging woman's place
within the family circle. Some of Verbitskaya's heroines even become revolutionaries, as in the novella "Istoriya odnoy zhizni" (The
Story of One Life, 1903). The novel *Dukh vremeni* (The Zeitgeist,
1908) portrays the fateful events of 1905–7. According to V. P.
Kranikhfel'd, one of the important critics of the day, in this novel
Verbitskaya "reached the summit of her fame."[1] *The Zeitgeist* de-

picts a multitude of events in a lively manner, and has numerous colorful and well-delineated characters. We read here about banquets, general and provincial strikes, intrigues, and even about the armed uprising in Moscow. The author's philosophy of life is expressed quite clearly: the goal of life is happiness and happiness is found in the fullness of experiences and sensations. This was the period when Verbitskaya advocated extreme individualism and neo-egoism. Verbitskaya's later works, among them *Klyuchi schastya* (The Keys of Happiness, 1909–13), with its rich and entertaining plot, and *Igo lyubvi* (The Yoke of Love, 1914–15), treat "free love" and sexual problems. Her works have hardly any landscapes or observations of nature in general. She was, however, very particular with regard to interior scenes, clothing, and the physical appearance of her heroes—sometimes, perhaps, even at the expense of their psychological portrayal.

Verbitskaya's reading audience was very large. Since she had always been interested in progressive ideas, she was especially popular with Russian students, who read her books with enthusiasm. They were attracted by her plots, which abound in adventures and excite the reader's curiosity, and by her concern with various questions much in vogue at the turn of the century. Indeed, Verbitskaya surpassed even Lev Tolstoy in popularity. Critical of Chekhov's and Maxim Gor'ky's plays because of their "remarkable poverty of ideals and their pitiful heroes," she strove to create "new ideals" and new people. This challenge, of course, had a strong appeal to the student population, also seeking fresh approaches for their continuing struggle with the traditions of the past.

Verbitskaya herself divided her work into two main periods: the first, of "asceticism" and "cold self-denial"; the second, of "the sun in its entire splendor." Eudaemonism, however, was characteristic of her entire creative work, and melancholy and vague dreams of happiness formed the basis of her whole literary output. During the first period, her eudaemonistic system of ethics was oriented toward utilitarianism; during the second, she adhered to egotistical hedonism. All of her favorite heroes within the second period strive for happiness, but they differ in their pursuits and the practice of pleasure and delight in life. Verbitskaya had a talent for selecting her protagonists from among average people and fathoming their particular problems—the family, occupation, ideals, or the "new consciousness." They genuinely suffer as both champions and victims of a changing time and mode of life; yet they stubbornly defend and even justify their interest in "new ideals." A Russian critic of the day, E. Koltonovskaya, praised "The Story of One Life" as a work portraying one such person, who appears before the reader at various stages of her life, full of disturbing undercurrents and events.[2] Verbitskaya withheld her own answer to the predicaments of her heroine; the artistic presentation enables the reader to reach his own conclusions.

K. Chukovsky, later an eminent Soviet writer, disdained Verbitskaya's grandiloquent language, the artificiality of her style, and her "cheap novels" which she "persistently compared to the works of Gor'ky, [Leonid] Andreev, [Fyodor] Sologub, Kuprin, and Valery Bryusov."[3] He strongly disapproved of her "frequent use" of such names as Nietzsche, Maeterlinck, Karl Marx, Zarathustra, and Goya. Another critic, A. Bartenev, joined the chorus of those contemporary writers whose attitude toward Verbitskaya's work was negative. In his article "Parazity literatury: A. Verbitskaya" (Parasites of Literature: A. Verbitskaya), he referred to her works as a clear manifestation of "exultant vulgarity"[4] which he felt was exhibited in her rich and expressive, but, at the same time, artificial and tasteless style. "And with what multi-colored Bengal lights does she illuminate contemporary man's soul in her novels!" exclaimed the indignant critic. "How vulgar are the devices with which she intentionally and crudely emphasizes her points of interest; how vulgar are her stupid sallies into the abstract realms of shallow psychological analysis! [. . .] Her topics include individualism, revolution, Modernism, arch-individualism, sexual pathology. [. . .]"[5] Bartenev was at a loss to understand why Verbitskaya's popularity continued to grow and her readers increased in number, now including not only students, but also many venerable members of the Russian intelligentsia.

With all due respect for the opinions of the above critics, it must be stated that Verbitskaya's presentation of some problems of the day was very effective. It is likely that Chukovsky and Bartenev were alienated by her emphasis on the problems of women in Russian life. This was a new and highly controversial issue at that time, and Verbitskaya's advocacy of equality, self-assertion, and

Anastasiya Verbitskaya

material independence for women was not welcomed by many men. Furthermore, in her works she revealed the emotional and intellectual capacities and the latent potential of women. On the other hand, her artistic presentation of woman's inadequate position and the latter's struggle for the realization of her ideals found many sympathetic ears at the turn of the century, and the social problems treated in her works were of interest to many readers, both male and female. At no time did Verbitskaya pretend to follow Dostoevsky and Tolstoy in their search for the ultimate truth, or to emulate the depth of their psychological analysis. Verbitskaya did not attempt (as did many writers of the time) to create variations of Raskol'nikov, Stavrogin, Ivan Karamazov, Andrey Bolkonsky, or Anna Karenina. Her heroes and heroines are less intense in their thoughts and emotions; they are less memorable and infinitely less tragic. Yet they fit the situations presented in Verbitskaya's books, and they are able to sustain the validity of the author's arguments. Her literary technique is traditional in that it uses the accepted devices and modes of narration and presents the main ideas at the outset of the story, yet she utilizes this technique with great success. Her skill may be seen, for example, in the play *Mirazh: Komediya v pyati deystviyakh* (Mirage: A Comedy in Five Acts),[6] selected for inclusion in an abridged form in the present volume. Verbitskaya's use of "skaz" and the careful individualization of the protagonists' patterns of speech are impressive; the characterization of her *dramatis personae*, the development of the plot, and the presentation of ideas and problems are natural. *Mirage* resembles Chekhov's plays in mood and dramatic situations, although it was written several years earlier than Chekhov's dramatic masterpieces.

Verbitskaya's play depicts Russian society in the 1890's, the period of the "blind alley" in Russian life. The members of the intelligentsia began working in various capacities in factories, trying to establish closer ties with workers. Egor is one of these people who wishes to live his life in accordance with his ideals. In his weakness, however, he fails. Vera, an attractive representative of those "new," strong-willed women in Russian literature who are incapable of compromising their own consciences, will not yield to temptation till the end of her life. Frustrated in love and personal happiness, she does not lapse into pessimistic moods but continually encourages Egor, the man she adores, to go forward, to join the progressive forces of the Russian intelligentsia and to work with them for the common good. She constantly reminds him of their new and important cause. But as a character, Vera is not well developed. She is the dullest protagonist; paradoxically, however, it is through Vera that Verbitskaya expresses her modernistic ideas. The most successful character is Varyagin, a zealot of Beauty. In *Novye lyudi* (New People, 1896), Zinaida Hippius portrays those proud, solitary men who indulge in lengthy conversations about beauty, harmony, and love as abstract ideas. They do not live life, always remaining confirmed individualists, guided in their actions by the selfish dictates of Ego. Varyagin is one of these men who avoids with disgust the seedier side of life and remains a dispassionate spectator of his fellow man's misery. Abstaining from any kind of struggle for a better future for mankind, he pleads the cause of the supremacy of Reason in human deeds, feelings, and desires. Conceived generally in the image of Verbitskaya's Varyagin, Mikhail Artsybashev's crude and instinctive Sanin (*Sanin,* 1907) was a far cry from this refined aesthete with a dreadful vacuum in his soul. Varyagin's "truth" and beauty are entirely rational, devoid of all intuition and religious feeling.

Lyolya, a flippant coquette, represents the woman conditioned by society to perceive a "profitable marriage" or a "romantic" love match as her only future. In general, Verbitskaya seems to express the complexity of her male characters more persuasively. Her heroines tend to be negative or (in Vera's case) "flat"; although we know of Vera's love for Egor, the emotional side of her nature is not well portrayed. On the other hand, the two old mothers, Pelageya L'vovna and Nadezhda Mikhaylovna, are drawn in bold relief. Their first conversation shows only two positions available for woman within marriage—dominant or dominated—both unhappy choices. Although possible equality within matrimony is timidly hinted at the play's end, the nature of Vera's and Egor's two personalities suggests that they will fail, too. Throughout *Mirage* the relationship between man and woman is treated as a serious game: one must know the rules, because everything is based on deception. Vera, who understands the "game of marriage" only too well, is anxious to find her fulfillment elsewhere.

To evaluate Anastasiya Verbitskaya's significance, the reader must keep in mind the period during which she was writing, or, more specifically, the image of woman and the relationship between male and female as portrayed in the theatre of the time. Verbitskaya's presentation of the "new" woman and her possible role in society, outside of marriage, was indeed very radical. As is true for the works of most Russian Modernist writers, in her novels and plays Anastasiya Verbitskaya revealed a contemporary restlessness, a social and individual fragmentation, an absence of faith, an anxious pursuit of personal happiness, as well as hope, despondency, and an attempt at adjustment or escape. However, in her literary technique Verbitskaya continued the tradition of nineteenth-century Russian literature in that she refrained from separating the formal aesthetic goals of her craftsmanship from social, political, psychological, and other purposes. Yet, in harmony with the *Zeitgeist*, she too desired to go beyond mere fiction and to create a new man, with a new consciousness.

NOTES

1. V. P. Kranikhfel'd, *V mire idey i obrazov* (St. Petersburg: Samoobrazovanie, 1912), II, 169. Also read V. P. Kranikhfel'd, "O novykh lyudyakh A. Verbitskoy," *Sovremenny mir*, No. 8, Sec. II (1910).

2. E. Koltonovskaya, "Iz zhizni i literatury," *Obrazovanie*, No. 3 (1902). For more details, read E. Koltonovskaya, "Istoriya odnoy zhizni. Povest' v dvukh deystviyakh" (Moscow, 1903), *Obrazovanie*, No. 1, Sec. III (1903), 74–77.

3. K. Chukovsky, *Kniga o sovremennykh pisatelyakh* (St. Petersburg: Shipovnik, 1914), p. 14.

4. A. Bartenev, "Parazity literatury (A. Verbitskaya)," *Zhatva*, Book 1 (1912), p. 234.

5. *Ibid.*, p. 235.

6. (Moscow, 1913.) Read more about Verbitskaya in Ya. Chimishlysky, *Zhenskiye tipy v proizvedeniyakh Verbitskoy. Opyty kriticheskogo razbora eyo proizvedeny* (St. Petersburg: N. M. Nakhumov, 1904), and I. Kheif, "Verbitskaya. Ocherk," *Priboy: literaturny sbornik*, Book II (1913), pp. 20–31.

MIRAGE

A COMEDY IN FIVE ACTS

Presented on the Stage of the Maly Theater in Moscow, 1895–96

(Moscow: "Pechatnoe delo," 1913)

> "Our goal is not to excite laughter,
> but to stimulate thought . . ."
> Jean Julian

Dramatis Personae

Pelageya L'vovna Trofimova. *Fifty years old or close to it. The widow of a functionary of middle rank with modest means, heavy-set and graying. She has an air of importance and speaks slowly, impressively, condescendingly. All her movements and her gait are smooth; her facial expression is intelligent and decisive. She wears shabby and outmoded dresses; her hair is pulled back and topped with a wiglet. She often removes it and casually replaces it when meeting a stranger.*

Lyolya, *also called Elena Nikolaevna, Elenka, Lyolechka, and Lyol'ka. Trofimova's daughter, eighteen years old; a pretty, graceful blonde.*

Vera Alexandrovna Ivanova. *Trofimova's niece, twenty years old. An attractive brunette; her curly hair is held in one flowing braid. Her movements are angular; her manner, curt. She wears a simple, dark dress, tight-fitting, with a leather belt, with no pretensions to fashion.*

Vladimir Arkadyevich Varyagin, *also called Vol'demar, Voloden'ka, and Volodya. Twenty-four years old, Lyolya's fiancé, very handsome and elegant. His face is pale and nervous; his smile is full of sadness. He wears no beard or moustache. He is dressed simply, but well. He shows great self-restraint, not a hint of foppishness. He laughs quietly and hardly raises his voice.*

Egor Andreevich Petrovsky, *also called Egorushka, George, Georgie, Zhorzh, and Zhorzhin'ka. Twenty-six years old, a distant relative of Varyagin. Strong, masculine, dark haired. He glares sternly, speaks curtly. He has an awkward air, like that of a shy person devoid of social graces. He has just completed a degree at a technical institute.*

NADEZHDA MIKHAYLOVNA PETROVSKAYA. *His mother, fifty-five years old, the very poor widow of a petty country squire, also from the petty bourgeoisie. Scrawny, as if withered; she has a meek and inoffensive air at first glance, but she is a vicious old woman. Her manner is servile.*

MARYA. *The Petrovsky's cook, fifty-five years old.*

ANISYA. *The Trofimov's cook; elderly, unkempt, rude, she speaks in a bass voice.*

VARYAGIN'S LACKEY.

Acts I and II take place at Trofimov's summer home outside Moscow; Acts III and IV, in Petrovsky's apartment; Act V, at Varyagin's summer house outside Moscow. Three days elapse between Acts I and II; four years between II and III; twenty-four hours between III and IV; eight months between IV and V. The action is set at the beginning of the 1890's.

ACT I

The summer house. Part of the park. On the left, a terrace and a door leading into the house. On the right, a small garden seat; before it, a table and two wicker chairs. On the left, to the front of the stage, a hammock is strung between two trees. In the background is a park. It is a July evening at twilight.

All stage directions are from the audience's viewpoint.

Scene 1

PELAGEYA L'VOVNA and NADEZHDA MIKHAYLOVNA. *Both are sitting on the right. Pelageya L'vovna is telling fortunes with cards. Nadezhda Mikhaylovna is sitting on the chair and timidly watching from the side.*

PELAGEYA L'VOVNA. Well, it'll turn out to be nothing but silly troubles for you, my dear . . . There won't be any position . . . You might as well believe me . . .

NADEZHDA MIKHAYLOVNA. (*Tearfully*) Have mercy, Pelageya L'vovna! . . . A friend of Egorushka works in that office . . .

PELAGEYA L'VOVNA. Big deal, your friend! . . . I'm telling you, it's a bunch of silly troubles . . . Or don't you believe the cards? . . . If that's how it's going to be, don't ask me to tell your fortune

121

. . . I'm not some kind of swindler from Zatsepa . . . (*Shuffling the cards with dignity*) All of Moscow knows me . . . When I lived in Oryol, the noblemen from fifty *versts* around would come to have their cards read . . .

NADEZHDA MIKHAYLOVNA. (*Maliciously*) That's practically incredible! . . . But then, what's with ya, Pelageya L'vovna? . . . Now, don't get huffy at me . . . But, well, how come ya didn't make a bundle on that? . . .

PELAGEYA L'VOVNA. Should I be just a plain, old fortune teller? . . . A cheat? . . . You forget my dear, that I . . . (*distinctly and with emphasis*) am a Tro-fi-mov, born an Ivanov! . . . I received my education at Smol'ny. My Lyolya is destined to move in such social spheres! . . . She'll play a role at foreign courts . . . And you're thinkin' that I should take money . . . It's obvious that all I ever accept is gratitude . . . Well, sometimes, maybe a few candies, a box at the opera, a brooch or bracelet . . . Not long ago, a merchant's wife brought a silver coffee service from Ovchinnikov . . . Through the cards I'd revealed she'd had a large theft . . . That was *comme il faut* . . . Yes, if you could only see, my dear, how they accept me in high society! . . . You see you can't impress me with importance . . . I can walk into a place just like they do, and glance around like that! I don't speak French any worse than they, and I'm never at a loss for words . . .

NADEZHDA MIKHAYLOVNA. What are ya sayin', Pelageya L'vovna . . . Please forgive me . . . I'm real ignorant . . . I've lived a whole lifetime at the pigsty and the oven . . .

PELAGEYA L'VOVNA. (*Haughtily*) And what else?

NADEZHDA MIKHAYLOVNA. As far as that goes, your income ain't so big. Just the other day your Anisya was saying . . . you ain't paid for your summer house yet . . . the landlord's gettin' fed up. And you're in debt at all the shops . . . (*She hurries, seeing Trofimova's indignant gestures.*) And you left Moscow without paying no one . . . They're always dragging ya off to the judge . . . (*She jumps up and excitedly runs across the stage.*)

PELAGEYA L'VOVNA. (*Scornfully*) Why are you so interested in the cook's gossip! . . . Besides, what sort of tone is that you're using? To whom are you speaking? . . . Is this the thanks I get for petitioning for a position for your Egor? . . .

NADEZHDA MIKHAYLOVNA. (*Immediately cringing*) What did I say? . . . Did I really say anything out o' place? Please, dearest, don't judge my ignorant stupidity too harshly . . . Look, what can ya expect from us? We live in ignorance; it's 'cause of our ignorance that we jabber on. (*She kisses Trofimova on the shoulder. Meekly*) What sorta position, my benefactress?

PELAGEYA L'VOVNA. Have you heard of Bryansky?

NADEZHDA MIKHAYLOVNA. (*Frightened*) That millionaire with the glass factory?

PELAGEYA L'VOVNA. Uh huh . . . I'm almost on a first-name basis with him. I merely have to say the word, and the position will be Egor's . . .

NADEZHDA MIKHAYLOVNA. Benefactress! . . . Then I'll see daylight! Egorushka's always assurin' me: "Wait a bit, Mama, you won't sit down to potatoes all your life . . . You'll be eatin' fish in my house." . . . I surely have suffered in my lifetime, dearie . . . My departed husband left me without any means . . . he was an honest man . . .

PELAGEYA L'VOVNA. You can't eat honesty. Is it really honest to leave a family poverty-stricken? My better half was also a liberal at first. But I nipped that in the bud, but quick . . . Back then he got a government salary of three hundred rubles a year, but we lived in style . . . Even now all Oryol still remembers my dinners and receptions . . . The governor himself practically ran errands for me. Ah, why remember this . . . There was a time . . . without settin' foot out of the house, I knew everything that was happening in town . . . I used to lay out cards for whoever needed it and reveal all the most well-kept secrets! . . . I could make and destroy a reputation in an evening . . . They all approached me trembling . . . My husband was an honest bumbler, may he rest in peace! . . . Well, I wasn't caught napping. I pulled him by the ears! . . . Later he himself thanked me. "You," he said, "are my counsellor . . . You could run a province! . . ."

NADEZHDA MIKHAYLOVNA. Well, dearest! . . . How was it my place, a dumb peasant, to tell my dear departed husband how to run things? When he was dyin', he ordered me never to get in debt to no one . . . not even for a kopeck. And see, Egorushka's just like his father. He's got a lotta this here same kind of pride!

PELAGEYA L'VOVNA. That's stupid too . . . How can poor people afford to have that kind of pride? . . . Your Egorushka, though he's an intelligent man, is a big dummy . . . He has to be guided . . . shown the way . . .

NADEZHDA MIKHAYLOVNA. (*Kissing her shoulder*) Guide him . . . Don't stop, my dear . . .

PELAGEYA L'VOVNA. Can positions in that office really be gotten? You gotta travel in the right company and not beg . . . God save you! You haf'ta look like you could spit at the job! Too bad I don't have a son—I'd show you how to look for a position! And, most important, how to catch the women . . .

NADEZHDA MIKHAYLOVNA. (*Waving her hands in horror*) Oh, no! Don't say such things . . . that Egorushka might hanky-panky with the ladies . . . or anythin' like that . . .

PELAGEYA L'VOVNA. Come on, every male knows the science of dame-chasin' without instruction . . . Besides, for that stuff they don't need any brains . . .

NADEZHDA MIKHAYLOVNA. Well, Egorushka fears them dames like fire.

PELAGEYA L'VOVNA. What have you got there? Some kind o' freak? . . .

NADEZHDA MIKHAYLOVNA. (*Offended*) What do ya mean, a freak? Thanks be t' God . . . He's a completely normal male . . .

PELAGEYA L'VOVNA. Then what's the matter with him?

Scene 2

ANISYA. (*Dirty, disheveled, she speaks in a bass voice.*) The butcher, there, wants to ask ya a question.

PELAGEYA L'VOVNA. (*With dignity*) Concerning what?

ANISYA. You know why them butchers is comin' around . . . Fer money. Everyone's comin' today, they promised, they was . . .

PELAGEYA L'VOVNA. (*Haughtily*) Who are "they"?

ANISYA. The baker, the milkman, the vegetable vendor . . . Tikhon the fisherman [. . .] All of 'em! Yestiddy they was sayin' in the shop . . . "We're comin' 'cause we heard the fiancé'll be there . . ."

PELAGEYA L'VOVNA. (*With indignation*) Fool! . . . Go say that there's a telegram from Vladimir Arkadyevich . . . He'll arrive today and tomorrow I'll square accounts . . .

ANISYA. 'Be better if ya showed the butcher the telegram itself
. . . Without that he won't go. "Cause," he says, "ya can't believe
their promises. I've heard plenty about 'em . . ."

PELAGEYA L'VOVNA. *(Taking the telegram from her pocket)*
Here, take it! . . .

ANISYA. By the by, ma'am, you ain't played straight with me fer
three months now . . . What kind o' treatment's that? *(Sticking out
her foot in a worn-out and ripped slipper)* Worn clear through . . .
I'm shamed in front o' people . . .

PELAGEYA L'VOVNA. All right, go on! . . . *(Anisya starts to go.)*
Listen, tell them all out there: if they have it in their heads to come
without being summoned or disturb Vladimir Arkadyevich, I won't
pay them back a penny! . . . Do you understand? . . . Let them get
it through the courts! . . .

ANISYA *exits.* [. . .]

———

PELAGEYA L'VOVNA. Pigs! . . . They've been told that the fiancé
will pay. No deal; they don't believe it . . .

NADEZHDA MIKHAYLOVNA. Well, what if he don't pay 'em?

PELAGEYA L'VOVNA. What nonsense! What's it to him to throw
away a couple of thousand? Look he has five m-i-l-l-i-o-n!

NADEZHDA MIKHAYLOVNA. *(Sinking to the ground)* Five mil
. . . Ugh! I'm even gettin' dizzy. Dearest Pelageya L'vovna, how'd
ya finagle such a catch?

PELAGEYA L'VOVNA. Very simple! . . . Vol'demar, you see, is a
distant relative of ours. You see, his uncle was my grandfather's
first cousin . . . somethin' like that . . . I only needed an excuse to
visit his home . . . Well, his widow of a mother got ill . . . Like a
flash, I snatched Lyolya from the institute . . . this was last year
. . . and went to their estate . . . "I've come," I say, "accordin' to
the dictates of family obligations, to fulfill my duty . . . You're all
alone . . ." and so on. She ignored me, of course . . . a society
grande dame, ya know. Well, it's not easy to get rid o' me unless I
wanna go . . . In August she died in my arms. And Lyolya returned
to the institute . . . already engaged . . .

NADEZHDA MIKHAYLOVNA. Well, that's real luck! . . .

PELAGEYA L'VOVNA. Not luck, my dear, brains . . . Yes indeed,
Lyolya's not some dowerless waif . . . *(Haughtily)* Have you heard
that I have a millionaire brother in America, and I'm his only heir?

NADEZHDA MIKHAYLOVNA. (*With poorly hidden envy*) Is that so? Saints alive! He's filthy rich! . . . Hah! Too bad them stupid men don't know how to use their dough!

PELAGEYA L'VOVNA. Varyagin—stupid? You forget yourself, my dear . . .

NADEZHDA MIKHAYLOVNA. (*Agitated and gesturing vividly*) I remember your Voloden'ka . . . Ya' see he's kin t' us too . . . He was a lazy kid . . . real teeny little runt . . . Seems t' me he and Egorushka studied together a year . . . Only your Voloden'ka didn't read any of the books he was supposed to . . . 'Cause of this he left the technicolor-school.[1]

PELAGEYA L'VOVNA. Heavens, you are vulgar, my precious! . . . "Teeny little runt" . . . "technicolor-school" . . . What's a technicolor-school? [. . .]

NADEZHDA MIKHAYLOVNA. Look, technical, technicolor . . . it's all one. The thing is, his mug didn't turn out so good, like my Egorushka's . . . So he's ignorant . . . didn't finish his learnin' nowhere . . .

PELAGEYA L'VOVNA. What nonsense! . . . At this very moment he's attending foreign universities, studyin' under the best professors. My, what can I say! Why they're such people, my dear, that you and Egorushka simply wouldn't understand. He's a remarkable man . . .

NADEZHDA MIKHAYLOVNA. Well, let me tell ya, Pelageya L'vovna . . . What's t' understand? . . . A while back ya bragged about that scarf the princess took off her back t' give t' ya.

PELAGEYA L'VOVNA. Real lace . . .

NADEZHDA MIKHAYLOVNA. Looks like a big rag t' our kind . . . I'd be embarrassed t' wear it . . . And then there's yer cup . . .

PELAGEYA L'VOVNA. *Vieux-Saxe*—it cost fifty rubles . . .

NADEZHDA MIKHAYLOVNA. And now it's a piece o' trash . . . the handle's broken off—and the saucer's chipped . . . I'd be ashamed t' offer it t' a guest, yet ya brag about it . . .

PELAGEYA L'VOVNA. (*With emphasis*) I told ya, it cost fifty rubles . . .

---

1. A mispronunciation of *real'noe;* in the original text Nadezhda Mikhaylovna confuses *real'noe* (technical high school) with *royal'noe* (piano school)—a nonexistent type of institution.

NADEZHDA MIKHAYLOVNA. *(Chuckling maliciously)* You and I were also worth a good bit when we was young . . . heh, heh . . . Pelageya L'vovna, dearie . . . but now, ya'll excuse the expression, we ain't worth a bent kopeck . . .

PELAGEYA L'VOVNA. *(Calmly)* I can see you and I won't ever agree . . . Just let me say this to you: I'm takin' the trouble to get a position for Egor, but for this I also expect you to do me a favor . . .

NADEZHDA MIKHAYLOVNA. *(Immediately shriveling up)* Your wish is my command, benefactress . . .

PELAGEYA L'VOVNA. *(Glancing around and lowering her voice)* You see . . . Vol'demar is returning from abroad today . . . Naturally, the fiancé would like to walk alone with his bride, sit a little . . . you know, kiss . . .

NADEZHDA MIKHAYLOVNA. That's only normal . . .

PELAGEYA L'VOVNA. But your Egor, God forgive me, drags after Lyolya like a tail. If you permit me . . . That's ridiculous! . . . How long can it be before there's a scandal? Look, Lyolya's a child . . . This attention flatters her . . . And what can your Egor count on? Is he really a match for my Lyolya?

NADEZHDA MIKHAYLOVNA. *(Her expression changing)* What sort of shinin' star is yer Lyolya?

PELAGEYA L'VOVNA. She's a Tro-fim-ov'! . . .

NADEZHDA MIKHAYLOVNA. What breed o' animal is that?

PELAGEYA L'VOVNA. I see you're utterly hopeless . . . I'm tellin' you in plain language that my Lyolya will be frequenting high social circles! . . . She's destined to play a role at court . . . *(Trying to ignore Petrovskaya's mocking grimace)* The point is, if you want Egor to get a position, tell him to get lost . . .

NADEZHDA MIKHAYLOVNA. *(Remembering her situation)* I'll tell him, I'll tell him, benefactress.

Scene 3

LYOLYA *enters from the right in a beautiful, dazzling outfit with a parasol;* VERA *also enters, without a parasol, with a book in her hands.*

LYOLYA. Lord, how tired I am! How hot it is today! . . . If only it were already nighttime! . . . *(She throws herself into the hammock.)* [. . .]

PELAGEYA L'VOVNA. Where have you been?

VERA. (*Curtly*) We ran to the station . . . Where else can we go? We only have one road . . . Thank God the bridegroom's coming soon! . . . Lyolya can go wherever she wants, but leave me alone! . . .

PELAGEYA L'VOVNA. Why do you speak in such a tone, Vera? A stranger might think you're jealous that Lyolya is engaged!

VERA. What's there to envy? . . . (*Lyolya starts to sing softly.*) As if getting married was such a joy! . . . (*Lyolya sings loudly.*) I'm just sorry for your fiancé . . . What kind of life awaits him, married to a flirt who makes eyes at anyone she meets? . . .

LYOLYA. Ha! . . . Ha! . . . Ha! . . . Vera can't forgive my flirting with this officer . . . Ha! . . . Ha! . . . Ha! . . . I can't recall his silly-looking face without laughing!

PELAGEYA L'VOVNA. What officer? . . .

LYOLYA. He doesn't live far from us. He's been running after us, the fool . . . Well, can I be blamed if I have laughing eyes? . . .

NADEZHDA MIKHAYLOVNA. (*With irony*) Elena Nikolaevna is a complete child . . . To them who ain't cried, everything's a joke . . .

VERA. Still a child at eighteen? Then why are you marrying her off? . . . Give her a doll, not a husband . . . If she beats the doll's head, it won't hurt.

PELAGEYA L'VOVNA. Vera . . . You will please stop your sermonizing! . . . Tell me, what's so criminal about making eyes? Look at yourself, dearest. We've heard all about your anatomy and botany. Complete depravity! Well, here you are—a university student, an educated woman, and well-spoken . . . and even beautiful . . . Well, just try to catch up to Lyolya! . . . Who'd lose his head over you? Who would, to use an elevated expression, lay his fortune and his heart at your feet? All this happens to Lyolya, though she's studied neither your physics nor your chemistry . . . But tell me, who gets any pleasure from you? . . .

VERA. What exactly did you have in mind? . . .

PELAGEYA L'VOVNA. Well, I'm asking you, what use are you? You're not in tune with women and you don't fit in with men. Are you really female?

VERA. Ha! . . . Ha! . . . This is truly becoming amusing . . . So, aunt, in your opinion, what am I?

PELAGEYA L'VOVNA. A cold fish. Have you heard of that kind of woman?

LYOLYA *and* NADEZHDA MIKHAYLOVNA *giggle.*

PELAGEYA L'VOVNA. Tell me, dearie, what kind of wife will you make? A man loves a gay face, witty conversation. A husband, when he comes home from work, likes to see an elegant, gracious creature, full of femininity, so that he's aroused . . . A wife must always stimulate this excitement in her husband; her strength lies in this . . .

VERA. Good Lord . . . What depravity! . . . This is practically an organized system of depravity . . .

PELAGEYA L'VOVNA. (*Not listening*) And what about when your husband comes to you with a kiss, and you give him physiology . . . He whispers: "What a tiny foot you have, Vera! . . ." And you answer . . . (*Putting her hands on her hips and assuming a stern expression*) "And what bones make up the foot? Hm?" Is it surprising that he takes his hat in his hand and makes a beeline for someone else, a real dummy? . . . We're lucky that the traditional institutes maintain accepted precepts and produce girls *comme il faut* . . . innocent doves . . .

VERA. Who, on the sly, have read all of Zola . . .

LYOLYA. (*Laughing defiantly*) That's true, Vera, I've read it all.

PELAGEYA L'VOVNA. Well, what if she has read it all . . . Big deal. It's not written on her forehead nor does it appear on her diploma. Anyone can see that the young lady's well bred . . . And that she knows how to blush and demurely lower her eyes . . . But would you ever lower your eyes before anyone? . . . To hear you talk, it's not proper to make eyes . . . But in hospitals those miserable doctors play all sorts of dirty tricks under the guise of science, and that's considered proper? If I had my way, I'd make all university women marry doctors and students . . . And bang! In a flash, the courses would be cancelled!

VERA. That means that in your opinion we attend classes only to find husbands? . . .

PELAGEYA L'VOVNA. Tut . . . tut . . . tut. Try arguing with anyone else, but not me. You won't convince me that in your classes you're not lookin' for the same thing we dummies chase after at the clubs. There you just cover it up with other ideas. Science, independence, this and that . . . But we simply admit:

one has to compromise . . . An old maid's neither a candle to God nor a torch for the Devil . . .

VERA. (*Calmly*) That's been said before you . . . that a woman's primary purpose is to nurse children, and cook . . .

PELAGEYA L'VOVNA. Actually, no respectable husband demands one or the other from his wife.

VERA. Well, at least here's something new and original! You mean to say a wife has no responsibilities? Then tell me, what is expected of her? . . .

PELAGEYA L'VOVNA. To make her husband happy . . .

VERA. And how is this "happiness" to be had? . . . What is this, a special science? Tell me, where is it taught?

PELAGEYA L'VOVNA. How can you working girls understand such fine points? . . . After all, this isn't along the lines of a medical worker's vocation. Well, why are you making such big eyes?

VERA. But that isn't being a wife, but a kept woman.

PELAGEYA L'VOVNA. You aren't gonna bully anybody with shocking words . . . It's been like that since time began and it'll be like that in the future.

NADEZHDA MIKHAYLOVNA. Not everyone, my dear young lady, seeks that path for his wife. Take my Egorushka. He's a workin' man, and he needs a workin' wife, sort o' like you [. . .]

VERA. (*Bursting out*) I have no intentions whatsoever of marrying . . .

PELAGEYA L'VOVNA. That's foolish. I also feel you and Egor are the same wild breed, and you'd make a good pair. Others have children, but you two, you see, in nine months would produce a new textbook on physiology. Now wouldn't that be helpful to society!

Scene 4

ANISYA. (*Barefoot, her hem tucked up, a rag in her hand*) Someone from Moscow's askin' fer ya out there. They've brought a whole box . . .

LYOLYA. (*Jumping up in surprise*) What kind of box? From where?

PELAGEYA L'VOVNA. (*Hurriedly pinning on her wiglet*) Anisya, for the fear of God! What are you trying to look like? . . .

ANISYA. Look, I'm washin' the floors in the house. Ya told me yestiddy yerself: scrub the floors extra clean for the bridegroom . . . 'cause mushrooms is growin' all over.

PELAGEYA L'VOVNA. Well, get along! . . . Finish quickly! . . .

ANISYA exits.

——————————

PELAGEYA L'VOVNA. That's probably a messenger with presents from your fiancé . . . Let's go, Lyolya . . .

LYOLYA. (*With disappointment in her voice*) Does that mean he's already in Moscow?

PELAGEYA L'VOVNA. He'll be here toward nightfall . . . He sent a telegram today . . . I kept quiet about it to surprise you, you little fool. (*She takes her by the chin.*) Well, aren't you pleased by the presents? Let's go . . . Ah! . . . I've also gotta do something about food for him. Most people get supper in the evening . . . but Vol'demar gets lunch! (*Haughtily*) That's 'cause he's an aristocrat *pur-sang* . . . (*She and Lyolya exit into the house.*)

——————————

The stage grows noticeably darker. A pause.

VERA stands in deep thought.

NADEZHDA MIKHAYLOVNA. (*Approaching her, she speaks in a lowered tone.*) Your dear little aunt has promised to find us a position . . .

VERA. Is that so? . . . She's got something up her sleeve . . .

NADEZHDA MIKHAYLOVNA. You bet she does! She's afraid that Egorushka'll compromise her daughter in front of her fiancé . . . What a card she is! She says I can get a job for Egor with Bryansky at the factory.

VERA. (*Calmly*) It's all a big lie. She's never even laid eyes on him, this Bryansky.

NADEZHDA MIKHAYLOVNA. Huh? . . .

VERA. Why should she help you? Does she really need you? Don't deceive yourself. We're all beggars—Egorushka, you, me —we're not people to her . . . We're outcasts, who can be scorned and duped if necessary.

NADEZHDA MIKHAYLOVNA. (*Offended*) Well, how can we compete with 'em, when they're completely surrounded by millions!

VERA. You're referring to the uncle in America and his inheritance? It's a lie . . . None of us—her relatives—are either rich or a famous part of the impoverished nobility. And Pelageya L'vovna has long since renounced us. If I find shelter here with her, while I'm studying, it's not due to her feeling for family. I pay her for room and board and have never agreed to any obligation toward her.

NADEZHDA MIKHAYLOVNA. (*With vicious satisfaction*) So, that means she ain't an aristocrat?

VERA. (*Imitating Pelageya L'vovna's intonation*) A Tro-fim-ov. Ha! . . . Ha! . . . Ha! . . . Have you ever heard of them?

NADEZHDA MIKHAYLOVNA. You're right! Never in all my born days have I heard of 'em.

VERA. It's some kind of delusion of grandeur. In lying, Pelageya L'vovna is a positive artist. She lies without cause, without purpose, unconsciously, through habit, with inspiration; she delights in lying [. . .]

NADEZHDA MIKHAYLOVNA. So, that's what they are! Uh, my poor Egorushka! (*She cries.*)

VERA. (*Upset*) That's enough! . . . Enough . . . They won't let Varyagin's millions slip through their hands. Lyolya will get married and then leave . . . But Egorushka is a man of character.

NADEZHDA MIKHAYLOVNA. (*Howling through her tears*) But what if he blows a hole clear through hisself?

VERA. (*She paces quickly and speaks to herself, not listening to Nadezhda Mikhaylovna.*) Now analyze this psychological puzzle for me. What could Egor Andreevich and this egotistical, spoiled young girl have in common? Moreover, they say that women must be re-educated, they must achieve the status of men . . . a wife ought to be a companion to her husband . . . Nonsense, lies! . . . What they need in a wife is a doll, a little idol. The kind that will play the fool all her life and, while joking, break his heart . . . (*She falls onto the little garden bench, covering her face with her hands.*)

NADEZHDA MIKHAYLOVNA. (*Approaching Vera and taking her by the shoulders*) Is this any reason to cry? (*Vera sobs.*) Ah . . . ho . . . ho! . . . I ain't lived here long, but I realize what's really up . . . No matter how I strain my brain I don't know what to do. A friend's invited Egorushka to the provinces for a visit . . . But I'm afraid to bring it up with him. Wouldn't ya speak to him, my dear . . . Could be he'll listen to you; he's always respected you.

VERA. (*With bitterness, slowly*) Always respected me . . . (*She shudders and quickly rises.*) Ah, here he is! For God's sake, don't tell him I was crying, don't tell him anything . . . (*She runs off to the left, behind the house.*)

Scene 5

PETROVSKY *is dressed in a modest day-suit and an even more modest coat. He wears a fedora. He has no gloves. His face is pale and tired-looking.*

NADEZHDA MIKHAYLOVNA. (*Coming to greet him*) Well, well, Egorushka. I been waitin' for you, today. What'd they tell you at the office?

PETROVSKY. (*He sits on the couch and wearily flings his hat on it.*) The same old rigmarole. Endless promises. No positions . . . Where's Elena Nikolaevna?

NADEZHDA MIKHAYLOVNA. She's expecting her fiancé . . .

PETROVSKY. (*Anxiously*) You don't say? When? . . .

NADEZHDA MIKHAYLOVNA. T'day, I reckon . . . He sent a bunch o' presents from Moscow. Our young lady flew the coop like a little bird and ran to look . . . (*A pause. Petrovsky is about to say something, but, clenching his teeth with an expression of acute pain, he lowers his head and buries his face in his hands.*)

NADEZHDA MIKHAYLOVNA. (*Affectionately, while stealthily wiping away a tear*) Merciful God, Egorushka! Why are ya so upset? There's lots of fish in the sea, and we ain't got the wallet or the looks for them kinds o' dames.

PETROVSKY. (*Wringing his hands*) Uh! Don't pester me! . . . Be quiet . . . (*With an effort*) That's what I'll do. Pack my suit-case—you know, linen, books, in a word, whatever's needed . . . I'm going away today . . .

NADEZHDA MIKHAYLOVNA. To the provinces, to yer friend? . . . Good thing, sonny! . . . There you can walk a little, stuff yerself, relax. Look at that, your cheeks is so sunken, one's eaten the other . . . I'll get ya packed in a jiffy . . . (*She exits.*)

The stage is dark.

PETROVSKY. (*Alone. He sits wrapped in thought. A short pause.*) And so, the end of a fairy tale . . . Well, so what? It's time. It's overdue . . .

Scene 6

LYOLYA *enters quickly, looks around, then throws herself headlong toward him, and stretches out both her hands.*

LYOLYA. Egor Andreich . . . You're here? Finally! . . .

PETROVSKY *stands up, pulls Lyolya to him, and greedily gazes into her eyes.* [. . .] (*Without releasing Lyolya's hands*) Today your fiancé will be here . . . and so I'm leaving . . .

LYOLYA. (*With alarm*) Leaving? For where? When? [. . .]

[*The lovers engage in a passionate, somewhat melodramatic scene, at the end of which* LYOLYA'S *will dominates.* PETROVSKY *is hopelessly in love with her and is willing to sacrifice all his ideals for her.* LYOLYA *is revealed as no mere child, but a capricious coquette indulging her frivolous willfulness. She is attracted to* PETROVSKY'S *fiery nature, but the relationship is a game for her.*] VARYAGIN (*hidden in the shadows*) *witnesses their passion and hears them plan a rendezvous for that evening. Then he comes out of the shadows. He is pale, but calm. He plays the entire scene with control, but with a noticeable shade of irony.*

LYOLYA, *upon seeing Varyagin, cries out.*

VARYAGIN. (*Gaily*) *Bonsoir*, Lyolya . . . It seems I've startled you?

PETROVSKY. (*Not moving, he remains in the shadows. Aside.*) Now you're too late . . .

LYOLYA. (*Confused*) Ah, Vol'demar, I'm so happy! . . . But you turned up so suddenly . . .

VARYAGIN. (*Catching the phrase*) Like the ghost of Banquo at Macbeth's feast . . . (*He takes Lyolya's hands and kisses them one after the other.*) My charming fiancée! Aren't you going to scold me because I arrived here by coach earlier than expected? I got fed up with the train schedules.

LYOLYA. (*Laughing nervously*) You're a whole hour earlier than the train. We didn't expect you so soon . . . [VARYAGIN *kisses* LYOLYA.] [. . .]

PETROVSKY. (*Taking a step forward, breathlessly*) Stop! You're not alone here . . .

VARYAGIN. Is that so? Who would be silly enough to be a third party at a lovers' tryst?

PETROVSKY. (*Approaching*) I am here . . .

LYOLYA *runs off to the left.*

VARYAGIN. (*Stretching out both hands to Petrovsky*) Egorushka . . . What a happy surprise! . . . Have you known my fiancée for long? . . .

PETROVSKY. (*Confused*) No . . . a long time . . . About three months . . .

VARYAGIN. Was it you who's infected Lyolya with the austere attitudes of a Cato? . . . Ha! . . . Ha! . . . But, well, we'll already be married in a week . . .

PETROVSKY. (*In a disheartened tone*) So soon?

VARYAGIN. I must hurry and live, Egorushka, while my taste for life is not yet dulled . . . hurry and marry, while I'm still so passionately in love . . . You're so gloomy, like Cassandra at the ruins of Troy . . .

Scene 8

PELAGEYA L'VOVNA, NADEZHDA MIKHAYLOVNA, VERA, LYO-LYA, *and* ANISYA *with a lamp in her hand; they all come onto the terrace from the house and descend into the garden.*

PELAGEYA L'VOVNA. Where is he, my little dove? Where? Let me kiss you! . . . (*She embraces Varyagin.*) At last! We waited and waited. Your bride kept peeking out, on the run to meet you. We were waiting for our dear guest [. . .]

VARYAGIN. (*Offering his arm to* PELAGEYA L'VOVNA, *he goes with her to the terrace.*) Now I trust no postponements of the wedding are foreseen. I would request it be held (*loudly*) within the week [. . .]

PETROVSKY. [*Now alone with* LYOLYA] Be careful, Lyolya! If he so much as kisses you once . . . Remember, you're bound to me by word and feeling . . . and I will not yield you alive to anyone!

LYOLYA. (*Aside*) I'm ruined [. . .]

Curtain

ACT II

The same set as in the first act. Three days have passed. On stage evening is falling. PELAGEYA L'VOVNA, *to the right, is laying out patience.* NADEZHDA MIKHAYLOVNA *is sitting on a stool next to her, with a woolen stocking which she is knitting.* VERA *is reading a book on the terrace steps.*

Scene 1

PELAGEYA L'VOVNA. (*Shuffling the cards with annoyance*) Phooey, nothing! . . . That's the third time everything has come out empty nonsense . . . I'm afraid, Lyolya may be falling ill . . .

NADEZHDA MIKHAYLOVNA. Yeah, we're all surprised at the young mistress. Her face has already grown so thin . . . What could it be from? In his joyfulness, her fiancé showers her with so much money. What a bunch he dumped on ya three days ago! . . . And weren't them merchants all over you! Like crows on a cow that's kicked the bucket, you'll excuse the expression . . .

PELAGEYA L'VOVNA. Vultures! . . . Throwing themselves on the money . . . As if they'd never seen it before. Yesterday we had seven hundred rubles, and today we can't even scratch together fifty . . . Well, that's why I've been living on credit since spring . . . Naturally, since I've lived my life like a lady, I'll want to kick the bucket like a lady, too . . .

VERA. That's all fine . . . Only it turns out you've been living an idle life at someone else's expense . . . A stranger wouldn't think you're so refined . . .

PELAGEYA L'VOVNA. I spit on how it looks from your point of view. (*To* NADEZHDA MIKHAYLOVNA) He still has to put some capital into the bank under my name. I'll probably be no stranger . . . as the mother-in-law . . .

VERA. So you're going to soak him three times over for that good piece of luck! Why should you begrudge him his money? . . .

PELAGEYA L'VOVNA. You haven't launched your little son yet, Nadezhda Mikhaylovna? I bet you're still waitin' for a position from those people, aren't you? . . . I thought he decided to go to the provinces?

NADEZHDA MIKHAYLOVNA. (*Shouts in agitation*) So he did. He says t' me: "I'm waitin' fer money fer the trip, a student's late in payin'!"

PELAGEYA L'VOVNA. Oh he's lying, my dear! . . . I've got a premonition. Look, I'll gladly stake his trip myself . . . How much does he need? . . .

NADEZHDA MIKHAYLOVNA. (*Waving her hands at Trofimova*) Tsk! . . . Tsk! . . . What's the matter with you? How'd I approach him? . . . With this here offer? . . . He'd chuck me out on my ear! . . . Don't ya know nuthin' 'bout his character? . . .

PELAGEYA L'VOVNA. (*Angrily*) What kind of mother are you? . . . You—noodle! How is it that ya can't get around your only begotten son? . . . Butter him up, work on him a little. Everyone has his weaknesses . . . You've only gotta dig 'em out, and then you can play on 'em like keys on a piano . . .

NADEZHDA MIKHAYLOVNA. (*With conviction*) He don't have none o' them weaknesses! . . . No siree! Ya' can look till doomsday, you won't find none! . . .

PELAGEYA L'VOVNA. What, is your brain shrinking from all this nonsense? Who doesn't have 'em! . . . Come on, does your Egor have two heads? He'd be like putty in my hands, if I took out after him! . . . It'll turn out badly for your Egor . . . if he doesn't go . . . For goodness sake, can it be long before we have a scandal! He paces day and night under Lyolya's windows. No matter how much in love ya are, that'd lead anyone to suspect something . . . and should it come to a duel, you'll have only yourself to blame. Abroad, Vol'demar always took first prize in marksmanship.

NADEZHDA MIKHAYLOVNA. (*Shrinking from fear*) Oh, how terrible! Saints alive!

PELAGEYA L'VOVNA. What's more, your Egor is cookin' somethin' up, I can feel it in my bones . . . You've only to look at his eyes . . . Yesterday I met him toward nightfall and he had me shakin' in my shoes . . . Well, Cain will always be Cain! . . . (*Glancing to the left*) And here he comes now, speak of the Devil . . . (*Quickly pinning on her wiglet*) Doesn't he look the brigand of Murom? All he needs is a club in his hand and to crawl into a ditch by the highway. (*She stands.*) Uh, get thee behind me, Satan! . . . I feel like I could curse him up and down . . . (*Quickly, almost at a run, she disappears into the house.*)

NADEZHDA MIKHAYLOVNA. (*Calling after Trofimova*) Take to your heels, dearie. The hands haven't been born that can handle my Egorushka . . . Lookee, how she cleared out! (*Immediately changing to a timid tone*) Maybe I should get lost, too. Ya should ask him about his trip to the provinces, my sweet. He'd confide everythin' t' you, my precious. I wanna stay outta his sight . . . "You bother me," he says . . . (*She quickly exits to the right.*)

Scene 2

PETROVSKY *enters from the left. His face is drawn.*

VERA. At last, Egor Andreich! Hello! Where have you been disappearing to these past few days? . . .

PETROVSKY *sits down to the right on the divan.* I don't know anything, Vera! For God's sake, don't ask! (*He hides his head in his hands.*)

VERA. (*Approaching him, she speaks with emotion.*) What? You've even forgotten what you considered your goal in life? . . . Then I'll remind you, Egorushka . . . You were striving to get a position at the factory, even if only a modest job, and devote your energy and knowledge to those who exist in hunger and cold, in perpetual darkness, injustice, and ignorance. You dreamed of championing the interests of the proletariat, battling the exploiters, awakening the consciousness of the masses. You sought to alleviate through your influence the burden of those who are ignored, for whom no one intercedes. It is necessary to invest much labor, selfless love, and energy in this endeavor . . . But you would not retreat before such a task, would you, Egorushka? Of course, you wouldn't settle for the easy ethics of a careerist . . . You wouldn't be content with compromises . . . A man such as you is easier to break than to bend! . . .

PETROVSKY. Vera . . . You're a wonderful soul! . . .

VERA. (*Excitedly, placing her hand on his shoulder*) Do you remember my dreams, Egorushka? Beside you like a faithful friend, I wanted to be a physician's assistant at the factory. Though my knowledge might be modest, still, how useful I could be in a place where there's only one doctor for many *versts!* . . . And there's so much to do! There's never an end to epidemics . . . And death, and filth, and poverty . . . I've seen all this, Egorushka; I myself have suffered through it all. In the provinces, it's not hard to find a goal and a task. It's right before your eyes . . . It strikes at your heart . . . It cries out desperately, appealing to your conscience—work, there's no time to rest . . . each day, each hour is precious . . . To lose heart here is shameful! . . . And to cry for yourself—sinful! [. . .]

PETROVSKY. (*Rousing himself*) Vera . . . my friend . . . arrange a meeting with Lyolya for me, and I'll never forget this favor! [. . .] Everything is in this meeting for me! Lyolya has been avoiding me for the past three days . . . Varyagin follows us like a police detective . . . It seems, he's guessed about everything.

VERA. You yourself see that she doesn't need you. Let her have Varyagin and his millions!

PETROVSKY. (*Enraged*) She loves me, not Varyagin!

VERA. (*With bitterness*) Perhaps, but you don't have any millions. In Lyolya's eyes only money gives one the right to happiness [. . .]

[VERA *reminds* EGOR *that he has forgotten about* VARYAGIN *and what his reaction to the relationship might be.* PETROVSKY, *being an old acquaintance of* VARYAGIN, *reveals the duality he has witnessed in the man's nature—his magnanimity and aloofness, his passionate yet cold nature, his vacillation between kindness and cruelty, and above all the pointlessness and vacuity of his existence. These qualities begin to emerge in the two subsequent scenes.* VARYAGIN *and* LYOLYA *return from an evening in town. They are cross with each other. He has obviously been plying her with liquor. While* LYOLYA *is changing her clothes,* VARYAGIN *reveals to* VERA *his knowledge of* PETROVSKY's *love for* LYOLYA. *He also confesses his own strong attraction to* VERA—*precisely because of her cold indifference toward him and her disdain for his money.* VERA *asks him to yield* LYOLYA *to* EGOR; *she is willing to sacrifice her love to make* EGOR *happy.*]

VERA. Do you love Lyolya very much?

VARYAGIN. If love is enthusiasm, the readiness to undergo sacrifice, tears of veneration, then I don't love her . . . and I've never loved anyone . . . I know what an orgy of sensation is . . . that's all . . .

VERA. Oh, that means it would be easy for you to give up Lyolya . . . What good is she to you? . . .

VARYAGIN. The cruel logic of a woman in love! . . . Petrovsky has had a cherished goal, practically since his early school days—he has friends, a mother's love, and your love, Vera. I have only sensations . . . Do you wish to rob the poor to give to the rich? Won't you have any pity for me?

VERA. (*Pulling away her hand*) I don't understand you . . .

VARYAGIN. For people like me, Lyolya is the same as hashish . . . I feel that it won't be long before my taste for life will be dulled, and to arouse my energy I will have to increase my dose of this sort of narcotic . . . It's as though I sometimes foresee all the horror of the future [. . .]

Scene 4

LYOLYA *has changed into an elegant blouse.*

VERA. (*Glancing at* LYOLYA) I'll leave [. . .] *She exits to the right. She is noticeably upset.*

————— • —————

VARYAGIN *looks after her for a long time.* [. . .]

[LYOLYA *notices* VARYAGIN'*s attraction toward* VERA *and is jealous. He hopes that* LYOLYA, *somewhat intoxicated by the liquor he has forced her to drink, will reveal her true feelings. To test the motivations behind her love, he poses a hypothetical question—would she marry him if he were bankrupt?*]

LYOLYA. . . . Poverty would kill me . . . How can one live in three rooms? Have five dresses? Never travel anywhere? . . .

VARYAGIN. (*Prompting*) And earn your own living . . .

LYOLYA. That's horrible! . . . Vera seems to me so pitiful with her cheap lessons, her dreams of living somewhere in the wilderness, among the peasants . . . Oh, it would be better to die! . . . Tell me you were joking . . .

VARYAGIN. (*Embracing* LYOLYA) Yes, my dear, I was joking. You'll have everything that money can buy . . .

LYOLYA. (*Pressing her head against his chest*) As if there is something that can't be bought! . . . (*She laughs scornfully.*)

VARYAGIN. Yes, my sweet cynic, there is one trifle—happiness . . .

LYOLYA. But we'll be happy . . . What could interfere with our happiness? . . .

VARYAGIN. (*Kissing her and smiling ironically*) Also a mere trifle—doubt . . .

LYOLYA. (*Coquettishly glancing at his face*) Tell me, do you love me very much?

VARYAGIN. Yes . . . Yes . . . I've figured you out . . . I need someone just like you . . . Lying, unfaithful, fickle, like a daydream . . . elusive, like a shadow [. . .] With you one wouldn't soon be satiated and bored . . . (*He kisses her.*) I expect much of you . . . I've arranged a great deal of bank credit for you . . . You won't disappoint my expectations? . . .

LYOLYA. How alike we are, Vol'demar! . . . I also am very afraid of boredom—and, to be gay, I'm ready to try anything . . . I will tell you confidentially: I'd definitely like to experience everything . . . everything in life! . . . We'll be glorious mates . . .

VARYAGIN. (*Sadly*) Yes, we'll live with ease, knowing no responsibilities, seeking only pleasure . . . Isn't that, essentially, the goal of life? . . . We have no future, Lyolya . . . therefore we're heroes of the day . . . Pitiful heroes, without any banners or heroism . . . But so what! . . . We were created for each other! Try to comprehend this thoroughly, Lyolya, and don't forsake me! . . .

Scene 5

PELAGEYA L'VOVNA, *then* VERA [. . .] [VARYAGIN *exits.*]

PELAGEYA L'VOVNA. (*Quickly approaching her daughter and grabbing her by the hand, in an undertone*) What's the matter with you, shameless hussy? Again romances? . . . What did you promise me? . . . Or have you forgotten how you trembled with fear last night while your admirer was prowling under the window? Ain't it obvious you're as wanton as a cat, but as cowardly as a rabbit? . . .

LYOLYA. Ah, Mama, where do you get all this? As far as I can see, there isn't even a trace of Petrovsky here . . . Besides, I gave you my word that I wouldn't kiss him anymore . . .

PELAGEYA L'VOVNA. Heh, you saucy thing, watch out! It's no good crying afterward . . . Leave off these shenanigans for just one more week . . . You'll get married, and then you can kiss whoever you please . . . Then it'll be none of my business. (*Exits*) [. . .]

VERA. Why are you avoiding Petrovsky?

LYOLYA. (*Wringing her hands*) Well, what else can I do? Tell me . . . I purposely stayed behind to speak with you . . . Tell him to leave me in peace, once and for all! He'll listen to you . . . I'd been hoping all this time that he'd come to his senses and leave for the provinces . . .

VERA. So that your game with him will go unpunished? What a petty scheme! . . .

LYOLYA. Have pity on me, Vera! . . . You know, I'm still—a child . . .

VERA. Look, what an excuse! Children play with dolls, not with the emotions and lives of people [. . .]

LYOLYA. (*Looking around in fear*) Oh, I fear this man! . . . I don't sleep at night from fear, seeing his shadow beneath my window . . . He's capable of anything . . .

VERA. (*Grabbing her hand*) Look, he's coming . . .

LYOLYA. (*Tearing away*) Vera, let me go! . . . Let me go . . . (*Having seen Petrovsky, she covers her face with her hands.*) Ah! . . .

Scene 6

VERA *quietly exits to the right, into the park.*

————

PETROVSKY. At last! . . . Don't you feel guilty for torturing me so? Or doesn't it matter to you? . . . Well, why are you silent? . . . How you're trembling all over! . . . My joy . . . (*He embraces her.*)

LYOLYA. (*Trying to free herself*) [. . .] Wait a minute . . . Egor Andreich . . . There's a misunderstanding between us. Hear me out calmly . . . I cannot . . . be your wife . . .

PETROVSKY. What? (*Backing away, he looks at her perplexedly.*) You cannot be my wife? . . . But why?

LYOLYA. (*Wringing her hands*) I'm—engaged to Varyagin. This cannot be changed . . . I can't fight them . . . They're stronger than we are . . . George . . . resign yourself to this! . . .

PETROVSKY. (*Forcefully*) Never! . . . Even if it costs me my life . . . Now, answer me truthfully! . . . (*He grabs her rudely by the hand.*) Are you making fun of me? . . . Did you feel engaged to someone else when you were kissing me? . . . (*Breathlessly*) When you said you loved me?

LYOLYA. (*Throwing her arms around his neck, frightened*) No, no, my precious! . . . I love you . . . you, alone . . . But don't you

see? I must marry Varyagin . . . But why are you turning so pale?
. . . Is everything really lost? . . . You little dumb-bell! . . . We'll
have meetings . . . I swear . . . I'll arrange it so you'll again be with
me . . . always . . . forever . . .

PETROVSKY. Be quiet . . . Be quiet! . . . Oh, how they've corrupted you! [. . .]

Scene 7

VARYAGIN *comes out onto the terrace. He's very pale and upset.*
Nevertheless, he plays the entire scene with great restraint.

VARYAGIN. (*With spiteful irony*) Stop! . . . You're not alone here!
. . .

LYOLYA *shrieks. In terror, she tears herself away from Pe-*
trovsky's arms and in a swoon falls onto the divan, face down.

VARYAGIN. What's the meaning of this tender scene, Egor
Andreich?

PETROVSKY. (*Gloomily, but with self-control*) Lyolya loves me
. . . That says it all . . .

VARYAGIN. You are making a serious mistake if you think you can
rely on Elena Nikolaevna's words . . . Half an hour ago, on this
very spot, my bride told me that I—am her first and only love
. . .

LYOLYA. (*With a groan*) Oh, Lord! . . .

PETROVSKY. (*Enraged*) You're lying! . . .

VARYAGIN. How can one comprehend such a misunderstanding?
Obviously, she is making fun of one of us . . .

PETROVSKY. (*With loathing*) All that's left for us to do is to rip
out each other's throats . . .

VARYAGIN. Why resort to such primitive means? . . . For such a
case, civilization has invented a more refined means . . . I suggest
an American duel [. . .]

LYOLYA, *with a groan, lowers herself onto the bench in an un-*
feigned swoon. [. . .]

Scene 8

VERA, *frightened, runs in from the right.* What's happened? . . .
Egorushka! [. . .]

[PETROVSKY *confronts* VARYAGIN *with (what he believes to be)*
LYOLYA's *love for him, and begs him to reconsider the marriage.*

EGOR *insists he cannot accept losing* LYOLYA *and will commit suicide if the marriage takes place.* VARYAGIN *remains coldly restrained and agrees to relinquish his claim to* LYOLYA.]

VARYAGIN. I was prepared for this outcome three days ago, when you were kissing each other before my very eyes . . .

VERA. You saw and were able to remain silent?! But why? [. . .]

VARYAGIN. Why this petty talk? We're all unwilling instruments of the passions governing our behavior . . . Yes, Egor Andreich, in the scheme of things you've come out the victor . . . But this time, woe to the victor! With this marriage you've dug yourself a grave from which you'll never arise! . . . Forgive me if I sound like I'm gloating. But I don't wish to be hypocritical by saying that I wish you happiness! You will never have it . . . Farewell. (*He exits.*) [. . .]

LYOLYA. (*Not opening her eyes*) Vol'demar! (*Having recognized Petrovsky, she makes a gesture of fear.*) Egor Andreich . . . Why are you here? Go away! . . .

PETROVSKY. (*Painfully*) Lyolya! . . . Lyolya . . . My sweet . . .

LYOLYA. (*Not listening, frightened*) Get up! They'll see us. You've gone out of your mind! . . . Where's Varyagin? [. . .]

VERA. (*Taking her by the hand*) Crazy girl! Come to your senses! You yourself chose Egor. And here he is before you . . . your future husband. Enough of playing blindman's bluff! Be serious, if only for once in your life . . .

LYOLYA. (*Wringing her hands*) How dare he leave? Who gave him permission? So he didn't love me? (*Stamping her foot*) He didn't . . . he didn't . . . he didn't . . .

PETROVSKY. No, he loved you, Lyolya . . . But he's noble, and he wished happiness for you . . .

LYOLYA. (*Maliciously*) Shut up! . . . Shut up! . . . How dare you defend him? . . . Tell me, what kind of nobility is this! . . . To abandon your bride . . . And for what? Only because she kissed someone else? Is that really a crime? (*She screams furiously.*) Why, I've kissed dozens of them! [. . .] Leave me alone, all of you! . . . Go away! . . . I hate Varyagin . . . I hate . . . all of you! . . . (*She falls onto the little garden seat, sobbing.*)

PETROVSKY. (*Confused*) You're angry? My sweet, about what? (*On his knees before* LYOLYA) Do you fear poverty? But I'm going to work like a bull. Happiness doesn't lie in money . . . Lyolya! I'll love you so passionately . . . so madly! I swear that you'll never shed one tear because of me! . . .

Scene 9

PELAGEYA L'VOVNA. (*At the door of the house*) What's this? (LYOLYA *begins to laugh hysterically.*) What sort of comedy is this? (*Enraged*) Hey, Lyol'ka, am I speaking to you or not? (*She steps down from the terrace.*) Hussy! . . . Shameless creature! You're engaged to someone else . . . And you're a fine one, sir! Sprawled out on your knees, as if you were at home . . . Get out! . . . As I was sayin' . . . You, Vera, why are your eyes poppin' out? . . . Are you gettin' a lesson in how someone else's bride gets in a clinch with every passin' guy? . . . Clever! And this, on the eve of the wedding? What did you do with Varyagin? Why isn't he here? . . . Can't you stop chuckling, you naughty thing? . . . Please explain, what's this uproar all about? And why are you slobberin' all over one another? . . .

PETROVSKY. (*At Trofimova's arrival, he gets up off his knees.*) I am Lyolya's fiancé . . .

PELAGEYA L'VOVNA. Wh-a-a-t? Fiancé? . . . Where has it yet been seen that one can marry two at the same time? . . . Well, sir, I'm not in the mood for jokes . . . Get lost for your own health and well-being! . . . While Vladimir Arkadyevich hasn't yet broken your legs . . .

LYOLYA. (*In a defiant tone*) Varyagin has gone, Mama. It was the only thing left for him, since I myself chose George! [. . .]

Scene 10

PELAGEYA L'VOVNA, *who has been standing as if in a stupor, suddenly tears herself from her place and howls.* What do you mean he's gone? . . . What's this consent? . . . And I . . . have you left me out? . . . Did you as-s-k me? I do not agree . . . (*She screams.*) Vladimir Arkadyevich . . . Where are you, my little dove? . . . (*Running around the stage, like someone lost*) Answer me! . . . Speak . . . Call out . . . Voloden'ka-a-a! (*She runs behind the wings.*) Halloo! [. . .] (*She returns from behind the wings, stops at center stage, and wipes the sweat off her face with a handkerchief.*) What are you doin' to me, you good-for-nothing wench? . . .

Huh? . . . Are you bent on killin' me? . . . Huh? . . .I can't get a
hold of myself . . . And where'll we get money for the house? . . .
They're comin' for it tomorrow . . . It's good that I wasn't caught
napping—I just now took a check from him for five thousand. It's
as if I'd had a premonition . . . But no! . . . No . . . This can't be
. . . What, am I sleeping? [. . .] (*With bitterness*) This is what I get
for all my love and troubles that she might grow up like a princess.
All my life I denied myself everything for her . . . (*With tears in
her voice*) Well, what of it . . . Get married! . . . But I'm going to
catch up with my Voloden'ka . . . Maybe, he won't drive me out,
old woman that I am! . . . (*She goes to the terrace, hunched over,
having difficulty with the step.*) [. . .] (*In a thunderous voice*) Out
of my way! . . .

*All involuntarily part. She goes, raising her head high. After
several steps, she turns around.*

PELAGEYA L'VOVNA. (*Scornfully*) Wretches! . . .

Curtain

ACT III

*Four years later. Poor and slovenly surroundings. A room with
two windows* [. . .] *Dust everywhere. A winter day.*

Scene 1

LYOLYA *is lying on the divan, her hands clasped behind her
head. She has on a dirty chintz blouse, worn down slippers. Her
braid is undone and unkempt.*

LYOLYA. (*Alone*) Oh my God! . . . How boring! . . . (*She yawns
and, while yawning, continues to talk.*) What if I could just get ill?
At least it would be some kind of change . . . I wrote to Mama
in Oryol . . . "If you don't come—I'm going to poison myself! . . ."
She'll probably come. (*Yawns*) Uh, damn! It seems you sleep
and sleep, and still never sleep enough . . . Granted—Egor was
terribly rude to Mama when he drove her away . . . But, after all,
it's been more than three years . . . And I did write to her to let her
know that in revenge against my little spouse I also drove out
his Mama; that way no one would be slighted. But what's most
important—I don't want to live this way any longer! . . . (*She
yawns and stretches.*) Well, shall I curl my hair out of boredom?
(*Shrilly*) Marya! . . . Marya! . . .

Scene 2

MARYA. (*Appearing at the middle doors, with the oven tongs in her hand*) What d'ya want?

LYOLYA. Give me the mirror, and find the curling iron! . . .

MARYA. (*Resentfully*) Phooey! I thought they tore me away from my work for sumthin' important . . . Well, and I'm a good one too! . . . It ain't the first year I've known ya . . . The only jobs ya have are windin' up yer curls, and lookin' at yerself in the mirror fer whole days at a time.

LYOLYA. (*Carelessly*) What a big fool you are! Get lost with your sarcasm! You've been told, hand me the mirror! . . .

MARYA [. . .] Yer ladyship! She's even too lazy t' walk 'cross the room. Here ya are, wrap up yer curls! That's all ya know how t' do anyways! [. . .] (*She exits.*) [. . .]

LYOLYA. (*Alone. She looks at herself in the mirror.*) How pale I am! How plain looking I've become! But for whom should I be beautiful? Surely not for my spouse? (*After a pause*) Why is it so cold? Marya! [. . .] Marya! . . . Marya! . . . Deaf devil!

Scene 3

MARYA. (*Behind the stage*) I hear, I hear, I ain't gone deaf . . . (*She appears at the doors.*)

LYOLYA. (*With disgust*) It seems you didn't heat the house today . . .

MARYA. And what should I heat it with? The wood's done with. I already told the master day 'afore yestiddy that we're runnin' low.

LYOLYA. Well that's nice! What then, do you want me to freeze now? A fine state of affairs! Give me a warm shawl! Can't you borrow wood from the neighbors? The master will bring money . . .

MARYA. You keep jabberin' the master this, the master that! Do ya think he's gonna mint us some coins? My heart already sinks t' look at him, the little dove, and how he nuzzles 'round the city for jobs. Poor guy, he jumps out o' bed even 'afore the cock crows. He's lost weight . . . The other day he put on a suit and it turned out lookin' like a bathrobe. You, mistress, oughtta pity him and give him lovin' . . .

LYOLYA. (*Bursting out*) You've gone completely mad, Marya! How dare you give me instructions? You've really put on airs. Get into the kitchen!

MARYA. You bet I'm goin'. I'm goin' to get some wood.

LYOLYA. Wait a minute, isn't there anything at all to eat? Maryushka, not one little sardine left? . . .

MARYA *takes a sardine can from the window and turns it upside down.* Empty . . . Ya finished it yestiddy. Wait a bit, I'll fix ya meatballs lickety-split.

LYOLYA. (*Stamping her foot capriciously*) I'm sick to death of your meatballs! . . . Lord! We can't even eat like real people. What kind of a life is this? (*She cries.*)

MARYA. (*Good naturedly*) Well, well, well . . . Tears already? Ah, mistress, mistress! How cheap they's t' ya! . . . them tears! Would ya like me to bring ya some salted cod from our store . . . greasy . . . sweet . . . you'll lick yer fingers all up . . .

LYOLYA. Ugh . . . Revolting!

MARYA. Salted cod—revoltin'? Just you give it a little lick first. Six kopecks a poun-n-d! And it's smo-o-ked! It's got such a smell to it, ya can nose it out 'cross three rooms. And I'll stick out the samovar and get five kopecks worth o' bomb-bons.[2] They was sayin' in the store—they bring 'em fresh, right straight from Apricotville[2] itself.

LYOLYA. (*Smiling through her tears*) Well, go ahead . . . get some . . .

MARYA. I'll go. But you listen here by the door . . . You watch out, somebody might sneak in . . . These days people is cheats . . . (*She exits.*)

LYOLYA. (*Alone*) How low I've sunk! My only dream is to eat well . . . They say I'm intelligent, good-looking, and talented. What's all that to me and in such a shack? It's just as if I'd been shoved into a grave. (*Tearing herself from her place and starting to pace around the room nervously*) To realize that all of this was merely a mistake . . . I never loved this repulsive man. But how dearly I'm paying for a silly flirtation! (*She wrings her hands.*) And it's all because of that hateful Varyagin! He should have challenged

---

2. Marya in her ignorance mispronounces the name of a famous Russian candy factory *Aprikosov*'s, as well as the French sweet *berlingot*.

Egor to a duel and killed him . . . But he ran away, like a coward. Did he really never kiss anyone but me? Egoist . . . Hypocrite . . . Oh, if only we could meet now! How I'd love to send him whirling! I'd spin him, I'd torture him, and throw him away like yesterday's bouquet . . . I'd pay him back for everything . . . for everything . . . for everything . . . (*With a sob she falls on the loveseat.*)

Scene 4

PELAGEYA L'VOVNA. (*At the middle doors with a huge suitcase and bag. Her coat and hat are extremely out of fashion.*) Fifty-five steps! I barely made it.

LYOLYA. (*Running toward her mother with a cry of joy*) Mama! Mama! . . . At last! . . . (*She smothers her in an embrace.*)

PELAGEYA L'VOVNA. (*In a voice shaking with excitement*) Oh, let me go . . . You're smotherin' me . . . Let me sit down! I'm completely out of breath [. . .] Umpt! . . . Well, you're really living high up! What kind of yard is that? . . . And this stairway? On each step sits a pair of dogs and seven pairs of cats. Stench, filth. From behind every door they stare at you, until you've counted off all those fifty-five steps. What a fine little house! . . .

LYOLYA. (*Ironically*) That's why it's cheap . . .

PELAGEYA L'VOVNA. That's obvious. (*Taking off her street clothes*) And your furniture! . . . Have you hocked all of it?

LYOLYA. Some we sold, some we pawned . . . Only the love seat is left . . .

PELAGEYA L'VOVNA. How can you let yourself look that way? Don't you even wash? Ugh, Lyolya, what a slob you've become.

Scene 5

MARYA. (*With packages*) And here we are . . . Good grief . . . Can it really be Pelageya L'vovna? [. . .] Our little mistress was joyfully expectin' ya . . . I'll set the samovar out for ya lickety-split, ma'am . . . It's boilin' already. There's fresh bomb-bons for ya. Here's salted cod for ya, too.

PELAGEYA L'VOVNA. (*Raising her eyebrows*) Qu'est-ce qu'elle dit?

LYOLYA. (*Bursting out*) I got those for her . . .

MARYA. Whadda ya mean, fer me? You eat 'em yerself . . . The grocer give me the best that he had . . . I'll go in the kitchen and beat it up so's ya can chew it.

PELAGEYA L'VOVNA. *C'est affreux ce qu'elle dit!* . . . Go, my dear, and take this revolting stuff away! And get us plates. I brought some snacks with me [. . .] There, Lyolya, get the sardines, cheese, caviar, lobster from the bag . . .

LYOLYA *squeals and bustles around the room with the bag in her arms.* Mommy, dear, how wonderful! . . . Oh what a spree we'll have! [. . .] I've been so famished that it's led to (*jokingly, in a tragic tone*) a complete moral collapse . . . to salted cod . . .

PELAGEYA L'VOVNA. *Quelle horreur!*

LYOLYA. You've saved me . . . On the edge of the abyss you've extended a helping hand [. . .]

Scene 6

MARYA. (*With the samovar*) Here's boiling water for ya to warm yer little innards . . . I'll bring some plates in a jiffy . . . (*She goes out.*)

PELAGEYA L'VOVNA. Innards . . . *Affreux!* . . . How vulgar she is in front of you! . . . (*She takes her fancy handbag.*) Well look, I've brought some candied fruit for your teatime . . . I remember that you've got a sweet tooth . . .

LYOLYA *kisses her mother.* Mommy, dear, little rascal! You've resurrected me! [. . .]

PELAGEYA L'VOVNA. And where's your lord and master?

LYOLYA. In class . . . He usually comes back late . . .

PELAGEYA L'VOVNA. So, he's still got no job? Well, why don't you do something about that? Or is it pleasant to starve? . . .

LYOLYA. Ah, Mama! . . . Is it really possible to make him see reason? I used to cry and cry, but he'd always play dumb.

PELAGEYA L'VOVNA. You're still stupid. Can one really get anywhere with a man by crying?

LYOLYA. Then what should I do?

PELAGEYA L'VOVNA. Gnaw at him . . . My, how I picked away at my dear departed! [. . .] You're just like your papa . . . That one would be after the girls the minute you looked away . . . Even when you weren't married, you were a sucker for a kiss . . . Because of your flirting, you let such an eagle as Varyagin slip through your fingers . . . Well, too late now to grieve over that . . . You'd better be on guard! . . . Is it really possible that you parade in front of your husband like such a slob? I don't recognize you, Lyolya . . . It's as if they switched you with someone else . . . You must always look like a stranger to your husband . . . this will excite him . . .

LYOLYA. Ah, Mama! God bless him and his excitement! To have children, then lose them, to suffer, to lose my looks . . . I don't want this anymore! . . . I don't . . . I don't . . . I don't . . . That's not life, it's slavery . . .

PELAGEYA L'VOVNA. But again, that's because you're a fool. A clever woman never falls into such servitude . . . So, both your sons passed away? . . . I'm so sorry for the eldest, Petya . . . (*She sighs deeply.*) What did he die of? [. . .]

LYOLYA. [. . .] For the whole year and a half of his life he wasn't well a day . . . I even got used to it and began to go out driving to amuse myself . . .

PELAGEYA L'VOVNA. Your spouse was jealous, no doubt?

LYOLYA. Can you imagine, not at all . . .

PELAGEYA L'VOVNA. You really do have a simple-minded one.

LYOLYA. Even to the point of boredom . . . They aren't any easier to deceive than he . . .

PELAGEYA L'VOVNA. (*Having winked*) And you, I dare say, didn't lose any time? You're a regular rascal, ya know! . . .

LYOLYA. I haven't been caught yet! Still, he couldn't forgive me for these outings. He was so egotistical and made such rigorous demands on me! . . . And when Petya died, it was as if he'd finally gone crazy. Whereas before he would only say over and over again: "You're a child . . . you're my virginal madonna" . . . Suddenly he noticed all my shortcomings at once [. . .] He said I'm an egoist, and heartless, and have a petty character [. . .]

PELAGEYA L'VOVNA. That's too much! . . . I'd have taught him a lesson for a month, the creep! He'd have tamed down, I'll bet . . . He'd have forgotten what his tongue was attached to . . . (*Pause*) And what great opportunities were in store for him! Surely if he weren't so hotheaded, he would have become headmaster in five years or so . . .

LYOLYA. How, for goodness sake? . . . He found it necessary to quarrel with Franzen because of some fines and salaries! "Why wouldn't they shorten the working hours of children?" He felt obliged, you see, to defend the interests of the workers! . . . As if he had no family of his own! As if he didn't have to *boire — manger?* . . . Oh, these lofty-sounding pedants!

PELAGEYA L'VOVNA. I've heard that story . . . he passed for a downright socialist . . . Why did he lose the second position?

LYOLYA. He was an accountant in a bank. They were supposed to set up certain business transactions . . . to show a different set of figures to certain people . . . And for this they offered him various percentages . . . Their former accountant built himself a home and left . . . Well, but how could Egor Andreich do that? . . . Honor . . . Principles . . . "I," he said, "would rather starve than work with a gang of robbers . . ." Well, wonderful, let him starve . . . But why should I have to suffer on that account?

PELAGEYA L'VOVNA. Well, you poor little thing! . . . Ugh! It makes me delirious . . . (*She fans herself with a handkerchief.*) Let's face it, I noticed long ago that he wasn't (*tapping her forehead with her fingers*) all there. (*After a pause*) How is Vera getting on?

LYOLYA. She works as a physician's assistant in one of the public institutions; she and Nadezhda Mikhaylovna live together. She picks up children off the street and fusses over them, and treats all sorts of beggars free of charge. We seldom see each other . . . But when Petya was dying, she and the old lady practically moved in with me. They took care of him at night . . . And Vera and Egor were so grief stricken over Petya's coffin that strangers thought she was the mother, and not I [. . .] They spent three whole days sitting with Egor, embracing, each with his arms around the other! And they even rode from the grave with their arms around each other . . . They'd cry and comfort each other. Whereas I was on the sidelines. It was even somehow funny! From then on they were on a first-name basis, and Vera now calls the old woman "Mama."

PELAGEYA L'VOVNA. Watch out, Lyol'ka, that she doesn't snatch your husband away! . . . What doesn't the Devil fool with? Here you have fights, and there harmony of souls . . . Can sin be far away? . . .

LYOLYA. Ah, what happiness that would be, Mama! Even in my sleep I dream of escaping to you, to freedom [. . .]

PELAGEYA L'VOVNA. Why is it you haven't asked me about Varyagin? . . .

LYOLYA. (*Blushing*) Hah, what concern have I with him? I've completely forgotten that he exists on this earth.

PELAGEYA L'VOVNA. And you've done the right thing . . . 'Cause he's also probably forgotten you . . . At least he's consoled himself magnificently . . . He squandered a million on one dancer in Paris . . . Can you imagine? . . . A mi-ll-ion in cash . . . Ugh! . . . It simply drives me out of my mind to think that that loot would be in our hands, if your nonsense hadn't . . .

LYOLYA. Ah, enough! I so passionately loved George then . . .

PELAGEYA L'VOVNA. Do tell me, if you please! "Passionately loved" . . . Is your love sweet in an attic, with dried cod as your only entertainment? . . . Last year, in Monte Carlo, Varyagin broke the bank . . . and the next day squandered his winnings on some sort of orphanage . . . In Paris he frittered away half a million on a scientific expedition . . . In Rome he got involved with an aristocrat, a beauty . . . The Italian woman's husband challenged him to a duel . . . Varyagin wounded him—he had to flee Rome . . . My dear, everybody took notice of him abroad . . . All the newspapers raved about him . . .

LYOLYA. (*Pale from anger*) I really don't understand, why are you telling me all this?

PELAGEYA L'VOVNA. I'm telling you so you'll bite your knuckles the rest of your life for your stupidity. And you thought he'd shoot himself for love? Like heck, he would! With his money and good looks the whole world's open to him . . . And as for the ladies? . . . As many as he wants! . . . Just give out a shout, there'll be no getting rid of 'em . . . Well, come on, see me out . . . (*Both exit.*)

———

Scene 9

LYOLYA *returns alone and, greatly upset, walks around the stage, wringing her hands.* That's how it is! . . . Oh that despicable, hateful man! And I imagined that he was suffering after losing me . . . I'm a fool, a fool! . . . (*She grasps her head.*) Is it possible they know how to love? It seems that it's only in books that people die for love . . . You wait, you hateful creature! . . . Just let us meet . . . (*With despair*) Oh God! . . . Could it be that I won't meet him? Haven't I suffered enough? . . . (*She falls down on the divan.*) [. . .]

[PETROVSKY *enters. He has changed greatly, grown visibly tired and poorer. He and* LYOLYA *have a bitter argument about the poverty of their lives. He meekly suggests their lives will be better in the future, but she threatens to leave him. The vacuity of* LYOLYA'*s existence and aspirations is expressed in the banality of her petty desires. She accuses* EGOR *of ignorance of the real meaning of love.*]

LYOLYA. (*In a frenzy*) Don't dare speak to me of your love! You're repulsive to me . . . You thought only of yourself when you dragged me with you into this unhappy marriage . . . I was a child, I didn't know life. You promised to devote your future to me, you promised me I wouldn't shed a single tear . . . You shamelessly deceived me . . . Your love gave me tears, poverty, sickness . . . children that I didn't want . . . Be quiet! . . . Be quiet! . . . Let me finish speaking! . . . What right did you have to berate me all these four years for my heartlessness, my shallowness? . . . I didn't promise you anything better . . . But you? . . . Remember your vows . . . How was your love expressed? Wasn't it by losing positions because of your detestable character and never even asking yourself: "What will become of my wife, if I condemn her to poverty?" (*She walks around the stage, greatly agitated.*)

PETROVSKY. (*Sullenly*) I acted on the conviction . . .

LYOLYA. (*Stamping her foot*) Of what concern are your convictions to me? Why must I suffer? Had I known that you would place your convictions above me, I certainly would have rejected you [. . .]

PETROVSKY *stares at his wife with despair, then goes to her and kneels.* [. . .] Oh, this laboring for bread only! . . . Without ideals, without enjoyment, just for the right to live [. . .] Do you think I haven't dreamed of giving you a bright, wonderful life, without a shade of worry? Ah, Lyolya, how cruelly life has ridiculed our dreams [. . .]

LYOLYA. You promise me a dozen children and console me with the thought that you and I have a whole lifetime before us . . . But I don't want the dozen and I don't want your love . . . All that has grown repulsive to me . . . And I'm leaving . . .

PETROVSKY. (*Gasping with emotion*) But . . . What's this? . . . May I dare to ask—where? With whom? . . . Is it for a long time?

LYOLYA. (*Trying not to show her agitation*) Where? . . . To Oryol . . . With whom? . . . With Mama . . . And for how long, I don't yet know myself . . . That remains to be seen . . .

PETROVSKY. Then what am I to do?

LYOLYA. Oh, you won't be left without work! . . . Solving learned questions, altering the fate of nations . . . You'll take Vera for your helpmate . . . Believe me, I won't be jealous [. . .]

PETROVSKY. (*Decisively*) I will not let you go [. . .]

LYOLYA. I despise you . . . You've spoiled my life . . . you snatched me away from Varyagin . . . I could have been rich . . . now I'm poor . . . I can't marry a second time, while you're alive . . .

PETROVSKY, *in horror, raises his hand, as if warding off a blow.* Oh, mercy! . . .

LYOLYA. (*Beside herself, wringing her hands*) How many times I've thought . . . "Die . . . die, you damnable creature! . . . Give me my freedom . . ." And yet I knew that I never again would be free, like the wind . . . that I'm bound to you by a chain to the grave [. . .] (*Seizing her head in her hands, she runs out, to the left, into the bedroom.*)

PETROVSKY *dashes after his wife.* Lyolya . . . Lyolya . . . (*He stops at the door, as if he's realized the futility of pleading. Staggering, he crosses the stage and, having begun to sob convulsively, he falls on the divan.*)

Curtain

ACT IV

The Petrovskys' apartment. The scenery is the same; one day has passed. It is twilight on a winter day. On stage it is growing noticeably dark. The stage is empty as the curtain is raised. Then PETROVSKY *and* MARYA *enter through the middle door.*

Scene 1

PETROVSKY. (*In his coat, putting a folder with papers on the table*) So you say the mistress hasn't come out of the bedroom all day?

MARYA. That's right, all day—sleepin' . . . How can she sleep all the time? I reckon that's enough sleep fer three workin' people . . .

PETROVSKY. (*Walking across the stage and rubbing his frozen hands*) Perhaps she's sick?

MARYA. Aw, go on with ya! . . . She's a healthy little thing! Just this mornin' when I give her coffee in bed, she'd gobbled up a whole box o' candy . . .

PETROVSKY. (*Anxiously*) And she ate nothing else, besides candy?

MARYA. At one o'clock I knocked at her door . . . She rattled the key . . . "Gimme," says she, "the snacks Mama brought! . . ." Whadda ya think, sir? She made a clean sweep of it all! . . . All these here lobsters, sardines, sausages—as if the French army'd marched through . . . I cleared away the empty boxes . . . Don't get yerself in a tizzy, sir, people don't kick off with such medicine . . . I'll give ya some nice warm cabbage soup lickety-split . . . (*Quickly she exits and returns with a tureen of cabbage soup. She puts it on the dining table, where one place is set.*) [. . .] (*Going up to Petrovsky, she speaks furtively, lowering her voice.*) And I got somethin' else I wanna tell ya, sir: 'seemed mighty suspicious t' me . . . It's as if our mistress is fixin' to go travellin' . . .

PETROVSKY. (*Alarmed*) What? . . . What did you say? . . .

MARYA. (*Glancing back at the locked bedroom*) After she finished stuffin' her mouth, 'soon as she locked the door, I'm to the keyhole, lickety-split. (*She sneaks up to the door and presses her eye to the keyhole.*) Lookin' like this here . . . I didn't hear nuthin' fer a half hour . . . Keys is jinglin', boxes is movin' . . . Then it dawned on me . . . Good gracious! Our mistress has suddenly got it in her head to put everythin' in order . . . Ya'd have thought doomsday was comin' . . . She's never as much as counted her hankies . . . She was packin' up . . . That's it exactly [. . .] (*She exits.*)

(*It is completely dark on stage.*)

PETROVSKY. (*Alone*) So it's true? I'm repulsive to her . . . I'm hateful to her . . . And she's leaving me . . . I've ruined her life. I, fool that I am, hoped this was a small outburst, a quarrel! . . . No, this is hate! . . . Yet I'm still alive [. . .] (*He exits, staggering.*)

Scene 2

For half a minute the stage is empty. Then VARYAGIN *enters and stands for a moment, looking around.*

VARYAGIN. What's happened here? A quarrel? Or something worse? He ran down the stairs with such a face, as if the Furies were pursuing him, and he didn't even notice me . . . So much the better! . . . No one to announce me! . . . Not a single soul . . . One can come in, rest, and leave unnoticed. (*He strikes a match; it goes out.*) How damp and unattractive! . . . So that's where my love is—in a hut! This is where my fairy princess lives! . . . (*He sits down on the chair by the divan.*) A presentiment tells me, I will see Lyolya . . . Oh, I know the old melody will no longer resound in my soul . . . Then why do I wait, fool? (*with a bitter grin*) Here, there is neither love, nor the caprice of a fantasy, nor jealousy . . . Then what has drawn me here? Could it be boredom? Or cold curiosity?

MARYA *peers through the door; she is in felt shoes and a shawl.* Ya come back, sir?

VARYAGIN. Yes.

MARYA. 's good . . . Just so's no one else come in . . . I'll be goin' to the shop fer kerosene. And by the way, here's yer change . . . Just so's I won't forget . . . Well, count it—kerosene goes fer fifteen kopecks . . .

VARYAGIN. Fifteen . . .

MARYA. Ya give me forty kopecks last night . . . figure it—this mornin' some buns fer the mistress fer coffee at five kopecks, and the coffee itself at ten kopecks . . . 'cause the coffee was all gone . . .

VARYAGIN. So [. . .]

MARYA. But isn't there somethin' in your voice like you was catchin' cold? Or d'ya have a tiff again? . . . Where's the mistress? Did she already leave?

VARYAGIN. I'd be very pleased, my dear . . . I don't recall your name . . . if you'd tell me, where is your mistress?

MARYA *steps back and upsets the chair.* Heavenly saints! Who's here? 'Pears it's a stranger! . . .

VARYAGIN. One of your own . . . one of your own . . . don't get excited . . .

MARYA. (*In a trembling voice*) What do ya mean "one o' my own"? What kindda lie are ya givin' me? (*She rushes around the stage, looking for an exit.*)

VARYAGIN. Allow me, my dear . . .

MARYA. (*Interrupting*) I'll go for a policeman . . . Good Heavens! It must be a cutthroat! . . . That's what people is nowadays! You go out for a minute . . . Saints! [. . .] Don't come near me, murderer! . . . I'll scream so loud all fifty tenants'll be here! . . . Leave without sinnin'! . . . It'll be the worse for you . . . 'sides, there's nothing to steal here . . . We're poor people. Both the silver and the mistress' cloak is pawned . . . ya come to the wrong place . . .

VARYAGIN. [. . .] I need neither your silver nor your cloak . . . But, in plain language, just open your eyes and look at me . . . Do you still not recognize me? (*He casts the light of a match on his face.*)

MARYA. (*After clasping her hands*) Good grief! . . . Isn't it the bridegroom? . . .

VARYAGIN. Of someone else's bride, fortunately . . . (*He throws away the match.*) The former fiancé of Elena Nikolaevna, Varyagin . . .

MARYA. (*Joyfully*) I remember, I remember you, sir [. . .] (*Making a gesture of helplessness*) Here's a fine mess! . . . I can't get my wits about me . . . Everythin' inside my belly's shakin' so hard, 'cause I didn't recognize yer voice [. . .]

Backstage, LYOLYA'*s voice booms,* "*Marya!* . . . *Marya!* . . ."

MARYA. There she is . . . Ya can hear her sweet little voice.

VARYAGIN. (*With a grin*) What's that? Can it be my heart is throbbing . . .

LYOLYA. (*Backstage*) Marya! . . . You deaf devil! . . . Get over here! . . .

MARYA. (*With a grin*) And how pleasant her sweet little voice is! . . .

VARYAGIN. (*Aside*) However, she doesn't shout quite in tune . . .

Scene 4

LYOLYA *is dressed in a short fur and hat. In her hand, a bag and a lit candle.*

LYOLYA. (*To* MARYA) Go get a cabby! . . . (*After seeing* VAR-YAGIN, in extreme confusion) Ah! . . . Is that you . . . you? . . . (*She stares at him in confusion.* MARYA *takes the candle from her hand and puts in on the table.*)

VARYAGIN. (*Going up to her and kissing her hand with a sad smile*) Alas, it is I again, cousin . . .

LYOLYA. (*Unable to find an appropriate tone; joyfully excited, but afraid to show it*) But where have you come from, tell me for God's sake? Why are you here? I can't understand this at all! . . .

VARYAGIN. A cruel question to someone who's been away for four years . . .

MARYA. So, ya wanna wait a bit for the cabby? . . .

LYOLYA. Go away! . . . It's not necessary! . . . Go away . . . Please sit down . . . (*She sits with Varyagin on the loveseat.*)

MARYA *exits.*

VARYAGIN. Are you planning to go somewhere? . . .

LYOLYA. O no, no! . . . I've had a migraine since morning . . . and I wanted to get some fresh air . . . How odd! I imagined that you were far away . . .

VARYAGIN. You're forgetting that I've spent all this time abroad, cousin, and so it's just possible I might be pining for Russia.

LYOLYA. (*Having recovered a little and trying to infuse irony into her tone*) Oh, please . . . You lived so gaily [. . .]

[LYOLYA *and* VARYAGIN *banter back and forth about his voluptuous and profligate life abroad and her "domesticity" with* EGOR *for the past four years. She begins to flirt with him. It becomes clear they are both willing to resume their alliance, when suddenly* VARYAGIN *declares he is thinking of getting married.* LYOLYA *is offended by his request for her help in this matter, and cools toward him. She goes to take off her travelling clothes.* MARYA *enters and* VARYAGIN *learns that the marriage has not been entirely blissful as* LYOLYA *has described; in fact,* LYOLYA *is deter-*

mined to leave EGOR. *She re-enters, now dressed provocatively in a bare silk blouse with her hair coquettishly arranged and her face powdered.*]

VARYAGIN. (*Taking Lyolya's hand*) I'm admiring you, Lyolya [. . .] What expressive eyes you have! [. . .]

LYOLYA. (*Coquettishly*) What is it you read in them? . . .

VARYAGIN. A poem, Lyolya . . . in the style of the *fin de siècle* . . . Full of brilliance . . . and sin . . . Tell me, Lyolya, is there anything for me in the future? . . .

LYOLYA. (*With excitement*) Oh, yes! . . . Yes . . .

VARYAGIN. Does that mean I haven't returned to Russia in vain? . . . You predict happiness for me? . . . I'm so tired of pursuing those mirages! . . . It's decided—I'm getting married [. . .] I returned suddenly, in obedience to this uncontrollable feeling . . . I don't know what to call it . . . Whether it's love, curiosity, a whim, self-delusion—I don't know . . . Can you guess who this woman is?

LYOLYA. [*At the table, preparing tea*] (*Bursting out*) How should I know that?

VARYAGIN. (*Seriously*) It's Vera.

LYOLYA. (*Dropping a spoon on the floor*) Vera? [. . .] You say—Vera? (*She begins to laugh nervously.*)

VARYAGIN. What's the matter, Lyolya? . . .

LYOLYA. (*With tears in her voice*) N-n-nothing . . . It's only . . . funny to me . . . Ha! . . . ha . . . ha . . . (*She stands up and goes to the back of the stage, where she paces in agitation.*) Vera and . . . and you? . . . Ha! . . . ha! . . . ha! . . . (*Her laughter suddenly stops.*)

VARYAGIN. What a lovely contrast . . . I—am an egoist, a pampered and immoral Athenian . . . She—is a Spartan, stern, proud, with staunch convictions . . . I've never met women of that type anywhere but in Russia . . . She's honest, Lyolya . . . That's such a rarity! . . . Yes, our marriage will be happy [. . .] To awaken such a Galatea would be undoubtedly pleasant . . . I hope that her attraction to Egorushka has disappeared with the illusions of youth . . . It's enough to see your family happiness at close range to make one go searching for one's own somewhere else, far away. Where is Vera now? . . .

LYOLYA. (*Hurriedly*) I don't know, somewhere in the South. We lost touch with her a while ago . . . (*Aside*) Oh! While I'm alive, she'll never set foot in my house! . . .

VARYAGIN. (*After a pause, extending his hand*) Lyolya [. . .] Tell me, are you a virtuous wife?

LYOLYA. (*With subtle irony*) Ah! . . . Very . . .

VARYAGIN. That's a fault, precious. That's an anachronism . . . You ought to break that habit. (*He kisses her arm near the elbow.*) [. . .]

LYOLYA. (*Laying her head on Varyagin's shoulder*) Vol'demar, are you really getting married? . . .

VARYAGIN. That depends on you, Lyolya. Entangle me so that I cannot leave, and I will stay [. . .] Let's take up flirting . . .

LYOLYA. And my husband? . . .

VARYAGIN. He'll only be a winner . . . Am I really infringing upon his rights? Am I really offering an eternal, unique passion? We both don't believe in that . . . and strong passions, in general, are not our lot in life . . . We'll search for pleasurable sensations, the sort which are noncommittal . . . And that's all!

LYOLYA. (*With a thinly veiled threat*) Ah! . . . So that's it! [. . .] What sorts of women have you had dealings with, that they've developed such a monstrous self-conceit in you? What if you lose this time, Mr. Seeker of Pleasurable Sensations? I challenge you! . . .

VARYAGIN. (*Seriously*) I accept with delight, Lyolya . . . And should you be able to arouse passion in me, I will tell you that, having lost, I will have won [. . .]

[PETROVSKY *returns and is surprised to find* VARYAGIN *with* LYOLYA. *He senses a renewal of their relationship. But she is now so kind to* PETROVSKY *that he refuses to admit to himself that* VARYAGIN'*s return may destroy his marriage. He swallows his suspicions and only weakly protests* LYOLYA'*s decision to go for a ride with* VARYAGIN.] (LYOLYA *exits to get her coat.*) [. . .]

VARYAGIN. *A propos* . . . During my return trip to Russia an acquaintance of mine was sitting in my compartment, a certain Matterson. You've probably heard of him? He manages a land bank, and he needs an agent to evaluate property, an honest man . . . That's no joke. He laughingly asked me whether I could provide him with such a specimen. All those so-called honest agents have bilked the bank for hundreds of thousands of rubles . . . I told him that I know of only one honest man—you, Egorushka . . . You are, incidentally, out of work . . . Wouldn't you like to have an interview with Matterson? You could make about five or six thousand a year there . . .

PETROVSKY. That's a fine occupation! Helping to enrich a handful of stockholders who are getting fat at someone else's expense . . .

VARYAGIN. I knew all your objections beforehand . . . But, you see, you've already proved your inability in the field of service to your fellow men . . .

PETROVSKY. What do you mean by that?

VARYAGIN. You worked in a factory, and things were, understandably, better for the workers under you than under anyone else . . . But the director wounded your self-esteem . . . And you, after committing yourself to the goal of fighting for the interests of the proletariat, you abandoned the workers to the mercy of fate and left just when the struggle began . . .

PETROVSKY. (*Bitterly*) I couldn't stay! . . . (*Controlling himself, he speaks sullenly and hollowly.*) Besides, you wouldn't understand me . . .

VARYAGIN. Oh, of course! . . . You sacrificed the welfare of hundreds of people for your own self-esteem. And you considered yourself in the right. Now you're again making a mistake . . .

PETROVSKY. (*Sullenly*) How exactly?

VARYAGIN. You don't consider yourself in the right regarding your wife, do you? People like her cannot endure deprivation . . . Hold on to her, while it's not too late [. . .] Take the position with Matterson and be happy . . . It's so simple!

PETROVSKY. (*Trying with difficulty to appear calm*) Be quiet . . . be quiet! . . . Let's speak of something else!

VARYAGIN. How is Vera getting along? Are you friends as before?

PETROVSKY. Oh, yes! . . . Ah, if it weren't for that friendship! (*Wringing his hands*) What a splendid person she is! . . .

VARYAGIN. (*Biting his lip*) Is she happy? . . .

PETROVSKY. I don't know . . . she must be. You see, she's—not at all like us. She's constantly working . . . She has no spare time, as you do, to analyze her own soul . . . But tell me about yourself, what did you do abroad? . . .

VARYAGIN. As before—everything . . . Or, more accurately, nothing. I was everywhere a dilettante—in science and in art, in philanthropy and in love . . . I snatched a moment of delight wherever I found it . . .

PETROVSKY. What a wasted life! With your talents? We all expected something outstanding from you . . .

VARYAGIN. In vain . . . First of all, where are they—these heroic deeds? Where is the arena for them? In our time? Among us? . . . Finally, you're forgetting the most important thing . . . In order to undertake these great deeds, one must believe in their usefulness and necessity . . . But for people like me, Egorushka, universal ideals are old fairy tales that have lost their magic . . . It takes great courage to admit this in front of such an idealist as you . . . As a compensation for my sincerity, believe me when I say that this distresses me . . . I'd give away my fortune to believe again these wonderful fairy tales, to love deeply—whether a person, or an idea—it doesn't matter which! . . . To live without anguish . . . to die without fear . . . And to gaze fearlessly at that boundary, beyond which all is darkness and silence . . .

PETROVSKY. I don't understand you! All you needed was the desire—to fill your own life with meaning, if not happiness . . .

VARYAGIN. That's it exactly, Egorushka, I had only to have the desire! But I'm incapable precisely of this . . . I don't want anything, I don't know how to want! . . . The energy of the life force has been dulled in me almost from the cradle. My fate reminds me of a fairy tale . . . The fairies put all the gifts in my cradle, but forgot to invite the evil sorceress . . . And she made it so that all these gifts have no value for me. Sometimes it seems to me that someone else has worn out all the power of my soul, and it came into my body already tired and sad, without passions or aspirations. From the time I began to live consciously, the thought always followed me that very soon I'd no longer have any desires at all . . . And I haven't rushed through life . . . I spent the best years of my youth studying . . . I wanted to establish an attitude which would reconcile me with a life without goals or passions . . . And, finally, I bowed before the scheme of things, before Fate . . .

PETROVSKY. (*Heatedly*) But you're forgetting, you have obligations . . .

VARYAGIN. (*Taking up his thought*) To the welfare of my fellow man and so forth . . . Oh yes, Egorushka! . . . I know that, in comparison to you, I'm petty . . . You have stock formulas for everything, readymade decisions with which you can console yourself . . . You have entered life with a wealth of tradition . . . You'll never be bankrupt . . . I, however, came without these riches. But from what I have acquired on the way, I won't give you one iota! Seek out your sacrifices and great deeds! . . . Take on far-reaching and difficult tasks! . . . But be tolerant of those who pursue the phantom of happiness in a different way . . . Perhaps, the mirage will deceive me . . . Let it! It's easier to live that way! . . . But leave me my moment of delight . . . Only one moment, that I might forget I am powerless and alone. And we'll call it even . . .

Scene 8

LYOLYA. (*Running in, in a fur coat and hat*) Here I am . . . Did you get tired of waiting? [. . .] Ah, what stars! . . . What a deep blue night! Let's drive outside the city, Vol'demar . . . There, so that the air might take away one's breath, the snow might squeak under the runners! God! . . . My God! . . . How wonderful life is! (*She runs out the middle door.*)

VARYAGIN. (*In his coat, shaking* PETROVSKY's *hand at the door*) Good-bye, George . . . (*Aside*) Here it is, my moment of delight, which I would not yield to anyone!! . . . (*He exits.*)

PETROVSKY. (*Alone*) She was in such a hurry, she didn't even glance at me . . . "God, how wonderful life is"! She said that in such a tone! . . . Poor thing! . . . How little she needs to make her happy! [. . .] But why is there no true heroism in me: Why do I stand like a coward at the crossroads and ask myself . . . "Which way?" No . . . It's not terrible to die . . . But terrible to live . . . To live for long years with the knowledge that you have killed in yourself your brother Abel. (*He covers his face with his hands.*) [. . .]

[VERA *enters. She has grown prettier, matured. She knows* VARYAGIN *has come and expresses her apprehension to* EGOR. PETROVSKY *tries to justify his decision to sacrifice his ideals and accept the position* VARYAGIN *has suggested—it is for fear of losing* LYOLYA. *He begs for* VERA's *forgiveness and continued friend-*

ship. Perceiving his weakness, she acquiesces and weeps "for the past."]

Curtain

ACT V

Eight months have passed. It is July, a sunny day. A beautiful, spacious room in VARYAGIN's *summer house, arranged elegantly and with artful taste* [. . .] *As the curtain rises, the stage is empty.*

Scene 1

NADEZHDA MIKHAYLOVNA *in a cape and scarf, in her hands an old parasol and a small bag. Arm in arm with her is* VERA. *She is dressed simply, but fashionably and elegantly, in a dark dress, straw hat, and blouse. All of this is dark, severe, but beautiful. When she takes off her hat, her hairdo appears in all its simplicity and distinctiveness. All of her gestures are free, full of power, assurance, and obvious graciousness. The expression on her face is sad, but firm and full of character. A lackey carries a suitcase and pillow behind them* [. . .]

NADEZHDA MIKHAYLOVNA. (*Sitting down*) Oof! Soft . . . 'Ain't fittin' fer my kind to settle in on such forniture! . . . Tell me, her mother get here yet?

VERA. She's already been here a week; and, it seems, she has no intention of leaving . . .

NADEZHDA MIKHAYLOVNA. That's hunky-dory! . . . Well! This is practically a palace! . . . (*Looking around*) I can't even believe my own eyes that Egorushka lives here . . . Look at this forniture [. . .]

VERA. This is Varyagin's summer house, and his furniture and servants . . . He invited Egor and his wife for the summer and gave him half the estate. Egorushka begged me so to be his guest for the summer that I hadn't the heart to refuse . . .

NADEZHDA MIKHAYLOVNA. Oi, I don't like his job! Ya know, since spring he's been on the road . . . evaluatin' property, ya see . . . And his wife's . . .

VERA. (*Interrupting, ironically*) All alone?

NADEZHDA MIKHAYLOVNA. It wouldn't surprise me for her to be alone, but she's always with that Varyagin [. . .] "Ah cousin . . .

Ah, Vol'demar, purlay françie, ariviewer" . . . Phooey! It was sick-
enin' t' see 'em . . . One time I could hardly stand it . . . Three
o'clock in the morning, and still no sign of 'em. Went to the
the-ay-ter, ya see . . . So what, they don't go on 'til dawn there,
do they? Ya gotta give even actors a chance to rest . . . "How long
are they gonna be drivin' around, Egorushka?" I ask. "Aren't ya
suspicious when your wife drags around 'til dawn with a strange
guy?"

VERA. (*Beginning to pace around the room*) What did he say?

NADEZHDA MIKHAYLOVNA. Saints alive! He nearly drove me
out o' my wits . . . He started to tremble so, and turned so white
. . . "You're my enemy," he says . . . "You want to kill me . . .
How can you tell," he says, "what I mull over alone during the
night? While I have faith in my wife—I'm happy . . . But the
minute I stop believing—I'm a lost man," he says . . .

VERA. (*With bitterness*) I thought so [. . .] (*Having looked
through the window*) Ah! . . . There, they've returned from their
horseback ride . . . They're coming here . . .

NADEZHDA MIKHAYLOVNA. (*Trying to hide*) Take me to your
room . . . Where shall I go? I don't want to see her shameless face
now . . . Everythin's boilin' up in me . . . Good grief! [. . .] (*They
exit.*)

[VARYAGIN *and* LYOLYA *return from an afternoon of riding. As
the conversation proceeds, it becomes clear that* VARYAGIN *has
grown tired of the affair. He wants to go abroad and end it. He
admits he is still greatly attracted to* VERA. LYOLYA *is fearful of*
PETROVSKY's *wrath, should he discover the affair, and confused
by* VARYAGIN's *envy of* EGOR, *of his ability to feel life so deeply and
passionately. She does not wish to release* VARYAGIN.]

VARYAGIN. Shouldn't you have foreseen that this strange existence *à trois* would at some time begin to bore me? I'm tired and
thirst for rest . . . or amusement. But you give me neither one nor
the other [. . .] Let's part as friends . . . We gave each other
several months of happiness and there's no reason for us to be
enemies . . .

LYOLYA. Aha! . . . Release you? . . . So you can go away with
Vera?

VARYAGIN. You're forgetting that I haven't yet proposed to her
. . .

LYOLYA. We have no choice but to run away secretly . . .

VARYAGIN. It's obvious that you've read a great many novels. But I'm an enemy of romanticism. And, after all, I don't in the least wish to have a deceived husband at my heels with a revolver in his hands. You see, by Egorushka's single standard, it would be fitting to act precisely in that manner . . .

LYOLYA. How cruel you are, Volodya! Do you want to destroy me?

VARYAGIN. Let me have a talk with your husband! I've been looking forward to this scene for a long time and promising myself a great deal of pleasure. In any event, it will be a powerful moment . . .

LYOLYA. (*With a sob*) But, surely he'll kill me . . .

VARYAGIN. Then stay! [. . .]

[VERA *interrupts their quarrel to discuss some unpaid bills that have arrived from the dressmaker.* LYOLYA *exits indignantly, and* VERA *demands that* VARYAGIN *leave immediately. She blames his presence for the deterioration of* EGOR's *marriage.*]

VARYAGIN. Vera Aleksandrovna, we are speaking two different languages . . . You are stubbornly seeking out a guilty party . . . But there is here only life with its eternal struggle for happiness . . . If, from your point of view, I am guilty of this before Petrovsky, then we—he and I—are now even . . .

VERA. (*She covers her face with her hands.*) But . . . Now I understand . . .

VARYAGIN. I'd wager you don't, judging by your tragic tone . . . There is no tragedy here . . . It's all inevitable, simple, even banal . . . Egor Andreevich is merely reaping what he himself has sown, when between the two of you he chose Lyolya . . . I am not a villain, nor a monster, but a very ordinary lover . . . Replace me with another person, and the comedy loses nothing [. . .] There is in this house, Vera Aleksandrovna, only one person before whom I would wish to justify myself, but it is not the injured husband . . . You, Vera, are the only being I respect. And it pains me to think that, leaving here, I will carry with me your undeserved disdain [. . .] I have no ill will toward Egor Andreevich, and there was never any hatred . . . Five years ago, when he took Lyolya from me, he was right, he was fighting for his happiness . . . I did not come back for revenge, Vera. I simply could not forget Lyolya. Our meeting awakened my dreams and my old curiosity. I was attracted by the game. Her love seemed to me such a poignant delight! . . . But . . . (*sadly*) that was a mirage. Reality, as always, turned out to be below expectations . . . There was no ecstasy . . . there wasn't even amusement . . . Everything was bleak and . . . unnecessary . . .

VERA. Vladimir Arkadyevich . . . The evil you have done cannot be repaired or justified by any kind of sophisms. But give up Lyolya now! You've cooled toward her . . . You despise her . . . Why do you want her? . . . I implore you! . . . (*She takes him by the hand.*)

VARYAGIN. (*Excited*) Vera [. . .] Why should I despise Lyolya . . . Am I really better than she? But you're right. I don't love her. I never have . . . This is all clear to me now. At your first word, I'd abandon Lyolya without regret and go away with a light heart, leaving Egor in blissful ignorance. (*Seeing Vera's indignant gesture*) But I will be logical, I will be consistent. I will separate Egor from his wife. This is my goal . . . yes! But don't consider me cruel and petty . . . This goal is my justification for everything. It's because I love you, Vera. I wish to bring about your happiness! [. . .] Yes, Vera . . . I love your proud, childlike soul . . . (*Seeing Vera's gesture of protest*) Hear me out! After all it doesn't obligate you in any way . . . How many times I've dreamed of coming to you, embracing your feet, putting my head on your knees, and crying . . . Crying because of the burning awareness of my impotence, my uselessness. I wanted to say: "I love you . . . Teach me to believe, to fight! Show me work, feverish and wideranging! . . . Share your strength and the fire which burns so brightly in you and warms those around you, with me! . . ." But you don't need me, Vera, you love someone else. And what is more dreadful than all this is that even if you'd fall in love with me, there would never be any happiness! You would demand my regeneration. But I'm already incapable of regenerating myself. I'm spiritually empty [. . .] Look beyond the present moment! If I leave alone, there'll soon be another in my place, and a scandal will take place sooner or later, granting no one happiness. Egor will perish—so save him! I want you to be happy in the end! I want this! . . . Vera, if I've been able to convince you, give me your hand! . . .

VERA. (*Stretching out her hand in confusion*) You haven't convinced me, no! But I can no longer hate you [. . .]

[LYOLYA *returns to find* VARYAGIN *passionately kissing* VERA's *hand. She is incensed.* VARYAGIN *bows coldly and exits.* PELAGEYA L'VOVNA *enters as* VERA *and* LYOLYA *are quarreling. When* VERA *has left,* LYOLYA *and her mother discuss the compromising situation in which she now finds herself. She is in debt, and, not wishing to obligate herself to* VARYAGIN, *asks her mother for money.* PELAGEYA *refuses and adds that* LYOLYA *has, in fact, already obligated herself by accepting expensive presents.* LYOLYA *suggests writing to her rich uncle in America; but* PELAGEYA L'VOVNA *finally confesses there is no such uncle.* LYOLYA *at last agrees to ask* VARYAGIN *to pay, and they both go to the garden to find him.*

PETROVSKY *returns unexpectedly, hiding a gun in his pocket. He tells* VERA *he has had the feeling* LYOLYA *needed him, and so ʰ ɹs returned for a few days. He notices the change in* VERA—*she has become even more beautiful. When he suggests it's because she's fallen in love with* VARYAGIN, *she can no longer contain herself and tells him* VARYAGIN *loves* LYOLYA. PETROVSKY *is determined to confront his wife with this accusation himself.*]

Scene 8

NADEZHDA MIKHAYLOVNA. (*From the door on the left*) Egorushka! My little dove! . . . (*She throws herself on his neck and cries.*)

PETROVSKY. Hello, my dear! I'm glad you've come, at last . . . You've seen Lyolya, of course? . . .

NADEZHDA MIKHAYLOVNA. I seen her from a distance . . . But I didn't—I couldn't speak to her . . . What's it to her? . . . She ain't got no time for us now . . .

PETROVSKY. (*With concealed irritation*) Again the old feud begins? If only you'd give me a little peace! Why do you use that strange tone when you speak about my wife? [. . .]

NADEZHDA MIKHAYLOVNA. Oi, sonny, sonny! It's not good to speak to yer mother like that . . . It's sinful! . . . Yer always fer yer wife and ya'd be happy t' slit my throat . . .

VERA. Enough! You're not coming to the point . . . Here's the problem, Egorushka—your wife has again incurred debts, and today they've demanded payment. I promised they would be paid by tomorrow evening . . .

PETROVSKY. That's all? I'm relieved . . . And how much is the debt? . . .

VERA. Five hundred rubles . . .

A gesture of astonishment escapes from PETROVSKY.

NADEZHDA MIKHAYLOVNA. (*Shouting*) An' can ya say "That's all" again? . . . Jus' try 'n pay it by t'morrow! . . . You're t' blame yerself! [. . .] Ya wet chicken! . . . What kind o' man are ya? And that's just half the grief—if wives would throw only their husband's money into the street . . . But what if they throw his name into the street as well [. . .]

PETROVSKY. How dare you? I won't allow you to insult my wife! . . .

NADEZHDA MIKHAYLOVNA. (*Shouting*) Lookee you! "Won't allow! . . ." No, sonny! Ya ain't big enough yet t' shout at yer mother . . . I, for one, lived my whole life honestly . . . I didn't shame yer father, nor you . . . See that ya teach yer wife not t' drag our good name through the mud! . . .

{ VERA. Get hold of yourself! . . .
{ PETROVSKY. (*Seizing his head*) What is she saying? . . .

VERA. Let's go away from here! . . . (*She drags* NADEZHDA MIKHAYLOVNA *to the door on the left.*)

NADEZHDA MIKHAYLOVNA. Why are ya grabbin' me? Won't ya let me say a word? You know I'm tellin' the truth. I'm offended for him, that he's makin' such a blockhead outta himself . . .

PETROVSKY. (*Enraged*) Will you come to the point? What are you hinting at? . . .

NADEZHDA MIKHAYLOVNA. (*Shaking all over*) There, she's comin' herself . . . (*She points to the park.*) Your hussy—all in a tizzy. Ask her! . . . I'm too old that such a puppy should pump me fer what's goin' on and yell at me . . . Let's go, Vera! Let him learn his wife how t' live in the world honorably, without deception . . . (*They both exit to the left.*)

PETROVSKY. (*Alone, he sinks into an armchair like a broken man. The monolog is carried on in a whisper.*) What did she say just now? . . . "How to live in this world honorably, without deception"? Did she say that? . . . My fair and honorable mother . . . And Vera did not refute her? . . . Vera was silent? . . . What's happened here? (*Raising his voice*) What's happened here while I was away? (*In a whisper*) Is it possible? . . . No, it can't be . . . (*He wants to stand up.*) I can't get up . . . I have no strength [. . .]

[PETROVSKY *is, at first, cautious with* LYOLYA—*trying to ascertain where the truth lies. He tries to perceive her true feelings by noting her reaction to two statements—that* VARYAGIN *is leaving and that* VARYAGIN *is in love with her. She is visibly upset by both, and this agitates him. The final blow to his self-control is his suspicions regarding the dressmaker's bills.* LYOLYA *lies that* PELAGEYA L'VOVNA *is paying them. This enrages* EGOR. PELAGEYA *appears, and she and her daughter continue to taunt* PETROVSKY, *finally suggesting* LYOLYA *should separate from him for the sake of her "delicate" health.* PETROVSKY *is livid and orders* PELAGEYA L'VOVNA *out of the house. He then turns to* LYOLYA *and confronts her.*]

PETROVSKY. I won't let you go anywhere! . . . Enough of this madness! . . . Enough bargaining with my conscience and senseless sacrifices! Tomorrow I'm going to look for another position . . . Deep in the provinces, at a factory . . . I'll break you! . . . Think before you mock me! . . . Let you go? Have you forgotten that you carry my name? . . . The name of honorable people? I won't allow you to drag it through the mud . . . (*He shudders and seizes his head.*) So that's it . . . now I understand . . . you want to go away with Varyagin? (*He approaches her slowly.*) [. . .] What's been between you? Speak! . . .

LYOLYA. N-n-nothing . . . I swear to you [. . .]

PETROVSKY. How horrible! . . . I can't trust her . . . She deceived me once . . . she'll deceive me again . . . What's to guarantee she won't? Wait . . . Look me in the face! [. . .] Oh, how much treachery is in that face! . . . Was I so blind? (*Laughing wildly*) What's it to you to swear? What's it to you to deceive? How could I forget that you're Trofimova's daughter? Ah! . . . If you've lied to me just now . . . (*He shoves her rudely.*) [. . .] Lord! . . . Lord! . . . Everything is crumbling! . . . That's what they were trying to open my eyes to! . . . But I, like a blind man, didn't see . . . How can I find out the truth? How? Death is easier . . . Death instead of this uncertainty! (*He exits through the middle door, stumbling, like a drunkard.*)

LYOLYA *lies in the armchair alone, sobbing.*) [. . .]

[VARYAGIN *has learned of* EGOR's *rage from* PELAGEYA L'VOVNA *and enters looking for him. He wishes to come to an understanding. Although he is in favor of* LYOLYA's *divorcing her husband (so* EGOR *may be free to marry* VERA) *and is willing to support her as his mistress, he firmly vows he will never marry her.* LYOLYA *is desperate.*]

Scene 12

PETROVSKY. (*At the middle door. For a second he stands as if struck, then with a hollow shriek he rushes at* LYOLYA.) So it's the truth? . . . So he is your lover? (*He grabs* LYOLYA's *hand.*) Answer me! . . .

LYOLYA. (*Involuntarily falling on her knees*) I'm ruined . . .

VARYAGIN. The answer is clear . . . Yes . . .

PETROVSKY. (*Choking*) Ah! . . . Then, die! . . . (*He rips the revolver out of his pocket.*)

VARYAGIN. (*Trying to tear the weapon from him*) Why? Why? Run, Elena Nikolaevna!

LYOLYA, *after shrieking, falls on the carpet, unconscious.*

Scene 13

VERA *runs in from the left with a piercing scream.* Egorushka! (*She throws herself at* PETROVSKY's *chest at the same moment as* VARYAGIN, *after a struggle, knocks the revolver from* PETROVSKY.)

PETROVSKY. (*Dully*) Leave me alone! . . . Go away! . . . Go away! . . . I haven't settled my accounts [. . .] A curse on all of you! . . . (*Weakened, he falls on the divan.*) [. . .]

VARYAGIN. Egor Andreich, I must say a few words to you . . . Will you hear me out? [. . .]

PETROVSKY. Oh, how I loathe you! Go away, go away! . . . I'm sorry I didn't kill you both . . . (*He lowers his head onto the table.*)

VARYAGIN. Yes, I'm leaving right away. And this time I'll leave defeated. You are happier than I, Egor Andreevich . . . In vain I s rch my soul to find hatred to answer your hatred . . . And I do. ﹒ find it . . . I will not begin to justify myself before you . . . I'll only remind you that five years ago, when you were in my place, I didn't take revenge on you, nor consider that I had the right to take someone else's life . . . and to punish people for their feelings . . .

PETROVSKY. (*Enraged*) Are you ridiculing me?! [. . .]

VARYAGIN. Oh, no! . . . I cannot mock . . . I cannot rejoice . . . I stand before what could have been a bloody drama, before these unnecessary sufferings, with revulsion and anguish.

VERA. (*After glancing at* LYOLYA) She's coming to . . .

VARYAGIN *shudders and a morbid smile steals across his face.* Look . . . Look . . . again . . . just as then . . . Five years ago . . . She regained consciousness, as I was leaving. (*As if in a daze*) Everyone's changed . . . Only I am the same . . . Everyone went on living . . . and only I waited . . . and deceived myself . . . (*Aloud, with anguish*) Vera! . . . Be happy! . . . And remember that I loved you . . . (*He exits.*)

VERA. (*Going up to* PETROVSKY) Egorushka! . . . Gather your courage and separate from Lyolya . . .

PETROVSKY. (*With horror and suffering on his face*) Separate? . . . Ah, I can't stand her . . . Let her go! . . . And quickly! Quickly! . . . Quickly! . . .

LYOLYA. (*Raising herself fearfully*) What's this? He's here again? He'll kill me . . .

VERA. (*Going to the middle door, she flings it open before her.*) You're free . . . Go! . . .

LYOLYA. Free? . . . Really? . . . Oh, what happiness! . . . (*She runs out.*)

VERA. (*Going up to* PETROVSKY *and putting her hand on his shoulder*) She's gone . . .

PETROVSKY. (*Who has been sitting, having seized his head with his hands*) Gone? (*With a shriek*) Gone! I'll never again see her face? (*He sobs.*)

VERA. (*After a pause, with deep emotion*) Cry, Egorushka, cry! . . . It's easier that way . . . Let these tears be in memory of those spiritual powers so shamefully wasted on the trivialities of life, on a superficial emotion . . . Cry! Let these tears wash away a seamy page in your life for which you've so often had to blush! All this was a mirage . . . Happiness isn't where you sought it . . . Look ahead and believe! . . .

PETROVSKY. (*Sobbing*) There is nothing ahead . . . For me, everything is finished!

VERA. (*With strength and passion*) Oh, Egorushka, there's a whole lifetime ahead!

Curtain

1896

Poliksena Solovyova

🖋 1867–1924

A sister of the famous Russian philosopher Vladimir Solovyov, Poliksena Sergeevna Solovyova (literary pseudonym, *Allegro*) was born in Moscow on March 20, 1867, where their father
was professor of history and rector of the University of Moscow.
Solovyova received her education at home, as was the fashion
among the Russian nobility at that time; she then studied at the
Moscow School of Painting, Sculpture, and Architecture. Among
her teachers were I. M. Pryanishnikov and V. D. Polenov, both
eminent Russian painters. Her first interests in literature included
the lives of the Russian saints, Andersen's fairy tales, Pushkin, Fet,
and Gogol'. She was particularly fond of Pushkin's *Ruslan and
Lyudmila* (1820) and Gogol's *Vechera na khutore bliz Dikan'ki*
(Evenings on a Farm Near Dikan'ka, 1831–32), for she loved Russian nature, the countryside of both the Russian South and the
North. Her early poetry glorified nature, and she wrote of the
"fatal suffering of the heart"[1] when she was eight years old! At
the age of ten she composed "Rassuzhdenie o zagrobnoy zhizni" (A
Discourse on Life beyond the Grave). Vladimir Solovyov showed
her youthful poems to Fet, who remarked that they had *"entrain."*
Poliksena Solovyova was gifted in many areas. She painted, played
the piano, and participated in various plays with considerable
success.

Her first poems appeared in 1882 in the journal *Niva* (The
Field). Later she contributed to *Russkoe bogatstvo* (Russian
Wealth), *Mir Bozhy* (God's World), *Zhurnal dlya vsekh* (The Jour-

nal for All), *Nedelya* (The Week), the Merezhkovskys' journal *Novy Put'* (The New Direction), *Vestnik Evropy* (The Messenger of Europe), *Severny vestnik* (The Northern Herald), and to the literary almanacs *Nashi dni* (Our Days) and *Yuzhny al'manakh* (Southern Almanac). From 1899, Solovyova's poetry appeared in separate volumes, often with her own graceful vignettes in pen and ink in the modernistic style. Her books include *Stikhotvoreniya* (Poems; St. Petersburg: Akinfiev, 1899); *Yolka* (The Fir Tree; St. Petersburg: Tropinka, 1907), a collection of poems for children with illustrations by Tatyana Hippius, Zinaida Hippius' younger sister; *Plakun-trava: stikhi* (Willow-Herb: Poems; St. Petersburg: Tropinka, 1909); *Novy God* (The New Year; St. Petersburg: Tropinka, 1910); a play in verse, *Svad'ba Solntsa i Vesny* (The Wedding of the Sun and the Spring; St. Petersburg: 2nd edition, Tropinka, 1912), which was put to music by M. Kuzmin; a collection of short stories, poems, and a play, all written for children, *Taynaya pravda* (The Secret Truth; St. Petersburg: Tropinka, 1912); a novella in verse, *Perekryostok* (Crossroads; St. Petersburg: Tropinka, 1913); a play in verse, *Beryozkiny imeniny* (The Birch Tree's Name Day; St. Petersburg: Tropinka, 1914); *Poslednie stikhi* (Last Verses; Moscow: GIZ, 1923); *Volshebnaya dudochka* (The Magic Flute; Moscow-Petrograd: GIZ, 1923), a folk tale in verse for children; and many others. Together with Natalya Ivanovna Manasseina, the wife of a Moscow doctor, Solovyova published a children's magazine called *Tropinka* (The Path), which appeared from 1906 to 1913 and met with great success in St. Petersburg. Solovyova was a close friend of Zinaida Hippius. They met in the mid-1890's, when Solovyova moved from Moscow to St. Petersburg, and their friendship continued until Solovyova's death in 1924 in a Moscow hospital. From there she wrote her last letter to Hippius, who was already living in Paris.

After the appearance of her first volume, Poliksena Solovyova was greeted on the Russian literary scene as a talented poet whose "elusive sensations" were comparable to the poetic gifts of Fet. A critic of *Russian Wealth*, for example, characterized her *Poems* of 1899 as revealing "some original, delicately sad, and femininely graceful coloring, which is typical of her art in general. Her poems are always brief and compressed to the maximum. Their motifs are the moods which flash in the young poet, but remain vague

POLIKSENA SOLOVYOVA

even to herself. Her poems are the memories of something beautiful and sad."[2] Solovyova's verse is very melodious, poetic, and refined in all respects, as are her own vignettes. One of the refreshing features in Solovyova's poetry was the absence of *grazhdanskaya skorb'* (songs about civic injustices), which was in style at the same time, continuing the tradition of Nekrasov, Ivan Savvich Nikitin (1824–1861), and Nadson. The center of Solovyova's poetry was "pulsating human feeling."[3]

In 1905 another volume of her poetry appeared, entitled *Iney: risunki i stikhi* (Hoarfrost: Drawings and Verse; St. Petersburg: Tropinka). This collection attracted the attention of many writers and scholars in Moscow and St. Petersburg. Alexander Blok, for example, highly esteemed the youthful and fresh qualities of Solovyova's verse in *Hoarfrost*. "There is nothing more contemporary, and there is no more lawful joy, than this harmonious and mature world outlook, which is portrayed with a childlike spontaneity of feeling against the illumination of noble nature,"[4] said Blok. Solovyova's attraction toward the depiction of Russian northern nature especially delighted him.

Despite its close relationship to the poems of Fet, Solovyova's work was nevertheless new, for it was very quiet, subdued, and peaceful. Her verse was also novel because of its spiritual and aesthetic qualities. It neither inveighed against Russian social conditions nor bewailed the unfortunate position of the Russian peasant, as was fashionable at the time. Rather, Solovyova's verse endeavored to fathom the spiritual depths within the human heart. Her poems, with their intimate character, "transparent sadness," "unexpected joys," and "thanksgiving and leave-taking motifs," are closely related to Blok's own poetry. And he believed that her "fiery words," born from the "fiery anguish" of solitude and clothed in her images by white hoarfrost in the silence of night, would be audible to the entire world. "There will come the day," Blok asserted, "when we will say the Word in a loud voice. At present, the Word is only a pale shadow which is, however, growing and gradually assuming the form of a white wing; it is still only the muffled echo of the Universal Word, which was prophesied in such a simple and clear fashion—yet so mysterious for many people—by the poet Vladimir Solovyov, who is related by blood and in spirit to the author of *Hoarfrost*."[5] Another eminent poet of the period, Innokenty Annensky, described Poliksena Solovyova's lyricism as *"intimate* and *daring,"*[6] and likened it to the lyricism of Zinaida Hippius and Cherubina de Gabriak, who also prophesied the advent of a new world and a new mankind. Annensky lauded these three poets for their craftsmanship and artistic tastes, observing that the refined simplicity of words and the delicate plainness of rhymes and rhythms were the salient features of Solovyova's poetry.

Poliksena Solovyova's poems are just as serious as those of Z. N. Hippius, but they are also different: they are subdued, as it were; there is asceticism in them; they reveal the most whimsical ineffability. The poems of Poliksena Solovyova are *not prayer-like,* as are those of Z. N. Hippius, but merely *lyrical.* Her poems reveal her lyrical experiences in varied forms. In her poetry, the fog "does not bring the sky down to the earth," but "aspires to make the earth into the sky." Moreover, Solovyova paints with chalk charcoal. Hippius lives in a strangely unsteady and an agonizingly symbolic world of words, in a world of abstractions which has absorbed the entire knowledge of this world in order to laugh at the contrast which exists between the black and the white. . . .[7]

Annensky admired Solovyova's unusually smooth monosyllabic rhymes, the graceful qualities of her verse, its content, and the nobility of its mood. It is true that Solovyova's poetic universe abounds in delicate and refined movements of the heart and thought; it reveals the poet's aspiration to the beautiful and unattainable, the world of bright hopes and lofty dreams. Her Muse is solitary, and her art is pure poetry. In its rhyme, rhythm, imagery, and content, her verse is "grace and beauty."[8]

Solovyova's poetic pictures of nature are supported by the musical quality of her poems. She used the beauty of nature as a springboard to soar into the world of mysterious dreams and revelations; yet her striving to attain the other world never resulted in despair and pessimism over her inability to achieve her goal. Frequently it resolved itself in a quiet prayer and her firm hope for God's mercy and help. Sadness, loneliness, memories of the past, timid anguish, and dreams about reciprocal love form the recurrent motifs and poetic images. *Hoarfrost* is ample proof of the poet's craftsmanship. The emotional effect of this volume rests largely on her symbols, built on the parallelism between her real and imaginary worlds. These symbols are ethereal, not clearly defined, given in half-hints, suppressed sighs, and light dreams, all of which create an atmosphere of nostalgia.

Solovyova's artistic method may be compared with that of Chekhov: simple on the surface, sincere, modest, and almost shy. But, in contrast to Chekhov, she portrays the eternal and the "essential." There are only a few poems in *Hoarfrost* which deal with the problems of everyday life. The tone is melancholic and elegiac, for happiness is but a reflection of the heavenly in the darkness of life on earth. Some other poems express the author's firm faith in the immediate future. All of them are in harmony with her drawings, full of mood and aspiration.[9] Each event in the life of nature is rendered in picturesque comparisons, unexpected sonorous rhymes, and musically arranged stanzas. Love for her fellow men, a joyous desire for self-sacrifice, and a striving for spiritual perfection in everything resound in many of her poems. The imagery includes the white flowers of the Annunciation, the white lily of Archangel Gabriel, the Virgin Mary and Mary Magdalene from the New Testament, the icons from the Old Testament decorated with flowers and verdure, the asphodel, and the snow-white young birch trees.

Valery Bryusov, the *maître* of Russian modernistic poetry in Moscow, availed himself of the opportunity to express his evaluation of Poliksena Solovyova's poetry. He related her work, in its presentation of "universal experiences," to the poetry of Fet and Vladimir Solovyov, and lauded her imagery and art of versification, especially in the poem "My peli solntsu v bylye gody" (We Sang to the Sun in Days Gone By) and those following it. In Solovyova, he saw a "real poet, *quiddam poetae.*"[10] He was also pleased with her novella "*Nebyvalaya*" (The Unprecedented One), which appeared in F. I. Bulgakov's *Novy zhurnal iskusstv, literatury i nauk* (The New Journal of Arts, Literature, and Sciences).

Poliksena Solovyova's characteristic melancholy permeates her entire volume *Willow-Herb: Poems,* which contains vignettes with perfect artistic finish, such as "Voskresenye" (Sunday), "Blagoveshchenye" (The Annunciation), and "Voskresshie doliny" (Resurrected Dales), to name only a few. They convey the poet's steadfast belief in the forthcoming end of all earthly sadness and the imminent beginning of a new life. The language and the exterior form of her verse are again lucid, deceptively simple, and firm. Other poems in the volume, however, appear somewhat labored, and their images occasionally lack the spontaneity and profound spirit of Solovyova's previously published volumes.

In keeping with the *Zeitgeist* of the period, Solovyova experimented with other literary genres—writing folktales, plays, and novellas in verse. For example, *Crossroads: A Novella in Verse* contains many lyrical episodes and poems, yet its structure is compressed, clear, and sustains the reader's interest. The heroine is a representative of a new Russian generation whose *Weltanschauung* may be described as that of "ideological denudation."[11] The mood of the Russian intelligentsia of that time, and their new philosophical problems and socio-political dilemmas, such as the women's liberation movement, give this novella a significance for our present-day world. Moreover, *Crossroads* may be viewed as Solovyova's successful resurrection of the genre of the novella in verse. Another noteworthy experiment may be found in one of the later collections, *Vecher* (Evening; St. Petersburg: Tropinka, 1914). In addition to her lyrical poems, Solovyova here presents pictures of nature and of the city which are juxtaposed in a curious artistic opposition. The theme of the metropolis had never interested the poet before.

Although unjustly neglected by today's reader and scholar, Poliksena Solovyova distinguished herself as an original poet in the history of Russian literature. Like the other poets of Modernism, she also experimented with imagery, versification, poetic atmosphere, and literary genres. The range of her literary endeavor is wide: Russian folksongs, songs about nature, religious meditations, and hymns; plays, novellas, and folktales in verse; genre painting of the city; poems and literary sketches for children; short stories; and so forth. In keeping with the concept of the truly gifted artist, as advocated by Maxim Gor'ky, she was entirely capable of passing from her personal, intimate poetry to the treatment of the "burning topics of the day."

NOTES

1. F. F. Fidler, *Pervye literaturnye shagi: avtobiografii sovremennykh russkikh pisateley* (Moscow: Sytin, 1911), p. 91.

2. "Allegro. *Stikhotvoreniya, s vinyetkami avtora.* St. Petersburg, 1899," *Russkoe bogatstvo,* No. 3, Sec. III (1899), 58.

3. L. Men'shin [P. F. Grinevich], *Ocherki russkoy poezii* (St. Petersburg: N. N. Klobukov, 1904), p. 346.

4. Aleksander Blok, "P. Solovyova (Allegro). *Iney: risunki i stikhi*, St. Petersburg, 1905," *Voprosy zhizni*, Nos. 5–6 (1905), 217.

5. *Ibid.*, p. 219.

6. In. Annensky, "O sovremennom lirizme," *Apollon*, No. 3 (1909), 29.

7. *Ibid.* See also Johannes von Guenther, *Ein Leben im Ostwind: Zwischen Petersburg und München, Erinnerungen* (München: Biederstein Verlag, 1969).

8. Evgeny Lundberg, "P. Solovyova (Allegro). *Iney: risunki i stikhi.* St. Petersburg, 1905," *Vestnik Evropy*, No. 7 (1905), 387.

9. For more details, read L. Vas-y, "P. Solovyova (Allegro). *Iney: risunki i stikhi.* St. Petersburg, 1905," *Obrazovanie*, No. 11–12, Sec. II (1905); Konstantin Konstantinovich, Grand Duke, *Poeticheskie otzyvy* (Petrograd: n.p., 1915), and Sergey Solovyov, "Russkaya literatura," *Vesy*, No. 3 (1909), 91–92.

10. Valery Bryusov, "P. Solovyova (Allegro). *Iney: risunki i stikhi.* St. Petersburg, 1905," *Vesy*, No. 8 (1905), 55–56. Also V. Malakhieva-Mirovich, "P. Solovyova (Allegro). *Plakun-Trava: Stikhi.* St. Petersburg, 1909," *Russkaya mysl'*, No. 11, Sec. III (1909), 260.

11. "P. Solovyova (Allegro). *Perekryostok: povest' v stikhakh.* St. Petersburg: Tropinka, 1913," *Russkoe bogatstvo*, No. 8 (1913), 363.

THERE

There it's now fragrant with mushrooms and lichen
In the gold-crimson quiet of the lowlands,
The air is filled with the intoxication of autumn,
The path of the spider's gray threads trembles.
If only I could see the quivering of the aspen,
If only a hare would dart through the bush,
If only I might greedily grasp
The fresh clusters of rowan-tree berries in my burning palms.
Here I languish, in the suffocating breezes of the desert,
The prophetic voice of the sea frightens me:
It foretells a difficult year
Approaching us like a terrible phantom.
If I only could retreat under the peaceful pine canopies,
If only I could be closer to my native skies,
If only I could be amidst dear, beggarly nature,
If only to be there!

Last Poems (Moscow: GIZ, 1923)

ТАМ

Там теперь пахнет грибами и прелью
В злато-багряном затишьи низин,
Воздух осеннего полон похмелья,
Зыбок полет паутинных седин.
Только б увидеть дрожанье осины,
Только бы заяц мелькнул через гать,
Только б прохладные гроздья рябины
Жадно в горячих ладонях зажать.
Здесь я томлюсь в душных ветрах пустыни,
Страшен мне моря пророческий глас:
Он возвещает о тяжкой године,
Грозным виденьем грядущей на нас.
Только б под тихие хвойные своды,
Только бы к бледным родным небесам,
Только б средь милой убогой природы,
Только бы там!

EARLY MASS

Pre-dawn's twilight has not yet broken,
My soul still lies between dream and vigil,
Yet the rhythmical chime, summoning and unanswered,
Falls like a drizzling rain beyond the slumbering window.
The light has just glimmered above the white bell tower,
The rope is trembling in the angel's hands.
Dawn—ever more sacrificial, ever more devout,
Pours its scarlet wine into the clouds of daybreak.
The veil is lifted from the temple's sacrament,
The blood has been shed, the chalice is rising,
And Someone, all-loving, in forgiveness, is blessing
This insane and unhappy world.

Last Poems

THE SNOWDROP

In the garden where the young birch trees had clustered
in a crowd,
The blue eye of a snowdrop peeped out:
At first, it slowly
Wiggled out its delicate green leg,
Then stretched itself with all its tiny strength
And quietly asked:
"I see the weather's warm and bright;
Tell me, can it be true that this is spring?"

The Fir Tree

ПОДСНЕЖНИК

В саду, где березы столпились гурьбой,
Подснежника глянул глазок голубой.
Сперва понемножку
Зеленую выставил ножку,
Потом потянулся из всех своих маленьких сил
И тихо спросил:
—«Я вижу, погода тепла и ясна,
Скажите, ведь правда, что это весна?»

Dry pines and shaggy black firs
  Bowed closely to the shore.
Their motionless gloom and heavy patterned branches
  Were mirrored in the drowsy water.
There, above the trees, the bright twilight sky
  Was all aglow with promises.
The water, though hearing the trees' indistinct invocation,
  Dared not answer the skies.
So, too, all my thoughts, enveloped in darkness,
  Threateningly encircled my soul;
My arms, which had been raised toward the distant skies, fall;
  The prayers have frozen in my heart.
Lord! I am asleep, but let me see the great and cherished miracle
  Upon my awakening;
Let my languishing soul answer with a new prayer
  Your ineffable word.

The Fir Tree

Сосны сухие и елки мохнатые, черные
  К берегу тесно склонились.
Мрак их недвижный и тяжкие ветви узорные
  В сонной воде повторились.
Там, над деревьями, яркое небо закатное
  Все обещаньями рдеет.
Слышит вода заклинанье деревьев невнятное,
  Небу ответить—не смеет.
Так, угрожая, все помыслы тьмою одетые
  Душу мою обступили,
Падают руки, к дальнему небу воздетые,
  В сердце молитвы остыли.
Боже! Я сплю, но великое чудо желанное
  Дай, пробудившись, мне встретить,
Томной душе дай на слово Твое несказанное
  Новой молитвой ответить.

We sang to the sun in days gone by,
We venerated its flame,
Pleading for refuge from dark night and foul weather,
We sang to the day.

Now we sing to the glory of the storm,
We weave garlands to the glory of darkness;
Beyond the storm is azure's rapture brighter,
And we know not the day—without night.

Hoarfrost

IN THE CRYPT

A ray of spring's sun slipped through a low window
Into the gloomy darkness of the mute crypt;
Onto the cold floor it threw
A spot of warmth, like a summons to forgotten merriment.

With a pale smile, the crosses responded,
Their dull silver showing white on the palls;
The wreaths' leaves, withered and decayed,
Sensed through their slumber the breathing of the laurel groves.

The door scarcely opened . . . with a rush of the breeze
Spring's greeting descended upon the silent graves,
And someone's delicate and slender hand
Laid spring flowers upon the tomb.

All again fell silent, but the bright blooms
Smelled even more delicate in the cold dusk,
Like forgotten yet eternal dreams,
And whispered to the dead of love and joy.

Hoarfrost

В СКЛЕПЕ

Весенний солнца луч сквозь низкое окно
Скользнул в угрюмый мрак немого подземелья,
И на холодный пол горячее пятно
Он бросил, как призыв забытого веселья.

Улыбкой бледною ответили кресты,
Померкшим серебром белея на покровах,
Венков увядшие, истлевшие листы
Почуяли сквозь сон дыханье рощ лавровых.

Приотворилась дверь ... с порывом ветерка
Привет весны слетел на тихие могилы,
И чья-то нежная и тонкая рука
Весенние цветы на камень положила.

И снова стихло все, но яркие цветы
В холодном сумраке нежней благоухали,
Как позабытые, но вечные мечты,
И мертвым о любви и радости шептали.

ST. PETERSBURG

The city of mists and dreams
Rises before me
With its indistinct mass
Of heavy houses.
With its chain of palaces
Reflected in the cold Neva.
Life hurriedly picks its way
Here toward an unseen goal . . .
I recognize you, with my former sadness,
Sick city,
My beloved, dispassionate city!
You torment me like a nightmare
With your timid question . . .
It is night, but the firmament glimmers with the dawn . . .
You are conquered
By that white dusk.

Hoarfrost

THE EVENING GLOW

Last night you were dying so slowly in the sky,
Glittering like gold, you smiled so at me.
Such joys and light did you promise
That all night I dreamed of a new and bright day.

But this morning was dismal and misty.
Having hung rain's gray net in the air,
It oppresses my soul, like an unexpected, malicious visitor,
With whom it is hard to live and worse to die.

Tell me, why did you promise me so much,
There, beyond the trees, glowing till midnight,
And paint with gold your pledge of rain,
My beautiful, inconstant evening glow?

But I won't grumble at you, my golden one;
Your deception, my bright one, I love as before.
And, remembering in my heart your vows,
I bless you for your beautiful lie.

Hoarfrost

ON A WINTER'S NIGHT

We went out, and the moon looked at our faces;
It was sad, cold, and distant.
The white halo around it, accompanying the moon
Along its solitary path, is dull.
    We went out through the heavy and hollow doors,
    Walking through the gloomy passage.
    The light of the lanterns flickers in the wind,
    The shadows tremble and sway.
Along the pale street, all life has died;
Only the windows barely glow with lights.
Everywhere—a blue, crystal darkness,
Nearby, far off, and above us.

Our farewell greeting rings out so timidly,
Our solitary path frightens us,
But the moon still gazes at our pallid faces,
Cold, sad, and distant.

Hoarfrost

THE OLD HOUSE

A lazy breeze, barely felt, roams along the grass . . .
The dew and shadows find their shelter here till midday,
Look how there, along the stairs, the sun ascends
Still higher, still warmer, up the ramshackle steps.

Above the stairs—a house completely overgrown with bushes.
Nobody lives there. It's long been deserted,
And the window, like an evil eye under sullen brows,
Is black and glints under the roof.

I so much like to walk along the overgrown path
Amidst the leaves and flowers of the neglected garden.
Here irises rise—a violet-colored family,
And dandelions in the smoke of their gray hair.

At evening, weary, I return to this place;
Here, barely seen, a bench awaits me in the grass.
Affectionately, I meet my memories
And ponder a long while—expecting something.

At such moments time appears to me merciless and evil,
And—completely clothed in misty silence—
My past approaches along those crumbling steps
To discuss with me the days to come.

Hoarfrost

Pre-dawn's twilight glances in the window,
The garden looms black like a gloomy wall,
The dismal hour, cold and dreary,
Like a ghost, glides above the earth.

My soul is filled with painful anxiety,
My tired head is bent,
While the blue dusk whispers overhead
The vague words of my last dreams . . .

Hoarfrost

I have not come to reproach you.
I have lost all reproaches in the fields:
The cornflowers called to me from the rye,
The corn's tall ear bowed deeply.
I've forgotten all my painful wrath . . .
The rye around me swelled in waves,
Like water from the rippling of oars,
And carried away—all my malice! . . .

Hoarfrost

Do you remember, we walked along the quiet river
At an early hour, like a pair of children.
I was filled with my fiery anguish,
You—with your white dream.
Wherever my glance lingered,
And wherever you gazed,
The world, sparkling with fire, flared up,
And white flowers began to grow.
People lived, were born, and died.
Their paths were alien to us.
Bending over the shore, we listened
To the slow river's peaceful fairy tales.
If the darkness breathed over the river,
We fought its vicious evil:
I—with my fiery anguish,
You—with your white dream.
Now, as the years are passing,
A narrow path leads us to the sunset,

Where the unfading vaults of heaven await us,
Where eternity sings for us its own song.
As in olden times, we walk hand in hand,
To others—an incomprehensible pair:
I—with my fiery anguish,
You—with your white dream.

Hoarfrost

Lidiya Zinovyeva-Annibal

〆 1866–1907

Lidiya Dmitrievna Zinovyeva-Annibal, born in Zagorye, Mogilyov region, was known mainly for four works, even though her literary output was far more voluminous. Her major works include a symbolist play entitled *Kol'tsa: drama v trekh deystviyakh* (The Rings: A Drama in Three Acts, 1907); a novel, *Tridsat' tri uroda* (Thirty-three abominations, 1907), and two collections of short stories, *Tragichesky zverinets: rasskazy* (The Tragic Menagerie: Stories, 1907), and *Net!* (No! 1918). The latter, published posthumously, contains a mystically colored and rather timidly formulated protest against Russia's social conditions at the time. During the uprising of 1905, Zinovyeva-Annibal participated in *Adskaya pochta* (The Infernal Mail, 1905–7). The illegal journal was patterned after the satirical monthly of the same name which appeared in 1769 in St. Petersburg under the editorship of F. A. Emin (1735–70) and was continued in 1788 by I. F. Bogdanovich (1743–1803).

Not much is known about Zinovyeva-Annibal's personal life. At the turn of the century she left her husband and settled down in Italy with their three children. Always extravagant, sensitive, and a great lover of life, she took along with her three Russian girls, her wards, who used to cluster around her on the floor of their Italian parlor and sing Russian folksongs. Their singing pacified somewhat the writer's nostalgia for her native land. Later, in Switzerland, Zinovyeva-Annibal became close to Vyacheslav Ivanov, at that time a scholar in the field of Germanic studies and an incorrigible dreamer, who secretly wrote "strange poetry." They were married in the Greek Orthodox Church in Liverno, Italy, where later (in 1912) Vyacheslav Ivanov was to marry his stepdaughter, Vera Konstantinovna Shvarsalon (d. 1920), Zinovyeva-Annibal's oldest child by her previous marriage.

Upon their return to St. Petersburg, the Ivanovs initiated the famous Tower group. Between 1905 and 1910 the literary and intellectual élite of St. Petersburg gathered at the Ivanovs' home every Wednesday evening to discuss Oscar Wilde, Nietzsche, Stirner, Eleusinian mysteries, and neo-Kantian philosophy. Prior to the political events of 1905, Zinaida Hippius and D. S. Merezhkovsky had also attended the Ivanovs' *soirées* regularly, since the topics of discussion at that time concerned artistic form and aesthetic principles, always of interest to the Merezhkovskys. After 1905, however, they were only occasional visitors at the Tower gatherings. They felt alienated because, instead of solving urgent socio-political questions, the host, hostess, and guests spent their time attempting to identify Dionysus with Christ and reconciling Solovyov's idealistic philosophy with Rozanov's sexual mysticism. With her characteristic wit, Hippius remarked that Ivanov, Zinovyeva-Annibal, and their visitors were engaged in nothing more than "dancing in a ring, singing bacchanalian songs, and wearing loose chlamyses and garlands."[1] Moreover, since the Ivanovs' "multi-dimensional" religion and neopaganism never appealed to her, Hippius often criticized the insufficiency of their faith in God. But on the whole, the poet respected Vyacheslav Ivanov's cultured and metaphysical verse. His ecstatic eroticism was not entirely distasteful to her; she admired its external decency and refinement of form. And, together with other writers of the time, she lauded Zinovyeva-Annibal's *Tragic Menagerie* as a remarkable and beautifully written book, although she was critical of her general literary endeavor, as well as of her eccentric demeanor.

Indeed, Zinovyeva-Annibal's impetuous temperament revealed itself in many vagaries. For example, she liked to wear red and white Greek chlamyses while entertaining, to decorate her rooms with the same materials in silk and velvet, and to burn incense and candles. She would often appear before her visitors with white garlands in her curly golden hair. The German poet and translator Johannes von Guenther described his Tower meetings with Zi-

LIDIYA ZINOVYEVA-ANNIBAL

novyeva-Annibal in these words: "Die dritte in diesem Musen-
zirkel war Lydia Sinowjewa-Annibal, Iwanow's zweite Frau, eine
imposante Erscheinung. Gross, ziemlich voll, mit einer rotblon-
den, uppigen Mähne und stets in farbenfreudigen griechischen
Chitonen gekleidet; laut, lustig, beweglich, entschieden—und na-
türlich ebenfalls Dichterin, wenn sie auch nicht Lyrik schrieb,
sondern kleine und grosse Prosa und Theater. Die gütige Frau
hatte ein warmes Herz für junge Dichter, so gewann sie bald ihre
Zuneigung [. . .] man konnte sie als den Motor betrachten, der
die turbulente Geistigkeit der Iwanowischen Mittwoch-Abende im
Gang hielt."[2]

Zinovyeva-Annibal was a compulsive talker. Her "decadent"
moods and eccentric behavior might have originated partially in an
anxiety for her children, who were left in Geneva with their governess. Her whims and daring escapades were in harmony with the
literary fashion of the day, when artists and poets wore masks
behind which they concealed their often tortured personalities.
The source of Zinovyeva-Annibal's eccentricities was in many respects quite different from that of the Russian Decadents: her vagaries stemmed from an intense manifestation of life in all its
exuberance; theirs, frequently from the vacuity and lack of vitality
of their inner lives.

Vyacheslav Ivanov and his vivacious wife soon lost interest in the
orgiastic celebrations at their Wednesday salons. Zinovyeva-Annibal allegedly said on more than one occasion: "Oh, these Decadents from the Apraksin market!"[3] The couple wished, in 1907, to
publish a journal which would be a literary and philosophical outlet
for Russian Symbolism. They no longer desired to contribute to
Vesy (The Scales), which in their opinion was "purely aesthetic."
The sisters Evgeniya and Adelaida Gertsyk, close friends of the
Ivanovs' for many years, were to take part in the creative and
technical work of their forthcoming publication.

These plans did not materialize. In the fall of the same year
Zinovyeva-Annibal died suddenly from scarlet fever in Zagorye,
where the Ivanovs were spending the summer. Evgeniya Gertsyk
recalls that during those summer months the Ivanovs were particularly happy, because of their intention to change their style of
life by plunging into "real work." Moreover, Zinovyeva-Annibal
was overjoyed to find herself again at home with her husband and

their children, who had returned from Switzerland. It was at that time that husband and wife recaptured the freshness of their former romance and developed a new, profound relationship. In Evgeniya Gertsyk's words, during that summer

> . . . all that which had deceived the heart
> Smiled at the heart anew:
> The sky, the green fields, and love.

> ... всё, чем сердце обманулось,
> Улыбнулось сердцу вновь:
> Небо, нива и любовь.[4]

In October, 1907, Zinovyeva-Annibal's coffin arrived on a freight train at the St. Petersburg railway station. The train was met by several distinguished writers, among them Alexander Blok, Mikhail Kuzmin, Sergey Gorodetsky, Georgy Chulkov, and Evgeniya and Adelaida Gertsyk.

Zinovyeva-Annibal's play, *The Rings: A Drama in Three Acts*, with an introduction by Vyacheslav Ivanov, was harshly criticized by contemporaries who missed her artistic objective. She aspired to create a new theatre of symbolic mystery-plays, in which there would be no stage and the actors would use their free imagination to improvise their roles. As Vyacheslav Ivanov explains in the introduction, the play was to present a new form of drama in the vein of Ibsen, as an "arena of profound spiritual experiences and crises of utmost significance."[5] Spectator, actor, and author were to be united in one common ceremony, simultaneously celebrating and serving the spiritual needs and pursuits of each participant. The tragic perception of the world inherent in the new drama would transfigure it into a mystery and thus return it to its original source, the liturgistic ritual at the altar of the suffering God. Ivanov concluded: "To die in the spirit together with the tragic victim, with the countenance of the dying Dionysus, and to be resurrected in Dionysus who is rising from the dead—this is the essence of dithyrambic purification."[6] In view of this definition of the art's objective, Zinovyeva-Annibal's identification of life with a series of deaths, and likewise of passion with death, is not surprising. She argued that real love belongs to the realm of eternity; there can be no place for jealousy in the most sublime manifestation of love on earth. The heroine, who seeks suffering as a step to the sublime revelation of love, throws her rings into the sea to free herself from all people and all earthly bonds. The play may be viewed as an approximation of Dionysian art, the utmost meaning of which is a dithyrambic solution of a personal tragedy. Zinovyeva-Annibal's three main symbols are related to the interior of the house, the sea shore, and the sea depth. They present the passage of the human personality through three fatal tests which attract the soul on its way to the mysterious goal. When this goal is achieved, there resounds a joyous exclamation: "Look, the morning has again arranged its *fête*—the sea resembles the sky. It shines, like a sapphire through the crystal of islands, and the horizon appears like a blue fog . . . And yesterday, and tomorrow, and again from the beginning, and again never—and so till the very end."[7]

It is true that there is a great deal of sensuality in the play; indeed, the Russian writer and critic A. V. Amfiteatrov claimed that Zinovyeva-Annibal's drama was no more than a "continuous babble of shameless impotence."[8] He was enraged that "Oberon was made to fall in love with an ass, while innocent Helene and Hermia were transformed into two licentious women and thrown to a gang of tramps for rape."[9] Amfiteatrov saw in this play a poor parody of Shakespeare's *Midsummer Night's Dream.* He failed to see that, parallel to erotic issues, there are also subtle psychological revelations. O. Mirtov, a critic of *Obrazovanie* (Education), accused Zinovyeva-Annibal of creating a "crude combination of artistic refinement and eroticism." An "insufficient equilibrium" in presenting the psychology of the protagonists was another fault, in her eyes.[10] She was joined by other critics of the day in her negative evaluation of Zinovyeva-Annibal's early works. Alexander Blok, for example, stated that in *The Rings* and in the novel *Thirty-three Abominations* the writer overindulged in her experimentations with "the word." According to Blok, these two works merely represented the beginning of her literary career: "This beginning was savage, impetuous, anxious [. . .] Here everything was filled with passion and suffering. Often the word itself controlled the writer."[11]

Analysis of these two works shows that Zinovyeva-Annibal was submerged in "living life on earth" to such an extent that her style acquired shrill, ecstatic tones. It strangely combines valid psychological statements, refined locution, and grandiloquent phrases with exaggerations and elements of crude sensuality and eroticism, also evident in *Thirty-three Abominations*. Here the attractive actress Vera and her young mistress (the latter is the narrator of the story) are priestesses of a religion of refined beauty from which also emerges their cult of the beautiful body. Just as Lyudmila instructs the boy Sasha about sensual love and physical loveliness in Fyodor Sologub's *Melky bes* (The Petty Demon, 1907), Vera develops her beloved aesthetically, revealing to her consciousness as yet unfathomed aspects of her physical beauty. Posing in the nude before thirty-three artists, Vera's mistress is horrified by their portrayals of her body; she sees in them thirty-three abominations, the thirty-three mistresses of thirty-three artists. "It is not our beauty, not Vera's!" exclaims the anguished narrator. "These are thirty-three abominations! Thirty-three monsters!" It is important to note that the love of these two beautiful lesbians is expressly physical, and not a spiritual idealization. One of them defines their love in the following manner: "I love your body because of its beauty, but I do not need your soul. I do not even know if there is any soul. Moreover, I do not need your soul, because your body is so beautiful."

The portrayal of sex and physical beauty in Russian literature stems from the works of Boleslav Markevich, a writer of the second half of the nineteenth century, and Ieronim Yasinsky (literary pseudonym, Maxim Belinsky), a writer of the late nineteenth and early twentieth centuries. Adultery became the unvarying theme in the novels and short stories of Yasinsky, one of the more talented of those Russian writers who indulged in the bacchanalia of pornography which was particularly prevalent during 1906–8. Anatoly Kamensky ("Leda" and "Chetyre" [The Four]), Sergey Sergeev-Tsensky ("Zhenskie trupiki" [Little Female Corpses]), Fyodor Sologub ("Lyubov'" [Love] and *Navyi chary* [The Sorcery of the Dead]), Mikhail Kuzmin (Krylya [The Wings] and "Kartonny domik" [A Small Cardboard House]), Leonid Andreev ("V tumane" [In the Fog] and "Bezdna" [The Abyss]), and Mikhail Artsybashev (*Sanin*) became engrossed in depicting sensuality and sexual perversion—homosexuality, hermaphroditism, onanism, nymphomania, incest, and bestiality. Having buried science, positivism, logic, a jubilant joy of life as relics of the past, these writers now celebrated a requiem for the Russian intelligentsia, with their hopes for a better future and a more perfect human being.

The general assumption that *Thirty-three Abominations* was rooted in this tradition caused Zinovyeva-Annibal to be criticized by her contemporaries. One of the leading critics of the day, A. A. Izmaylov, denied any intrinsic value in the novel.[12] Anastasiya N. Chebotarevskaya, Fyodor Sologub's wife and herself a poet and translator, saw something different in *Thirty-three Abominations:* namely, an original and significant idea which, unfortunately, was distorted by the author's "pretentious attempts at symbolism."[13] The aforementioned critic Amfiteatrov rejected the work altogether, likening it to Gaston Dubois Dessaule's *Etude sur la bestialité au point de vue historique, médical et juridique* (1905).[14] Zinaida Hippius directed her objections to Zinovyeva-Annibal's style, describing the novel as an uncultured work, and its language as awkward, clumsy, poor, and banal. "This anti-style," Hippius complained, "is sustained throughout the novel, with the exception of those rare cases when two or three good lines would occur to the author of their own accord."[15] In general, Hippius proceeded to say, Zinovyeva-Annibal's prosody resembled the lines:

> Evdokiya, Evdokiya,
> Which way are ya.

> Евдокия, Евдокия,
> Какия.

Zinovyeva-Annibal's art of versification was inadequate in Hippius' eyes, and she found her poetry devoid of all meaning.

With all due esteem for Zinaida Hippius and other critics, it should be emphasized that Zinovyeva-Annibal did herald a new concept of love which was to enable man to escape the exterior world of vulgarity and ugliness. She argued that only by revering love more than any other value can man create his own private world of harmony and beauty. Beauty is the essence of the spiritual world of inspiration, the world of joy, happiness, and peace. But beauty, she warned, can be easily corrupted through contact with the exterior world—as was the beauty of Vera's beloved (in *Thirty-three Abominations*), which was at the mercy of the thirty-three clumsy artists. Zinovyeva-Annibal's metaphysical con-

197

siderations form the aesthetic theme of the novel; this distinguishes it from those other works which were written in response to a literary vogue that had as its sole purpose the portrayal of sexual love.

The Tragic Menagerie is altogether different from Zinovyeva-Annibal's symbolic play and the novel. In this collection of short stories she seems to have found her real world and its adequate artistic expression. The reader may shy away from the wild and terrifying aspects of Zinovyeva-Annibal's poetic universe; one could easily be intimidated by the graphic depictions of the interplay among the wild elements of nature and life, "singing about freedom and whistling like the wind blowing into one's ears."[16] Alexander Blok was one of those writers who admired *The Tragic Menagerie* as a book about youth, ecstasy, and compassion, a protest against cruelty and the human proclivity for criminal acts. Zinovyeva-Annibal's pictures of children and animals are not refined or sentimental, but almost barbarous and insolent; yet at the same time they are affectionate and mysterious. The collection has a strong appeal to all readers, both to "simple souls" and to those "decrepit under the weight of literary experience."[17] Hippius joined Blok in his eulogy by saying that *The Tragic Menagerie* is a book rich with the warm, sincere, and graceful pictures of the author's own distant past.[18] Hippius particularly liked the stories "Medvezhata" (The Bear Cubs), "Zhurya" (The Fledgling), "Volki" (The Wolves), and "Chudovishche" (The Monster), all of which appear in this anthology. Another much celebrated poet, Marina Tsvetaeva, referred to the "unforgettable, affectionate, and picturesque stories" of *The Tragic Menagerie* in her reminiscences. She vividly recalled how Maximilian Voloshin had presented her with Zinovyeva-Annibal's "exquisite and very feminine book."[19]

The narrator in *The Tragic Menagerie,* the young Vera, grew up independently, submerged in the atmosphere of the Russian landed nobility's established traditions. Her sense of independence and her instinctive nature are in the foreground of the book. Vera's varied experiences are depicted against many (frequently tragic) collisions with the lives of other people and animals. However cautiously, the conflicts of interest between the nobles and their servants are indicated. Some critics professed to see in Vera an ever-growing tendency to accept some of the principles of revolutionary socialism; this development they detected in such stories as "Glukhaya Dasha" (Deaf Dasha), "Tsarevna Kentavr" (The Tsarevna Centaur), and "The Bear Cubs."[20] If there are any manifestations of social protest in Vera, they are clearly limited to her increasing awareness of isolated instances of social injustice and a vague consciousness of the dishonesty of the more privileged Russian classes toward their subordinates. While becoming aware of these social problems, Vera undergoes tormenting doubts, perplexity, and a lacerating feeling of shame.

The book abounds in psychological insights. Vera, a wild yet poetic and compassionate child who is deeply sensitive to and in harmony with nature, reveals a capacity for profound love. This feeling of love is evoked through the beautiful image of Vera's mother, especially of her warm blue eyes. Although endowed with a stormy and turbulent temperament, Vera can be meek when experiencing a pure joy in life, or affection for her sick mother, or warm sympathy for their servants and animals. The book is rich in content, mood, poetry, and unusual situations and scenes. The dialogue is equally impressive, always idiomatic, picturesque, and gripping in its expressiveness. The narrative technique is powerful in its stylization of the author's childhood reminiscences, which are interwoven with the more reflective perceptions of her adulthood. Characteristic of each story's structure is the shift in manner of narration at the end, where Zinovyeva-Annibal suddenly derives the spiritual from the material.

Zinovyeva-Annibal achieved harmony, unity, and artistic equilibrium between the young, hotheaded girl with her unbridled heart, and the melancholy adult enriched with diverse experiences. *The Tragic Menagerie* is an unmistakable example of artistic talent.

NOTES

1. Z. N. Hippius, *Zhivye litsa* (Prague: Plamya, 1925), II, 62.

2. Johannes von Guenther, *Ein Leben im Ostwind: Zwischen Petersburg und München, Erinnerungen* (München: Biederstein Verlag, 1969), p. 123. "The third person in this circle of the Muses was Lidiya Zinovyeva-Annibal, Ivanov's second wife, an imposing personality. Tall, rather full-figured, with a red-blond, luxurious mane and always dressed in Greek tunics of appealing colors; loud, gay, lively, resolute—and of course also a poet, although she did not write lyrics, but short and long prose works and plays. This good-natured woman had a warm heart for

the young poets, and so quickly awakened their sympathy [. . .] one could view her as the motor sustaining the turbulent spirituality of the Ivanovs' Wednesday *soirées.*"

3. The Apraksin market in St. Petersburg was a place of shabby shops and petty merchants.

4. Evgeniya Gertsyk, *Vospominaniya* (Paris: YMCA Press, 1973), p. 46.

5. L. Zinovyeva-Annibal, *Kol'tsa: drama v trekh deystviyakh.* Vstupitel'naya statya Vyacheslava Ivanova (Moscow: Obshchestvo rasprostraneniya poleznykh knig; September, 1904), p. iii.

6. *Ibid.*, p. ix.

7. G. Ch. [Georgy Chulkov], "L. Zinovyeva-Annibal, *Kol'tsa: drama v trekh deystviyakh.* Vstupitel'naya statya Vyacheslava Ivanova. Risunok oblozhki P. Fiofilatova. K-vo 'Skorpion,' M. 1904," *Voprosy zhizni*, No. 6 (1905), 258–259.

8. A. V. Amfiteatrov, *Protiv techeniya: zametki* (St. Petersburg: Prometey, 1908), p. 147.

9. *Ibid.*

10. For more details, read "L. Zinovyeva-Annibal. *Kol'tsa: drama v trekh deystviyakh.* Vstupitel'naya statya Vyacheslava Ivanova. Knigoizdatel'stvo 'Skorpion,'" *Obrazovanie*, No. 8, Sec. III (1905), 96–98.

11. A. Blok, "Literaturnye itogi 1907 g.," *Zolotoe runo*, No. 11–12 (1907), 96.

12. A. A. Izmaylov, *Pomrachnenie bozhkov i novye kumiry: kniga o novykh veyaniyakh v literature* (Moscow: Sytin, 1910), pp. 111–115.

13. Anastasiya Chebotarevskaya, "L. Zinovyeva-Annibal. *Tragichesky zverinets: rasskazy.* Izd. 'Ory,' Petersburg, 1907," *Obrazovanie*, No. 7, Sec. III (1907), 128.

14. Amfiteatrov, *Protiv techeniya: zametki*, pp. 149–150.

15. Anton Krayny, "Bratskaya mogila," *Vesy*, No. 7 (1907), 61.

16. Blok, "Literaturnye itogi 1907 g," p. 96.

17. *Ibid.*

18. For more details, see Krayny, "Bratskaya mogila," p. 61.

19. Marina Tsvetaeva, *Proza* (New York: Chekhov, 1953), p. 147.

20. E.g., Chebotarevskaya, "L. Zinovyeva-Annibal. *Tragichesky zverinets: rasskazy,*" and Yu. A., [Yury Aykhenval'd] "L. Zinovyeva-Annibal. *Tragichesky zverinets: rasskazy.* Izd. 'Ory,' St. Petersburg, 1907," *Russkaya mysl'*, No. 8, Sec. II (1907), 148. See also Andrey Bely, "Zinovyeva-Annibal," *Pravda zhizni*, No. 1 (1907), 2.

Lidiya Zinovyeva-Annibal

THE TRAGIC MENAGERIE
Dedicated to Margarita Vasil'evna Sabashnikova

THE BEAR CUBS

My brother returned from the hunt. They'd killed a large she-bear. They were carrying three tiny suckling cubs huddled to their chests.

It was still winter, and the bear cubs were raised in our large, warm kitchen, in the basement of our country house. I remember the first time I saw them. There, standing before me, was some kind of deep basket. Someone tipped it. I peeked in. It smelled sharply of an unpleasant odor. At the very bottom of the basket on some hay, tiny, fuzzy little bodies were wiggling. Those were the funny little bear cubs.

We must have returned to the city for the remainder of the winter, because the next time I remember the bear cubs they were already free, strapping, beautiful animals with fluffy, sleek fur and kind, clean muzzles. Their gay little eyes gazed with playful eagerness. There were were two of them left; the third had died while still suckling.

Then began a joyous country summer for me and my two friends, the bear cubs.

I remember the courtyard in front of the entrance to our large old wooden house, flooded with sunshine and covered with sand. There was a swing—a long, supple board suspended on two poles at both ends. I would sit in the middle of the curved board under a wild, luxuriant, and fragrant sweetbriar. I would gently push myself upward with my foot, then try to make myself heavier so that the swing would bounce closer to the ground. The board would creak, bending underneath me. The bear cubs, laughably bobbing along from out of nowhere and swaying on their broad, turned-in paws, would prance toward me at the sound of that familiar creak.

They'd rush along, those huge creatures, like guard dogs, sit in front of me on the sand and plop their paws on my knees. And sticking their paws into their kind mouths, they'd begin loudly sucking, slurping, and grunting all the while.

I remembered the proverb "In the winter a hungry bear sucks his paw." But it's not winter now; it's summer. And our bears are not at all hungry, yet they're sucking their brown, shaggy, broad paws. Our bears eat oatmeal to their hearts' content. They've grown tame on oatmeal. Look how one of them has forgotten about me and runs away when he spies our little dachshund, Krotik. Krotik yelps at the bear. The bear leaps at Krotik. In a jiffy, Krotik is in the bear's teeth; but his teeth are gentler than my caressing hands, and with a joyful yelp the dachshund squirms out of the bear's jaws and again barks tauntingly, nipping at the luxurious brown fur of his big, free friend.

I'm jealous. I tug the other one, my faithful playmate, by the paw. I jump off my board, and we chase each other. It's not long before we're also romping in the soft, fragrant grass. It smells of springtime's earth and warm fur, and the bear's hot breath right in my face makes me laugh and rejoice, while his sturdy flat paws tumble down on me. We jump up, still chasing each other. The bear leaps onto a tree like a monkey. His ponderous paws clasp the bough tightly, while his silly and kind head, that dear head of God's creature, hangs down, and his devilishly mirthful little eyes sparkle at me.

Dear, joyous, sunflecked spring! God's gift—my forest play-mates!

At four o'clock, after dinner, on the large semicircular balcony with the white wooden columns, tea would be served, as well as coffee and heavy cream, buns with caraway seeds, soft gray bread made from our own northern wheat, homemade honey-cakes, soda pop, hothouse strawberries, and, as an accompaniment to them, figs and jam. The whole family would gather together—my two older brothers and their former tutor (my little brother was still in the nursery with his nanny); our guests—friends of my brothers, my sister and her girlfriend; Mama; my governess—the same person who had instructed me: "In winter the hungry bear sucks his paw."

How delicious were those honey-cakes! The wife of the old cook baked them masterfully. They were fragrant with honey and well-baked flour. Yes, and the bears thought so, too. The bears' noses could pick out odors even more keenly than people's. Of course, they kept a very close watch in this area. They climbed along the little side steps which led from mother's cherished possession—her thick and resplendent flower bed—to the balcony. They would peek at us. We'd shout at them, they'd disappear, and again amuse us with the sight of their curious little eyes and sniffing nostrils.

But those muddle-headed young people, when they'd ended their feast, would blithely wander about their business, while the bears, having awaited their chance, would scramble straight to the table.

"Oh, the honey-cakes!" mother would recall. She'd run, and I'd be after her. The huge bears would be awkwardly piled in the middle of the round family dining table. They'd be greedily grabbing the honey-cakes. The jam would be overturned. They'd be licking off their sweet paws. Slurping, snorting. Their little eyes would dart back and forth craftily.

They'd notice us, and start to rush about. The heavy table would sway; glasses, plates would scatter in all directions. You'd hear the bears plop on the floor, and see only plump little bottoms with short fluffy tails waddling off, then bolting down the steps. Mama wasn't annoyed.

Mama was a gentle soul, and loved those silly bears.

Summer moved on. The bear cubs grew not by the day, but by the hour. They became much larger than the average guard dog. They played with our dachshund as before, frolicked with me as they used to, and (as was their unchanging custom) not only kept a close watch over any unwisely placed sweets, but also gobbled their oatmeal with grateful grumblings.

However, our harmless friends began to arouse the fears of the peasants who came to the farmhouse. The bears — those wards of the landowners — seemed to them a villainous business, and with disapproval the peasants glanced cautiously and avoided the bears in fear. Later I heard that the foreman came to complain to my brother. He asked that we get rid of the bears.

"At any time one of them might attack someone, crush him. Or the livestock, too . . . They're still wild animals, even if you did bring them up on a bottle."

They took the bears away to a stone pen. The gates were kept locked. The bears roared pathetically, begging for freedom, for sunshine, to play with their friends . . . I walked around like a lost soul, fussed, was rude to my governess, cried . . .

Our family council met together with the chief forester to decide the ultimate fate of the bear cubs. The summer was half over.

Towards fall the bear cubs would be full grown. To set them free was already impossible. To keep them locked in the shed was also unthinkable. And it would already be time to feed them meat.

"Why not shoot them?" suggested the chief forester.

I started to howl from the corner of the big old couch where I'd wedged myself in unnoticed. My older brother began to waver.

"That's sensible . . . Of course, that's sensible . . . And it's possible to do it painlessly . . ."

My second-oldest brother, the Fierce Hunter (as the family nicknamed him because of his love for solitary adventures in the forest), didn't agree . . .

"We've grown used to them, we raised them. They've been reared on the bottle. We will not raise a hand against them!"

I gave out a trembling howl, when I heard this. My sister sobbed: "Mommy, think of something!"

"They will be released in the forest!" Mama said.

I ceased my loud howling and shut my mouth. Everyone was silent. My eldest brother shrugged his shoulders. The forester expressed his opinion: "All the same, it's unwise. They're still wild animals—they slaughter cows."

I hated him. My bears were not "wild animals."

"It's unwise!" my eldest brother repeated, but hesitantly.

My sister looked at my mother with moist, pleading eyes. I got ready to howl. I'd already opened my mouth. But the Fierce Hunter said vehemently: "Mama is right. That's what should be done. Take them into the forest. We haven't the right to shoot the bear cubs."

And mother added quickly: "We took them out of the forest. If we hadn't, they'd be roaming there right now."

My eldest brother wanted to agree, and he did. The forester was defeated, and we all began to discuss how to go about freeing the bears. This is what we decided: We would put them in big nailed boxes and carry them into the forest beyond Devil's Swamp. It was remote and wild there. After we dumped the boxes off in the forest, we'd hammer out the nails and gallop away. By the time the bears had fumbled with the boards and freed themselves, the cart would already be far away. They wouldn't find their way back in a million years. And there, free in that dreamy pine forest, they'd grow wild . . .

The Fierce Hunter began to laugh: "Then, don't let me catch them again. We won't recognize each other. I'll shoot them."

They were taken away.

So terrible had been that moment when their fate was decided, and after that despair so poignant a joy was the hope for freedom and life for them, that I forgot to pine for my departed playmates. Besides, I had other things to do. Then, something terrible crept close to my soul, and my soul shrivelled.

I don't know how many days passed. Perhaps only one or two in all, not more, when I learned the final, evil news. I don't recall how I found out, or where, or the exact words. All the words fused into one word, or rather, one feeling, because I was able to define it by a word only much later. Betrayal! Someone betrayed someone. A certain kind of love, a certain joyous, childlike, no, even more basic, animal-like trust had been betrayed . . . betrayed.

Beyond Devil's Swamp the peasants and their wives had been mowing a clearing in the forest. Suddenly they caught sight of two bears running straight at them out of the forest. In their terror they thought them to be full-grown wild bears. The peasants and their wives became frightened and fell upon the bear cubs with their scythes . . .

The bear cubs used to run lovingly to people, to friends at the sound of beloved voices. Their playful little eyes would light up eagerly with gaiety; their broad bottoms would waddle laughably on sturdy, turned-in paws. That is how I pictured them.

The farmers, in terror, met the bear cubs with scythes. They were mutilated. Only one was caught still alive. He was taken to the tsar's park to be sold for the hunt. They would fracture his paws before the hunt, so that it would be easier to shoot him, and safer. The other one, slashed, lacerated, covered with blood, dazed and oblivious to everything, somehow escaped back into the forest.

My brother, the Fierce Hunter, rode there with his gun on his shoulder; he had pondered his love for the bear. He heard someone moaning, just like a man . . . Guided by the moaning, he crawled into a thicket. Our dear bear lay there dying. He looked once again at my brother. My brother lowered the gun from his shoulder and emptied all of his shots into the bear's ear.

That's how our bears ended their lives.

That it happened precisely in this way, I remember and am sure. But who told me, and where—I can't recall, nor is it important. Of course, the Fierce Hunter must have told us. But I do remember my mother's face. Most likely, it was just when my brother told us of the death of the bear cubs. From that moment I recall exactly that expression more vividly than anything else about my mother. She was so pale and her full lower lip twitched so oddly. In her eyes—so large and luminous—there was horror. Suddenly, she stood up and swayed. I sprang up. My brother also ran to her. Then, with a quivering lip, she said softly, apologizing: "It's nothing, Mitya. I was just a little sad about our bears. I'll return in a moment."

And she left . . . I grew very still. Apparently everyone had left. But suddenly I overheard words which were then still unclear to me, but which I recall with absurd accuracy. My brother's old tutor spoke them while seemingly quite close to me, with a tone of reproach.

"Well, that's what happens when man interferes in the realm of nature."

And my pragmatic governess replied: "Well, what would you do, order that those wild bears be spared, so that they could destroy the peasants' cattle?"

I wanted to cry. I didn't understand any of it. I wanted to cry, but I couldn't.

I remember—it was already dark. I was already in the nursery, in bed. But I wasn't asleep, and still there were no tears. The weathervane on the roof softly squeaked its metallic squeal. An unbearable heaviness fell over my heart. Evil had been done. A great injustice. Trust and love had been deceived. A betrayal had been perpetrated. The betrayal of love and trust. And . . . no one was to blame.

No one was to blame. That night, under the metallic screech of the weathervane, a thought was formulated in the silence and nearly spoken. I didn't weep. That unuttered question pressed against my heart too terribly. It pressed against my heart beyond endurance.

I crawled out of bed. I groped before me in the darkness. I made my way down the long corridor to mother.

Mother will tell me. Mother will answer the question. Mother, Mother . . . Mama must know everything. Mama can save us from everything.

"Mama, Mama! Why did God permit this?"

"My little child, there is no justice on this earth! There cannot be! . . . But you must still love the earth, wish justice for it, pray for justice, burn in your heart, my little child, for justice, and a miracle will have to happen. It will come about, a world of justice. Whatever the soul desires so deeply—will come true!"

"Mama, you said, it cannot be on this earth . . ."

"A miracle, my little child, a miracle. It's a heavenly gift. But it's worthless living only for this earth. It's worth living for the gift, little one, for the gift alone. And one must suffer and weep. One must strive and pray!"

"But living, Mama, how can one live when it's so sad?"

"Live? . . . Here's how, my little child, listen: One must love. That's how one ought to live. More than this I don't know. Love will teach you. It is strict. The greater and more sacred the love, the sterner it is. This stern love will teach you not to excuse injustice. Your hand will be firm, and your heart strong . . . Grow farther than I have, and understand more . . . *Love Greater Things, and Demand Greater Things!*"

I was kneeling on the small rug next to her bed, my face buried in her hands, and suddenly I found those tears and wept into Mother's dear hands . . .

I felt relieved . . . Then I wanted to sleep.

She wouldn't let me go back alone, through the long, dark corridor to the nursery. She laid me down next to her. It was warm and caressing. There was security and salvation in that caressing maternal warmth. And so I fell asleep . . .

Mother died when I was still a small child. I wouldn't have recalled her words so distinctly, but there was left, after her death, a small, blue envelope with this inscription in her handwriting: "For Verochka, when she turns sixteen." In the envelope, dated that same day that my brother shot our dear, tortured bear, was a short letter; no, not even a letter, but a note. Mama had that night recorded our conversation for my lifelong memory.

Dedicated to Olga Aleksandrovna Belyaevskaya

THE FLEDGLING[1]

I once had a fledgling crane. My dear brother—the Fierce Hunter—gave him to me one spring, pulling him from his hunting bag. He had wandered with his pair of setters for two days and nights in the forest and had brought back two sacks—one filled with dead birds, with their heads drooping on limp flaccid necks; and one of five hares with dimmed, murky-dark little eyes. And a third sack, from which, standing in the hall, he had plucked out and presented me with a live crane. The crane was still an awkward little fledgling on long, clumsy legs with a small, beady-eyed head high atop a crane's neck.

At first my fledgling grew up in the well-lit pantry in our house, where the little canaries lived later on. Already that summer, when he'd grown sturdy and strong and was covered with smooth ash-gray feathers, I took him to the apple orchard.

The orchard was separated from the park by a high fence. The fledgling had one weak wing, and besides that the feathers had been clipped on both his wings so he couldn't fly away. There he lived. There he fed on the marvelous worms that lived in the luxuriant beds of raspberries, and on caterpillars. There I shared with him the blessed hours of our friendship. He was so lively and mischievous.

We used to walk right out of the apple orchard, beyond the fence and all over the park. I'd run along the paths. The fledgling, fluttering his wings, would fly beside me among the trees. I'd lie in the grass. The fledgling would nip at my dress; he'd tug me by the hair 'til it hurt, and then he'd sputter something throaty and incomprehensible.

The crane was my winged puppy, my ethereal, free friend, my pride. I'd walk around smiling.

"What are you thinking about?" my governess would ask, and most likely it would be my fledgling.

Like someone caught with her hand in the cookie jar, I'd blush.

---

1. The original title, *"Zhurya,"* is a diminutive of "crane" in Russian and implies deep affection.

One day the crane did not appear in the apple orchard. I called and called, shouted 'til I was hoarse, skinned my knees on the gooseberry bushes, and cried. My heart sank somewhere deep and painful, contracting into a knot.

The day passed—gray, lonely, hopeless; I was evil tempered and obnoxious. That night I cried and didn't sleep . . . I gathered all my courage: I got up stealthily, crawled out the window (my room was on the second floor), made my way along the boards of the trellis to the nearby roof of the large balcony, and slipped down its columns, blanched by the moonlight, into the garden.

I wasn't afraid of anything; I knew where I'd be—in the park. And there in the orchard, beneath the apple trees which had long since bloomed, there along the unfamiliar moonlit garden beds amidst those shadows, so fiercely immovable, so distinctly de-fined—I ran and searched and called and cried.

The next day in the evening they brought back the fledgling alive—alive, but pecked all over and with a broken wing. The cranes had done this. The others, wild ones, were there in the fields where the oats were ripening. My fledgling had flown there to them. They didn't recognize their little brother, didn't accept this unfamiliar friend and beat him with their beaks. The Fierce Hunter was riding Little Eagle home from the forest at twilight and decided to shoot the cranes gorging themselves on the oats. Cranes are clever: when you're without a gun, they'll let you come right up to them. But if they see a gun, they'll scramble half a *verst* away with a squealing whoop. They took off, but one started to fly and tumbled down. My brother made his way to the edge of the field . . . It was my fledgling!

The crane was locked in the greenhouse. He was bored there among the hand-tended rows of pampered plants. There weren't any wonderful worms or caterpillars in the pea plants. The frogs didn't lazily hop about after the rain along the silly well-trodden paths.

But every day I came for him. He'd rush to me with a welcoming screech, and we'd escape to freedom. He became headstrong and powerful.

We used to go to the stables. But he didn't like the road between the meadow and the dried-up pond. He had his own fantasies! Why didn't he like it? I didn't understand. I'd push that stubborn one forward, pressing my hands with all the strength of an eight-year-old against his tall, smooth, unyielding back set on those long, sturdy legs. I'd push him. We'd run about three steps forward, and then one back.

I'd be all in a sweat and out of breath from my efforts, angry and laughing at my stubborn, strong friend.

In the stable courtyard, along the shed on the brown earth glossy with pungent and vital-smelling dung, planks were spread. And next to that, beneath the shed, was a gutter for liquid waste. There it was deep and boggy under a metallically iridescent film of mold.

It was frightening.

We'd make our way along the narrow planks, pushing and struggling. We'd press against the fence. One plank was a little shorter. I'd stoop down, fiddle around with it, and manage to flip it over. My crane would stand there, angry and silent. Suddenly he'd start to chuckle wildly at the top of his voice. Worms! Worms! Ooo, what extraordinary worms! Pink, no, they were so fat, they were even yellowish, like the salmon we eat during Lent. They'd lie on the manured earth, scarcely moving. My crane would swallow them one after another with a ravenous gurgling. What a feast! Too bad I can't join in! Well, even so—I still understand how delicious it is, how terribly delicious!

Autumn was long and boring. Strolling with the crane became inconvenient and . . . I was somewhat tired of that. I'd gotten used to him and my heart no longer longed for that friend, now all alone there, in the far-off, unheated greenhouse.

There were pots filled with earth there—surely worms could be found. There were tubs of water buried in the ground, too; why wouldn't frogs live there also? I thought—of course, yes.

Nevertheless, I'd bring the crane some barley. He loved grain. He'd be glad to see me and would beg to be let out. But, more and more often, I began to have less time! Of course, it was my lessons—with autumn I had more lessons. My governess was stricter. I was lazier, more obstinate, often rude, and often punished. After that I was in no mood for the crane. At least nobody punished him. I envied him. I would have been glad to be with him; but, of course, how could I see him every day? Wait 'til spring. Then we'll be friends again.

I hadn't visited the crane in three days. I went and brought some grain and poured some water into his pot. The most important thing was the water, because the tubs in the greenhouse were deep, and, although buried level with the ground, often after a watering they would be only half filled, and they were narrow. If the crane fell in—he wouldn't be able to get himself out with his wings . . .

I didn't go for about four days. I remembered—and brought food.

Then a rather serious mishap occurred. I ran away to join Marya in the fields and carted potatoes with her all day, standing on the wagon and driving the horse. I returned that evening covered with the dirt of the harvest and having lost one shoe in the fields. I had to stay inside for two days. I became evil tempered. My heart turned to stone, and my memory failed me.

A week passed. I was sitting, forgiven but still implacable, preparing my lessons. Opposite me sat Elena Prokhorovna—my governess, worn out, pale, spiritually and physically exhausted by me. Suddenly . . . the crane! My fledgling has no grain! My crane has no water!

I tore away from my seat without permission, galloped along the hall; I scrambled down the staircase, another hall and another staircase, the dark and stony one, into the basement, where we had our large kitchen. The scullery maid brought me some barley in a pot, over which she poured boiling water. My crane loved it that way. I fetched the wheelbarrow. The pot went on the wheelbarrow. Elena Prokhorovna called me from the porch—I sauntered by, not answering, down along the path to the greenhouse.

I was grinning from ear to ear. He'd be thoroughly starved. To make up for that, today he'd have his favorite grain, and soaked in hot water. How delicious that would be in his hunger! And never, never again would I forget him. Today my whole heart is overflowing with love—it's even gotten heavy in my breast; it's even hard to run with my heart bursting so. I want to stop and cry, and whisper at the top of my voice: "I love you! I love you! Forgive me! I'll never again forget! I love you! I love you! Ah, how I love you! . . ."

In the greenhouse it was silent and empty. Unpleasantly silent.

"Chickie! Here, my little chickie!"

Silence. Ah, that malicious silence!

"Chickie! Come here, my little chickie!"

I ran everywhere. Did the gardner take him? Did he die of starvation? There's not one worm in those repulsively clean pots! It's not true that frogs hop along paths like these, with no sky or rain.

I ran back to the door. By the door there was a tub, buried in the ground. In that deep tub something gray with a long neck floating up from the depths, limp and flaccid, lay still in the water. Someone's glazed, murky-dark eye rose from the depths to meet my approaching eyes . . . I screamed. I screamed. I hadn't the strength to come close. I knew everything was ended.

I ran to the gardener. I screamed. I screamed.

The gardener came to the tub with me. He pulled out my crane.

"He wanted to drink. What is it, Verochka? Did you forget to bring him water? He drowned some time ago. See, he's already stiff."

I couldn't look. I couldn't speak. From out of somewhere, despair crept into me; I heard him and I screamed. I stifled my despair with a wild shriek, and slowly wandered along the path up to the house, and wailed and wailed, not once closing my mouth. My mother, the governess, my sister, the housekeeper, my brother, and also my other brother, came to meet me.

But I kept wailing without hope and without comfort. Someone had squeezed my heart with pincers, had tied it in a knot, and my hot blood raced, and raced, and raced.

Too late. Too late. Too late . . .

Winter came. We were back in town. Was it forgotten? It was forgotten and remembered. I didn't pray well that winter. My sin was unforgivable, and I didn't know how to ask God's pardon for it.

A new spring came upon us. On Good Friday and Easter Sunday we went to the country.

For the first time I fasted and prepared myself for confession and communion. I went to church quietly, earnestly, whereas before I had been lazy and tired. I prayed on my knees by the hour, and wept. I was meek and gentle.

On Good Friday in the evening I went to confession. I trembled with a slight, gentle shudder when I passed through the dark church to the place where the choir normally stood and where now the old priest awaited those confessing. I stood, my head bowed. I answered all his questions: "I have sinned, Father!" Then, when he asked if there was anything special, I told him about my fledgling, that I had drowned my fledgling because I'd gotten bored with loving him. I was silent, I waited . . . Would he forgive me? Was it really possible to forgive me? Never, never, oh, of course not. I was damned for being bored with loving . . .

And rare, bitter tears began to flow.

"Verochka, don't cry anymore. Man is weak in his love. How can it be otherwise! That's why Christ loves. That's why Christ, our God, forgives. He will forgive you, too. He came to complete fully His work. We ordinary people cannot manage this. But we can pray, and ask for help. And if He forgives you and has mercy—He will take your soul and resurrect you. Then your soul will learn to love. He can do all this, because He died and was resurrected!"

And the old priest ordered me to get on my knees, covered my head with his rough vestment which smelled of incense, and whispered something. A shiver ran down my spine; my tears ceased. Such a silence fell that all my thoughts vanished and faith alone remained.

Then came Easter night. Snow was falling. It dripped from the roof. There was a rustling, a sense of expectancy, a whisper from the whole earth and an echo from the sky, wafted by a warm sigh from those lofty, fiery stars . . .

The sledge slipped along the packed, melting snow without squeaking. It shuddered across the thawed patches as it touched the still-slippery earth. Silence. The air was scented with spring's sap. And each tree, still dark, severe, distinct in the starlit haze —was a vial of incredible, magical fragrance . . .

The whole village was bustling . . . Something was reaching completion. Something was being fulfilled. The stars knew, and the wind, and the earth, and the people.

I was sparkling clean. I had scrubbed myself, my head too, until my hair squeaked. I even brushed my teeth with lemon, so they'd be white. My dress was also white. And I uttered not a word, not a single word. Since Friday evening I had counted my words, that my soul might remain pure after the pardon of my sins and Holy Communion.

It was bright, and the light of the candles flickered and wavered. The people sighed silently, crossed themselves, and bowed. They waited with bright, flushed faces; they waited with expectancy . . . that humble and silent crowd parted; the priest and the deacon passed through, and the choir with their banners and crosses . . . The crowd gushed after the procession. The fresh air wafted in from the courtyard, and the incense and the wax were perfumed with the inconceivable scent of birches.

"Christ is risen! Christ is risen! Christ is risen!"

And three times came the eager reply: "Truly He is risen!"

Truly, of course! My heart had arisen in my breast. My weak heart, which hadn't known how to love, had arisen that it might surrender. It has surrendered to You, my Christ and my God!

Life and Death in some strange way became a single entity in my young breast. It had only seemed that they were different. Nothing could frighten this heart which was resurrected in love; nothing that I nor anyone else might do could cause it pain.

You're alive, my sweet fledgling! Did I not love you? How can that be . . . indeed, if you wished, I would die for you this moment, here, that you might live instead of me.

You're alive, my sweet fledgling, you're with Christ. We'll meet there. Have you forgiven your stupid, weak, forgetful little friend? She's changed. Today, just now, she's changed. She's stronger than Death. Stronger than Life. She is today *fulfilled*, and you are today *fulfilled*. This is the meaning of Christ.

Is that really what I then *thought*? That's how I *recall* it now.

And so, when this dreary earth is transformed, this sick earth, this flickering earth—from death to life, from life to death; when this earth, which begs to stop, but rushes on, always rushes on in its self-annihilating whirlwind (that's just how I had been, as if in a whirlwind), is transformed—and Easter eternal is realized, then you, too, will be fulfilled, my silly little fledgling. And standing with me before Christ, together, we'll gaze into those forgiving eyes.

Lidiya Zinovyeva-Annibal

Dedicated to Maximilian Voloshin

THE WOLVES

It was late autumn. My brothers and sister had long since gone to town to study and attend balls. My aunt was living there with them in our apartment to supervise my sister and manage the house, since Mama was ill. Mama's legs were not well and she couldn't walk. The doctor had ordered her south to get out into the sunshine in her wheelchair, but she preferred to stay in the country a bit longer, where she would have gladly spent the whole winter in our large, warm old house.

In late autumn the tsar's hunting party came to our country house. There were many packs of beagles and greyhounds, many horsemen. A severe and taciturn German was the head huntsman, and with him, as a sort of guest-companion, a handsome, elegant gentleman with whom I fell in love—Vladimir Nikolaevich.

That evening in the village some of the very long troughs were filled with bloody entrails (I found out that the hunting party had slaughtered the farmers' old horses) and pieces of raw horseflesh. Then they allowed the skittish, hungry dogs, trembling and squirming, to approach the troughs. The dogs, growling and whining, rushed at the entrails. The hunters stood next to the troughs and lashed left and right with long whips to prevent scuffles . . .

The leader of the tsar's hunt and Vladimir Nikolaevich stayed at our country estate. I fell in love with that wonderful, refined Vladimir Nikolaevich at supper, when, upon the early departure of the tight-lipped German head huntsman, he described for Miss Florry—my English governess—how the tsar's hunting party captured live wolves.

The hunters usually close off one section of the forest with tall, strong nets, on all three sides of which peasants by the hundreds, summoned from local villages, are stationed at a short distance from one another. The peasants, armed with clubs and pitchforks, shout loudly, their cries preventing the wolves from slipping past them out of the forest. The mounted hunters and their packs of hounds gather in the forest. The hounds sniff out the wolf and chase him toward the net with their shrill yelps. The wolf flings himself against it, while from above a second net falls. He thrashes about, inextricably entangling himself. The hunters rush in. They pin the animal's neck to the ground with a wide two-pronged fork and tie his legs like a sheep. After turning him on his back, they pass a short, thick stick between his gaping jaws, fasten it with a rope to the back of his neck, and lift the animal on a thick pole by its tied legs. Two men, hoisting the pole onto their shoulders, carry the wolf hanging upside down to the main road, where covered carts as huge as market wagons await those captives.

"Where do they take them?" Miss Florry curtly asked Vladimir Nikolaevich, who liked her severity and who teased her.

"Ah, my God, to the tsar's park for the tsar's hunt!"

"But why hunt for wolves that have already been captured?"

"For amusement. Do you know, they fracture one leg on each animal so it won't run away too quickly . . . and also so it can't attack."

"What a vile thing! It's commendable that you worry over the well-being of the people by removing the wolves. But why this barbaric cruelty?"

That's approximately what I recall of that conversation between Vladimir Nikolaevich and Miss Florry, overheard while I was as yet very young. And I fell in love with him not for myself, but for my sister who had gone to the city. Vladimir Nikolaevich related much about himself also, about how he had brilliantly passed some examinations for which he hadn't been at all prepared, and how impudently he answered his examiners with anything that popped into his head. While he spoke, he moved his full, handsomely formed lips with gusto, and I envied him, and delighted in them . . . thinking about my sister.

On the evening of the arrival of the tsar's hunt, after my usual evening prayer at her bedside, Mama said: "Verochka, tomorrow at dawn Fyodor will harness the long flatwagon. Several ladies— the teacher, the physician's assistant and others, as well as our Emma Yakovlevna" (she was our housekeeper) "would like to be in on the hunt at Kerbokovsky Forest and watch how they catch wolves alive. If you wish, I'll let you go with Miss Florry."

Of course, I wanted to go. And with burning enthusiasm, turning her palms upward, I kissed Mama's delicate, white hands and the lids of her large, extraordinary blue eyes.

I hardly slept from anticipation and was in the stable much too early.

The stableman led the horses from the stable to the carriage house, where two small kerosene lamps still burned in the predawn mist. Beauty neighed and stamped his foreleg, tangling his traces. Fyodor shouted, in a delicate tenor, "Prankster! Watch your leg!" and hit Beauty on the leg with his fist, freeing the trace from under his hoof.

I echoed, but in a hoarse bass, "Watch your leg," and hindered Fyodor's work, fearlessly slapping Beauty on the leg while Fyodor had his back turned.

Chestnut-brown Beauty neighed with a joyful, delicate voice and, throwing his head on Laddy's unruffled, dark russet neck, he nipped and scratched him on the withers with his large, blunt, yellow teeth. The clatter of footsteps along the wooden floor of the shed arose; the bustle and swearing of the coachmen, the smell of horses' hide, manure, and sweat. The autumn morning chill began to drift in, and the sharp scent of rotting leaves and rye from the nearby barns came wafting in. This was the smell of autumn, my favorite, brisk, fleeting autumn.

The coachman, Fyodor, left to get dressed. I pushed Laddy's tail under the breech-band of his harness and wasn't afraid of anything, feeling twice as spirited because of my fearlessness . . . Then I put the bit in Beauty's mouth—he was clicking his teeth and splattering spit, shaking his sleek head—and I bellowed, "Prankster!" I bit my lip anxiously and frowned tensely.

Fyodor, a really handsome lad with gleaming black hair, stern, eager eyes, a thin, dark, serious face (those summers Fyodor was for me the most powerful and most adored creature on the whole farm), returned in a dark blue sleeveless caftan over a red shirt. He jumped immediately onto the coach box, and I into the wide cab which was slung on top of the huge, sturdy flat-wagon. In the cab there were three seats on the back bench, three in the front, and three lengthwise. Wide flat splashboards extended in back, and there were splashboards to the front as well.

The horses pulled us along the lane leading to the house up to the porch.

Miss Florry and Emma Yakovlevna sat down, and I jumped onto the rear splashboard. We galloped along to the village to collect the "local aristocracy," who wanted to observe the tsar's wolf hunt.

In the field, dawn was palely approaching. At the big blue shed, where in the vigorous autumn freshness it was unseasonably fragrant with the honeyed scent of last June's mowing, we caught up with the hunt and settled into a light trot. Through the distinct tramping of the mounts along the road, already frozen hard in the autumn-morning frost, and the glass-like crunch of their hooves piercing the newly formed ice patches, I heard the unfamiliar scraping rustle of a great many dogs' paws.

The long whips cracked, lashing the dogs' supple backs mercilessly. The dogs cowered under these blows. Through the clear, transparent air of the fields the shouts of the riders echoed in the distance. The dogs were tied off in pairs, and the pack, like a multi-headed, multi-bodied snake, dark and glossy, writhed and slithered quickly along the gray, icy road between the two rows of horses.

Vladimir Nikolaevich pranced along next to us, constantly irritating his dapple-gray horse by tugging the reins, and teased the young ladies of our "aristocracy."

"Sometimes it happens that the wolves rip through the net, and then watch out!"

The teacher with her braid to her knees, whom I worshipped for her feminine charm; the daughter of our steward, her hair close-cropped, with an African mouth and gray, piercing eyes, whom I feared and loved with a pining, secret love; the priest's daughter, a redhead, evil and obsequious, of whom her father (our cheerful old widowed priest) had said with complete incomprehensibility that for five years already "pilgrims" had been calling on her and still no one had taken her; and the rather masculine physician's assistant—all these young women, and the old postmistress and communion-bread baker, listened to Vladimir Nikolaevich and were frightened.

"Especially if it's a full-grown wolf; such wolves are extremely strong and terribly evil . . ."

I would often jump off the rear splashboard, rush by the passengers and clamber onto the front one, next to Fyodor. Both splashboards were set above the narrow wheels and provided me with convenient, although wobbly, little platforms for my gymnastics.

"Fyodor, whip Beauty; over there, the right trace is slack."

"That's because it's downhill here, Verochka. Can't you see? He's being very diligent. It's Laddy who's shirking, but Beauty's a forthright horse!" (It amused me that Fyodor spoke of the horse as "forthright." This was because Fyodor was from an orphanage, and had been brought up by some Karelians. That's what I heard my brother tell a friend. And he added something I didn't understand at all: "Perhaps he might even be a prince. That's the reason for his delicate features.")

Soon it began to smell more sharply of pine needles and swamp. The fields ended, and the forest crowded around us. Here, where it was still completely dark, one suddenly felt that the sun was rising somewhere beyond some far-off field. The cold, distant light suddenly tinted the treetops amber. The birches trembled in the wind, tangling their bare twigs in one another. The pine trees were dark and dull, the firs, green and elegant; along the brown earth the leaves—yellow, red, bluish-gray, purple—were turning silver with frost . . . A hut! . . . One could build a hut! And over there the brushwood lay strewn so thickly it was impassable . . .

The horses slowed to a walk . . . Then they stopped. The hunters crowded around the dogs and dismounted. Soon after, the freed dogs, shaking themselves off and yelping, broke away from the crowded pack. Shouts, commotion, barking, blows . . . Then, as before, everything was silent . . . The hunters and dogs had vanished into the forest. We were alone on the road.

I went to look at the carts with the big iron cages for the wolves. Then I strolled closer to the high wall of bare birches and dark pines which were covered by the nets.

Stealthily, I wandered from the group which had crowded together timidly near the wagon. In the forest I'm bored around people. In the forest I like to be alone.

And quickly my imagination carried me away from this tame and orderly life into a different one—wild, free, nomadic . . . I was the tsarina of a nomadic tribe . . . I was on a hunt. My people had to be fed, but suddenly today the enemy had surrounded our encampment—they wanted to capture and eat us. The enemy were cannibals. I alone, alone crawled out of the hut and fearlessly made my way through the bushes, searching for paths of escape, for a plan of rescue so I might secretly lead my people into the forest to freedom and evade the enemy . . . But the wolves . . . All the wolves in the forest had gone mad . . . What could be more terrifying than a mad wolf? He fears no one; he'd throw himself into a crowd and bite one man, and then another . . . and they too would go mad . . . they'd have to be tied up . . . It was the enemy who had infected the wolves with this madness, so they would torment my people. But in defense against the wolves we had hung nets on the trees, and now I stood guard, while all my people slept . . .

How strong was the scent of mushrooms! Ah, a death-cap! A useless toadstool! But what a beauty, what scarlet magnificence! And those tiny white stars set in royal purple . . . What's more, he's not a bad fellow, either: he guards the captive Boletus mushrooms.[1] The death-cap is a terrifying guard! He sprinkles poison on the daredevil who tries to approach his mushrooms. They are the enchanted tsarevitches, and the death-cap is the fiery dragon. Here they are! O, they're magnificent! A family—father, mother, and seven, eight, nine, eleven children. Where's the twelfth? There are always twelve sons, if one has only boys. How strong and healthy! Like an oak leaf in the autumn—dark brown, and they gleam and are so fragrant. How cold and gay they are, as I put them to my chilled nose. Ah, barking! That's the enemy. They're searching for me with dogs . . . I run . . . and run . . . But the mushrooms! It's shameful to abandon that treasure. It would be better to die. Besides, without them my people will surely die of hunger.

The wolves! The wolves! The tsar's hunt. The barking—high-pitched, harmonious, howling—continued uninterruptedly and

---

1. A type of mushroom considered a great delicacy in Russia.

grew as it came nearer. I could already distinguish individual voices—some sounded deeper, some shrill. And wild howling. My heart stopped. Who was howling? Oh, this was no longer a game. This was truly, truly the wolves! Who were they tearing apart? Who had begun to wail so wildly? There were many, many voices. Those were the peasants chasing the wolves back into the forest. And suddenly I heard the tramping of horses and snapping of twigs, as if a fire were crackling and sputtering through the forest.

"Aool, aool, aool!"

"Vera! Vera! Vera!"

It was Miss Florry's dear voice. I rushed to her, my arms outstretched and mouth agape, howling like a wolf in terror of the chase . . .

The dogs suddenly fell silent. I sat in the wagon with our "local aristocracy" and was ashamed . . . None of them were afraid. They were laughing. Ashamed and feeling rude, malicious, and stubborn, I would not answer their questions.

They came carrying something. Two people were carrying something. This was he. This was the terrifying wolf. Perhaps he's mad? The aristocracy huddled more closely into a lump; they all sat practically in the same place on one lengthwise seat. He was carried past us upside down. His head hung toward the ground. All four of his legs were lashed together, and a thick club had been passed through the rope. The hunters' shoulders sagged. A full-grown wolf is heavy. And over there they carried another, and yet another . . . Then somewhere in the distance that crystalline barking began again, at first like the buzz of a mosquito in one's ear. Once again the dogs had been led into the forest. Or was that a second pack?

Vladimir Nikolaevich came riding up to the cages.

"There's no danger. They're tied up! And I'm here with you!"

Surely with him around no one and nothing was in danger!

So we approached the cages.

Through the thick poles of the grating I stared at the wolves. The entire floor was covered. Five bodies . . . Yes, five . . . They were lying there like sheep, with their legs drawn up and lashed together. The ropes around their necks, which had held sticks in their jaws, were now cut through; but their teeth were still fiercely and stubbornly clenched, piercing the wood. They would not release their wooden bits.

I felt sorry for the wolves. A distasteful, slimy, limp feeling crept into my breast. I tried to reason it away—wolves are wild; they eat sheep; they devoured my donkey foal and Mama's old Little Dove, the horse she'd ridden as a young girl . . . Wolves are evil and nasty cowards! They prey upon a single animal in packs . . . What nasty eyes!

"Look at that ugly snout," said Vladimir Nikolaevich. Of course, ugly! Vladimir Nikolaevich was always right. Those beady little eyes stared with malicious terror, like coals—of course, like smoldering coals! They probably glow at night, like little green lanterns, those wolf eyes.

Horrible, horrible! At that moment the door of the cage was opened; they dumped in yet another one and pushed him even further down.

"Ugh, how disgusting!" cried the physician's assistant. "He has a wound in his side. Why don't they kill him? An animal has it better than a man—it's all right to kill him."

I looked at her tall, masculine figure. I wanted to be a doctor.

"That wasn't the order, miss. We were ordered to get them alive!" the hunter, short of breath, explained to her.

"The poor animal!" Miss Florry whispered in English, and immediately she walked away from the cage, with disgust on her face.

"What a stench in the cage!" said Emma Yakovlevna.

"Such repulsive animals!"

And the rest of the ladies walked away.

"Terribly interesting."

"The dogs are close by again. A new party will arrive soon."

"It's time to go home!" Miss Florry called. "I don't like such hunts. If it were on horseback with a shotgun, I'd go shooting myself. But this way—it's unpleasant and pitiful!"

I had taken a look and cried for a long time. The wolf's side has been pierced with a pitchfork. He was breathing through the hole in his side. I heard the air sputter, it seemed to me, through the hole. The edges of the wound moved up and down. It was horrible. The wolf bit the stick in his mouth with his teeth; and a short distance from my face, which was pressed against the grating, were—his eyes. I saw the whites of his eyes at each corner. He was covered with blood. His pupils strained straight into mine. Compressed in them were unbearable pain, furious hatred, anguish, and that final, hopeless, halting terror. Those pupils mesmerized me, and, like him, I clenched my teeth, grating them, and strained the wild pupils of my eyes, now dried of my recent tears. I felt my own grimace. My skin stretched drily. At the very tips of my ears I felt my own repulsive wolflike face convulse with the hatred, terror, and pain in my pupils and my grimacing lips . . . The breath continued to sputter, rushing from the bloody hole in his side, and the edges of the wound splattered up and down with his quick, feverish panting. How awesomely a body is constructed. When it is pierced, one finds here some kind of bloody flesh, and there something completely separate—the liver? The lung? What is that naked bloody thing which lies in the living body of the wolf? Why doesn't he howl? Why doesn't he scream or howl?

The horse snorted and gave a jerk. The wolf swayed at the sharp tug. Were they going to jerk and toss him like that for a hundred *versts* all the way to the tsar's park? I began to scream wildly, with a frenzied, animal-like howling.

"Vera, Vera!"

Someone was running toward me. Everyone was running toward me. But I ran from them, right into the forest. I leaped a wide ditch filled with water, tore through the bushes, and collided with the net. I fell. What was that which fell on my body? I heard steps close by. I wanted to leap up and run farther from them, from the people. But my arms were held fast, my legs entangled. The net, the net had fallen on top of me. The net entangled me.

Then a mad terror took hold of me, and I began to thrash about, roaring and shrieking, kicking and pulling my arms, gnawing at myself. At first laughter welled up around me, then everything fell silent. They were frightened. Someone said: "She's gone mad!"

Miss Florry's voice was heard: "That's not a little girl, but a wild animal. At least once every full moon she turns into an animal."

These words shocked me, and I suddenly quieted down. Perhaps it's true that I even am a little bit of an animal. Not only a little girl, but a little bit—animal. Once every full moon—I am an animal. I became sad, and suddenly tired in every drop of my blood and every inch of my skin. They untangled me. They were already joking. I was submissive and silent as they led me to the wagon, and they were joking.

I asked to sit with Fyodor on the splashboard by the coach box. I felt better with him. We were silent for a long time. I forgot to ask my friend if I could hold the whip. I sat wrapped in thought.

Then: "Fyodor, it's right that they capture all the wolves. It's a good tsar who ordered such a thing."

"I should say so!"

"Well yes, of course. Certainly. They're very evil—wolves. They tear apart the peasant's sheep, and they even killed Little Dove . . ."

I began to cry.

"Fyodor, I really don't like wolves. They shouldn't be pitied."

"Why pity the wolves, Verochka? Hey, you prankster, Laddy! Do you want the whip?"

"Fyodor, give me the whip?" I asked timidly. He gave it to me. I waved the whip at Laddy in such a way that Beauty wouldn't notice.

"Fyodor, will it really be better in the forest now without the wolves? Now no one will eat anyone else?"

"Eat? But aren't animals supposed to gorge themselves? They all gorge on each other. That's the way it's supposed to be."

Fyodor looked at me askance and laughed. He was joking with me. I lost interest. But Fyodor took a liking to the subject and continued to ponder it in a low voice:

"There are certain little animals that look unimpressive and quiet, but they too would gobble up anybody. That's because, if they didn't, they'd die of hunger. Even the grass smothers other grass. That's how it's supposed to be. It's the same with men. Only an animal gorges itself for no reason; but God has revealed to man what is clean meat, and what is unclean . . ."

I was curious: "Why has God done this?"

"It's very simple. Because God put man over all the animals and revealed to him all he should know about the animals."

I lost interest again, because I already anticipated I would understand none of this. Fyodor knew how to speak intelligibly only about horses.

"Fyodor, hey Fyodor!" I lashed Beauty, who kicked up his hind leg and fell between the traces. Fyodor got angry. He had to get down. The horses were jerking the reins. Beauty neighed.

The entire aristocracy, together with Emma Yakovlevna, scrambled out of the wagon with cries of terror.

Only Miss Florry remained imperturbably seated.

And I, on the platform next to the empty coach box, held the reins and pulled them with all my strength. I had very strong hands.

"Watch your fo-o-ot!" Fyodor shouted at Beauty in his delicate tenor voice.

"Watch your fo-o-ot . . . Your foot," I bellowed in a bass voice from my platform, lending my support.

We started out again. I no longer dared ask for the whip, guilty as I was.

"Fyodor, hey Fyodor, do you know what? I don't think it's nice that we all have to eat each other. It makes me sad, Fyodor."

"Well, never mind. There's no reason to be sad over that. That's how the situation is supposed to be. He, the animal, is without sin. We're the only ones that are sinful."

I didn't understand.

"Well, so what if we're sinful?"

"That's why we have to repent."

"And then what?"

"That only the Lord Himself knows. Death is not terrifying to an animal, you see, because, as I've explained to you, an animal is without sin. Only man has to worry about death."

I had never before carried on such an important conversation, and Fyodor's words so preoccupied and amazed me that all my thoughts turned in this other direction. Now I was silent because I couldn't find any words to convey these strange, important new thoughts. Everything revolved around only one question, although I was embarrassed to ask it of my severe Fyodor.

"Well, so what then, if we're sinful? So what if we're sinful?"

I thought his answer would be: "Well, that's all there is to it. We're sinful, and that's all there is to it!"

The road to our house ran up a mountain, and the closer we approached, the steeper it rose. But the horses sensed a rest nearby; they knew the stable, with its spacious stalls and corrals, was close at hand. They sped upward with the heavy wagon. "How offended they'll be when they've let us farm folk off at the main house, and realize they can't go to the stable right away, that they still have to carry the local aristocracy to each of their homes."

Old Elenushka, the housemaid, and the nurse had already wheeled Mama's chair onto Mama's sunporch. She sat in it, wearily leaning against its high back, and lowered her delicate eyelids over her huge blue eyes. I sneaked up to her and began to kiss her delicate eyelids. She wasn't surprised. Her heart must have told her that it was me.

"Mumsie, did your heart tell you it was me?"

I also kissed her hands, then her palms, and thought: "How beautifully I said that to Mama." She smiled.

"What happened on the hunt?"

My face darkened a little.

"Oh, nothing special. They caught many wolves. Only it was very unpleasant. They stabbed the side of one wolf with a pitchfork. He was breathing through the wound . . ."

But I stopped myself: Mama was very ill. Mama could have another attack like the one that took äway the use of her legs . . .

"Poor animals!" she said pensively, and her face was so pale, so pale.

"But it's wonderful in the forest so early in the morning, Verochka! Did the morning frost nip? I used to love it so."

"Oh, Mama what mushrooms I found! I'll bring them right away."

I ran to fetch the mushrooms. They were wrapped in a handkerchief. Mama untied the handkerchief with her awkward fingers, admired them, sniffed their fresh, rooty scent, as if they were a bouquet.

"I was never able to gather mushrooms. I'm so nearsighted."

"How come your eyes are so blue? Mama, I see myself in your pupil. In both your pupils, Mama!"

"Isn't Maria Nikolaevna waiting to give you your lesson?"

That was the local teacher with the braid who gave me lessons in the summer and fall.

"Not yet! She comes after dinner . . ."

"Of course. Even my memory is getting worse, Verochka. I confuse so many things. Perhaps I'll soon become a dunderhead . . . But you'll remember your other Mama, won't you, Verochka?"

The corners of her mouth were quivering. How frightened I was when the corners of her mouth quivered! I was just about to cry. I was ready, but I remembered that it was harmful for Mama to be upset. I summoned my strength and whispered, barely trusting my own voice: "Yes, yes, Mama. I do know you so well. Mama, why did Fyodor say that animals are not frightened of dying?"

"Does he really know that?"

"He says they're without sin."

"Oh! That's true."

"And people?"

"Sometimes there are also people who have no fear of dying . . . If they understand."

"Understand what?"

"If they've suffered a great deal and understand that there's no reason to lust after things . . ."

"What does that mean?"

"Ah, Verochka, I want to speak with you, as if with an adult! You try to remember, anyway; maybe my life, useless as it is, may be of help to you. I must hurry and tell you everything, because my sickness is such that it is gradually destroying not only my legs, but my mind as well . . .

"Do you know what it means when two people live in the same person?"

"Two . . . in the same? . . . Mama, is it always so? . . ."

"Even in you! It's always been so with me. One person coveted everything, was greedy and miserly, wanted everything for herself, and did not know how to give. She might yearn for a flower garden . . . like a huge carpet; or maybe for coffee with thick fresh cream; or for a little feather pillow under her head; or for Little Dove or Voloden'ka—your dead brother, and for his little grave; or for the old house where your father was born and raised, and where she'd been . . . happy . . . before he abandoned us . . . well, even for old Elenushka, so that she could always prepare white dresses for her . . . clean, comfortable . . . and for our ravine, for Abramov Springs . . . even for the linden tree in front of the wing of the house! . . . It's all one and the same thing. All of this is selfishness; that first person clings to it all. Yet there's a second person, who is very free and knows only how to love, but is free of selfish desires. That person rarely spoke within me. I rarely knew how to listen to her, when I was well. But when I became bed-ridden like this forever, then I heard her. And the flower garden became dear to me, and Elena became dear, and Volodya's little grave with its tiny flowers or even simply with wild grass was dear, and your papa who is far away was also dear and blessed, and our old house, and you, my little children still living—everything became dear to me for its own sake, and not for my own gratification. My love was no longer filled with selfishness, but with a greater freedom. You see, there is nothing else which holds me here."

Mama began to laugh quietly, as if she were cooing.

"All this seems silly to you? No? Not yet. It's still the pure truth. But now I'll begin the silly part. Only believe me still, if only for the last time, believe me. You know I can't even reach the railing of the balcony by myself. If I tried to get out of this chair, I'd start to sway right here, and fall. Nevertheless, not only can I get down to our ravine without the use of my legs, or to the hay harvest; I will wander throughout all of Russia, through the entire land, in the mountains and villages and cities, the monasteries and wild forests . . . I'll travel as a beggar, homeless, with no belongings nor any sort of ties, and I'll help people with a word of wisdom and my strong and free hands. Nothing will frighten me, neither cold, nor hunger, nor death. Every tree will be my father, and every old woman I meet—my mother, and every animal, innocent and obedient to nature—my brother, every blade of grass—my little sister . . . All of God's children on this earth will be my sons and daughters, and you, my beloved ones, will also be in my heart. Because man has endless space within his heart, and the fire of love is greater than necessary to inflame the entire world. But this fire of love does not consume; it is just like the fire which left the Burning Bush untouched, yet kept burning and never burned out . . . That's the second person, Verochka. She loves, but is free of selfishness. And my soul depends not on my legs to reach out, but on my love. That's why I say that, though I can't even reach the railing, I have travelled, and still travel, the whole world. You know, Verochka, I've become a completely different person since my illness. Verochka, I've reevaluated many things here, alone, but now I've told you everything all at once. It's not important that my illness is taking its course, and that my soul will again grow dark. Whoever has glimpsed just once, will enter his own new world . . . But why are you crying?"

"I feel sorry . . . for the wolf . . ."

"Silly!"

Mother kissed me.

"Is it really so terrible to suffer? To watch and pity the sufferer is even more terrible."

"I'm sorry . . . that you will die."

"So that's what you've been hiding, foxy little Verochka!"

And Mama laughed.

"Is dying really so important? Or living? One lives, you see, only to gain understanding. Once one has understood, that's enough. The little spark has flashed and passed on . . . From where? To where? How joyous it is not to know and to entrust oneself. That's what it means to love God . . ."

Mama suddenly began to cry. She was silent for a long time. Something in her face grew hard. And again she began to cry, and in a completely strange, old, rasping voice, she began to call: "Elena! Elena!"

The nurse came, but Mama angrily waved her hands at her . . . Her lips grew tired and heavy, and quivered. The skin around her eyes wrinkled; she became an old woman, and tears gathered in those tiny wrinkles and ran down them . . . it was a fit of darkness . . .

Or is it from later years that I recall this conversation? I couldn't have retained such words at that age.

But now I'm an adult, and my life, baptized with pain, guilt, the bliss of happiness, and bitter partings, has brought these dim, faraway words into focus from my memory . . . There are just such pictures for children (I loved them as a child)—magical little pictures. A tiny, dingy piece of paper—you can't discern anything showing under that haze. You plunge it into water, put it on a note pad, rub on top of it with your hand, and peel it off—and from its enchanted mystery spring delicate and vivid flowers.

Dedicated to Konstantin Aleksandrovich Syunnerberg

THE MONSTER

In the spring I caught a monster in the swamp, with a net.

It wasn't caught all alone. I carried it home in a little bucket, poured my whole catch into a jam jar, and put the jar on a little round table by the window in my room.

There, if you looked through the cloudy water toward the light, an entire miniature swamp world appeared.

Some kind of lively, whirling little creatures, delicate, practically transparent, with tiny heads and whiskers, twirled about daringly. Small, shaggy splinters, swaying to and fro like tiny fragments of the finest twigs, would move and suddenly thrust a mossy little head from one of their ends. A little snake would cut through the murkiness with sharp twists, first gathering its minuscule body into a rosy lump, then stretching it into the most delicate of threads.

And still more vague and improbable creatures, scarcely seeming alive, which I can now hardly recall, swayed among the little weeds at the bottom of my jar.

Lying there in thick clusters were jelly-like frogs' eggs. In each frail, murky-green berry was a tiny black seed—an embryo.

Soon those tiny black seeds began to grow and the jelly in the little berries melted away somewhere. And suddenly I noticed that each delicate seed had grown a tiny tail.

Often I would go up to my swamp jar, watch the swamp life, and wait. Look, look, I see it; look, it's beginning! But nothing was noticeably out of order. Nevertheless, I constantly awaited a new appearance of the monster.

I had seen it only for one moment that morning when a ray of sunlight had suddenly illuminated the swampy murk in the net, which I had raised above the water but had not yet drawn out completely. It came to the surface and again dove into the shadows.

It didn't appear to me vaguely, as sometimes happens in dreams, but in the most vivid reality: A yellowish-brown, stiff little body, fashioned out of joined flat sections, a powerful little rudder-like tail, and from its head two claws, huge, strong, round, with sharp joined tips! All this I glimpsed in that sunny moment, despite the fact that the monster was no longer than one-tenth of my ten-year-old pinkie.

For three days or more it remained hidden, and finally I almost ceased believing I had caught it. The net had probably been ripped somewhere, or it had died in the jar. I started to lose interest . . .

I had wanted to see a monster. And so, of course, I had seen one.

One day it appeared from out of the depths of the frogs' eggs, so completely unexpectedly that I screeched piercingly: "There it is!"

Startled, my governess asked with severity: "Who? . . . You frightened me."

I said nothing. For some reason I never liked to talk about the monster.

"Why were you so pleased?"

Had I really been pleased? I didn't realize that I'd been pleased, and glanced again at that foul, flat, sectioned little body with its claws, swimming slowly with malicious confidence and aptly steering itself with its powerful, pointed tail.

"I wasn't pleased about anything," I finally answered decisively.

"Well then, why did you shout like that?"

"I found the monster."

My governess was by that time laughing at me with her condescending, mirthless laugh. She came up to me.

We stood side by side in front of the jar and examined the monster.

It was repulsive to me, and at the same time my fear and revulsion drew me to it.

"That's a nasty little grub!" my governess said after a long silence. "Throw her away. She'll make mischief here."

But I didn't throw *it* away, and *it* again disappeared.

The jelly-like frogs' eggs melted not by the day, but by the hour. Instead of those tiny, indistinct seeds next to those broad, transparently gray and (in my opinion) rather elegant little tails, there appeared plump miniature black heads, indisputably ugly and awkward.

These gave rise to tadpoles. They swam out to freedom, sluggish, benign, squishy through and through, and ridiculously slow, despite the zeal of their broad, elegant, flailing little tails. Naïvely and stupidly, they bumped against each other with their tiny, awkward heads, and their gossamer little tails became entangled. I loved them tenderly.

They grew innocently, fed themselves innocently, on what and how—I didn't know.

In them I sensed something akin to myself. I envied them; I despised them; I loved them tenderly, even their silly, plump little heads (in which, of course, backs and tummies were hidden somewhere), and their elegant, rather overly delicate tails.

They grew not by the day, but by the hour.

My yellowish-brown monster began to fade before this copious, luxuriant black array.

Only it seemed odd: My tadpoles grew fatter and larger, but their number incomprehensibly decreased.

And then for the third time I saw *it,* and at first I didn't comprehend what was happening.

Now a third the size of my pinkie, *it* seemed gigantic. The spine of its stiff, flat body, linked together in sections, was arched upward crookedly. *It* hung its powerful tail downward like a stake and, flapping against that stiff tail, yet another tail thrashed back and forth, its delicate gossamer torn like so many rags.

Then I saw both its head and claws. The plump, awkward, silly head of a tadpole was caught in the stiff, sharp, powerful claws of the monster. And I understood.

My eyes stared at those two brothers of the swamp in their terrible embrace.

"Here's the evil which *it* will bring," I recalled my governess' words.

Suddenly my heart stopped completely; it became still, heavy, like a bar of gold, frightened and yet hypnotized, strangely rapacious.

Now calm, I stared in this way for a long time. And for a long time the silent activity of the bog continued there, in the swampy haze of the jar.

The tiny black body-head turned gray, and began more and more to resemble in color its delicately gray tail. It was shrinking, and the ragged little tail trembled more weakly . . . then ceased trembling at all. The gray membrane slowly descended to the bottom of the jar.

In our pond there was an island, rather small, completely covered with ancient resinous poplars which hung down to the calm, dark water itself.

On the shore, under a poplar, I sat by the calm, dark water. My little boat, now old and with its once bright paint peeling, stood perfectly still. One oar had been thrown aside. With the other I had pushed myself here along the bottom of the shallow pond from the nearby shore.

I sat above the water in the shade and cried. There, in the water, sleepy little fish drifted lazily. At noon or later, when the poplars no longer cast their shadows over it, all the water is covered with a dense midday light.

There are slender and silvery little fish there; those are the more lively ones, and there are also small black ones with plump heads and floppy bellies. They look very much like my tadpoles, only they're about five times larger, but just as awkward, only a bit more sleepy, and their tails are not of gossamer.

I cried and cried. Not very bitterly or abundantly, but like everything else there, with midday languor.

My soul was somehow sour.

"Vera! Vera! Again!"

That was the angry, slightly squeaky voice of my older brother.

"Bring the boat back right away! Are you allowed to go to the island alone?"

"Mama let me yesterday."

"Well, yesterday is not today."

"She allowed me to go today, and tomorrow, and anytime."

However, shouting all the while at the top of my voice, I still got into the boat, and with a strong push to the left from the stern I turned the nose of the vessel to the right, like a wing, and pointed it straight toward my brother. All in a tizzy, I seized the long oar and turned myself with it. A push to the right, a push to the left.

Right, left.

Jerkily, impatiently, shuddering violently, like my violent, impatient, headstrong will, the boat flew toward the shore.

The boat had almost touched the shore. My brother squealed: "Where do you think you're going? Where? And they let you go alone!"

"You have the dogs!"

Two sleek setters, Piron and Boyar, and a proud shaggy dog with a long, flowing coat, Bertha, whined with nervousness and excitement at the water's edge.

"You just now noticed?"

"Are you going to take them swimming?"

"Yes."

"May I come?"

I looked pleadingly into the boat, because it had already floated to the planks of the dock, but my brother settled down there, in the boat, in my place.

"That's impossible; someone's looking for you back home. You haven't practiced your scales or something again."

Vasen'ka, Vasen'ka, let me come!"

"I said, 'No.' Now I remember: Emiliya L'vovna was looking for you. She's in the main hall, terribly angry. Otherwise, I'd take you."

And suddenly, with a deep, profound tenderness unusual for him, my brother added: "What's the matter with you, Vera? Have you been crying? You're all puffy from your tears. Were you punished?"

I exploded. "Exactly the opposite."

"What exactly is the opposite of punishment? Reward? Well, do such things ever really happen? Let's ask, let's ask Emiliya L'vovna at dinner!"

Oh, how I hate that Emiliya L'vovna, the lazy creature. She only came to the country to give me music lessons, and she gets nasty from boredom and flings the sheets of music into my face.

But I didn't want to speak to my brother about *them* and *it*. And yet, I feared to remain silent—though he wouldn't believe me anyway; that is, he'd still believe all the same that I'd been punished. Shame! Shame! And he's so kind today, although he's teasing me as unpleasantly as ever. His voice is affectionate and he's become just like Mama.

"Vasen'ka, it's the tadpoles."

Again I cried and told him about *them* and *it*—the monster.

Vasya listened to me attentively, leaning one foot against the bottom of the boat, and putting the other on the high edge of the dock. Then he was silent for a rather long time.

Suddenly he said very seriously: "That's nature, Vera."

I was perplexed.

"A normal person becomes attuned to nature. That's what it means to adapt to the scheme of things."

I was puzzled.

He noticed my ignorance. He smiled at it condescendingly, but with a look of sadness.

"You understand that all this around us," he traced a wide arc with his hand, "in the water, on the land, you understand, even in the earth—everything lives according to nature's laws, you see, and that means it can't be any other way. Consequently, it must be this way. Well, sometimes people try to live in a way they can't. That means they try to complicate things unnecessarily, you see, and even disobey God, God, you understand. Now, don't you cry . . . Piron! Piroshka! . . . You'll get used to it . . . Boyarka! Bertha! Get over here! There's no use trying to avoid it . . . Get in the water, you cowards, you rascals! . . . Don't cry now, you silly little thing!"

Standing on the bow in order to watch the dogs better, he quietly worked both oars, steering along the pond toward the dam, where the water was deep. And the two dogs' heads, with their ears laid back, swam close behind the stern.

Only Bertha still whined and yelped on the shore. She'd run into the water up to her belly, scamper out, and from her long, flowing fur shake off a mist of diamonds. She'd cast her huge brown eyes at me, filled with guilt and fear, pleading ardently and excitedly. An exhausting and fearful desire was in her whine and in the unpleasant convulsions of her wet and suddenly abnormally thin body.

My brother shouted angrily.

"Bertha! Come here, you bitch's daughter!"

With a single leap Bertha was in the water. Her long back, white sprinkled with yellow, irregularly bobbed above the water. One could see that her paws still touched the bottom as she walked along. But then her back sank, with only its hump still bobbing out slightly. Bertha swam effortlessly, with a steady pace, and her luxuriant tail, like a trustworthy rudder, swished along the water. Soon I could barely see a white head in the distance, and even with my exceedingly farsighted eyes I could scarcely distinguish how her reddish ears trembled timidly, their long fur shining in the sun.

"You know what to do? Throw out your jar!" my brother bellowed too loudly across the calm, echoing water. "Hurry up, Bertha, come on! . . . Throw it into the garbage pail . . . Halloo, my friends, follow me! . . . Why keep that rotten stuff in your room!"

"Why haven't you thrown that repulsive grub out of the jar?" my governess asked, rather unexpectedly interrupting her explication of Schiller's ballad "The Goblet."

I began to look straight into her eyes, but I neither saw them nor answered her. She repeated her question.

"Because . . . that's the way it should be."

"What's the way it should be?"

"Like that—so *it* can eat."

"But why must it be that way?"

"God arranged it like that."

"And who explained that to you?"

"Vasya himself!"

My eyes, still oblivious to the tall, wiry woman sitting opposite me, became deeply insolent.

I added sarcastically, drawing out the words: "Because that's nature."

"You certainly do not have nature in that silly rotting jar. That's simply your whimsy."

She was very indignant. She was right and wrong, because it was true that there were more places in the swamp for them to hide, but by the same token there were also more creatures to attack them.

I answered angrily: "Well, so much the better."

Now I saw her eyes, into which I had stared so long and insolently, not really seeing. But her pale eyes, glaring unpleasantly, were unusually anxious, almost frightened. My strict, just, and very nearsighted governess was frightened by the reliable signs of another approaching rebellion. Something compelled me to rebel; certain words that I didn't even understand pressed up against my lips.

Again she asked: "What's better? Why is it better?"

"It will end sooner."

"Lord! What will end?"

I didn't know *what* would "end"; I didn't know *what* or why it was "so much the better." But I knew that I would no longer read and discuss Schiller's "The Goblet," with its repulsive sea monster. I stood up very insolently from my chair, which was opposite her, and with complete composure I slowly strutted out of the schoolroom.

I decided to go to the pond . . .

Of course, after my jaunt to the pond she punished me—three days without play.

Now only thirteen tadpoles remained, and nothing, except them and the monster, was left alive in the swampy murk.

Not less than two weeks must have passed since the day of my lesson on Schiller's ballad, and the reprieved tadpoles were essentially no longer tadpoles. From each plump head had grown four splayed paws with tiny webbed fingers. And the head itself was not just a head, but had a soft tummy and a frog's hunched back.

I laughed loudly now—at these frogs with tails. How come in the wild, in the grass, the frogs have no tails, but in my jar they do?

My lovelies, my delights!

But the monster, having devoured everything that had swarmed in my catch from the swamp—like the Pharoah's seven lean cows which devoured the seven fat cows and did not grow fat—still remained just as flat, stiff, and segmented as before with its powerful, evil tail and rapacious claws. Only it had become longer.

I began to like the monster.

It seemed to me to be dressed in a coat of armor, and in the soundless murk of that swampy water, where the soft-bodied, muddle-headed, completely defenseless tadpoles crowded and tussled each other at random, *it* alone, aloof, strong, aggressive, held unquestioned mastery over those lives.

And, being the master, it fed itself.

I scorned the tadpoles.

Nevertheless, I ran to the river and then the pond. Squatting down, I stared into the water for a long time. I thought about splashing *it* out there. Then I wouldn't have to watch anymore and I could spare at least those thirteen young frogs which still had their tails.

In the pond I again saw the black, drowsy little tadpoles. Perhaps it will start to suck them, too? It's grown to half the length of my pinkie; it's so monstrous!

I returned to the jar without reaching a decision. There I watched how the satiated, languid monster rested at the bottom among the drained gray membranes.

The monster was mysterious.

My governess and I discussed it a great deal. We looked through three little books where all kinds of monsters were described. We applied this information; we compared. But still we couldn't be sure of either its past or its future.

"You know, I still think your grub will turn into a water beetle!" my governess said decisively.

Then we both stood at the window and looked into the jar.

"I thought water beetles were black and round."

"Well, what does that have to do with it?"

"It doesn't look like one at all!"

"Lord, how foolish you are! Do mosquitoes, which is what those funny little twigs that were swimming in your jar before would have become, look like their larvae? Or butterflies?"

I wasn't convinced.

"Water beetles are good."

"How do you know?"

"A lot of them swim at the bottom of the tubs, you know, under the pipes."

"Well, so what? Have you swum with them like a beetle or a little fish?"

"What of it?"

"How can you be so sure that they wouldn't eat you?"

"Well, I still don't believe that it is a water beetle."

"I'm not sure either. What a strange, mysterious little grub!"

The monster had to change. But into what, exactly? Into what? Such evil, such brownish-yellow, clawed, armor-plated things with stiff tails that steer like rudders straight after the enemy—what could they turn into?

How terrifying that the monster had to change!

Still, perhaps it might change into a water beetle—black, round, glossy, and possibly, even probably, good.

But then where does the evil go?

Is it possible it can completely disappear? Go nowhere at all, but simply disappear? Like steam . . .

No, steam condenses into clouds in the sky from the cold, and forms rain . . . Isn't that so?

Only one little frog remained. His tail had already dropped off. He'd become so wonderfully youthful, so fresh. Such a dear, dear thing! My little green creature! With a strong back and webbed paws, covered with tiny bumps, and his eyes bulging.

He tried to get out of his tiny swamp home, crawling along the glass. He panted rapidly, the way little pocket-watches whirr; his plump, squishy tummy rose and fell, touching his stodgy neck. He was so green, so green, and always fresh—as though he'd just finished a bath.

He stared out of little bulging eyes with soft, folded lids. He didn't slip into the water.

He was tame!

And the monster?

What can I do with the monster?

I can't put him in the river. Or the pond. Into the swamp? There are also frogs there.

I brought a rock to the jar, a long narrow one that I'd found, and placed it as a platform so that my frog could crawl out on top of it. He had lungs by now; outside of water he breathed with lungs, and not gills. Both lungs and gills—whichever he needed at the time. That's what my governess said.

But he'll crawl off the rock. He liked the water. And then . . .

Murder.

I must kill the monster and save the soft, tame little frog, my last one.

But how can one kill such a stiff, armor-plated creature? One can't crush it, for it will crunch. Impossible. Disgusting.

Simply catch it and splash it out in the sun? The sunlight hit the balcony. Close by, a door led from my room to the balcony, or, more properly, to the roof itself, which was fenced off by a railing and covered with sheets of metal. The metal got almost as hot as the miniature irons with which I ironed my dolls' clothing. (I had even tried to heat them there in the sunlight.) It faced south. But, of course, it still wasn't enough to heat them . . .

If I dumped it there, it would roast. It would die, the foul thing.

Yes, Vasya had been right. It would have been better just to splash everything all together into the garbage pail before. Ah, my God, my God! Why is it so hard for me to do?

The little green frog sat on the small rock until nightfall. His mouth resembled an archer's bow, and he was covered with warts. He just looked around. Then he lowered those tiny soft folds over his eyes, and two gray bulging beads appeared.

Malicious, impatient, I paced. My heart was tormented.

I loved and hated the monster.

No, I hated that little green frog.

I went to bed, without resolving my dilemma. Besides, toward the evening the sun leaves my balcony.

I laid down and dozed, but did not sleep. It was awful.

Should I light my candle? Should I look at what's going on in the jar? What if it doesn't sleep at night either? Does it have eyes? I didn't notice any behind the claws. Anyway, it doesn't make any difference. At night one can't see too well.

It'll suck him dry. Oh, it will drain him by morning.

But he was still sitting on the rock . . . He'll slip off, oh, he'll slip off the rock into his beloved murky little pool of water, into his life-giving swamp water.

I had made a special trip to bring water from the deep ditch overgrown with that special slippery grass. Only this time I tried very hard not to scoop up any new animals with the water . . .

I gave a start and my feet were already on the floor. Suddenly I remembered with anger: "Nature! Nature!" "Man desires what cannot be." "That means he's not obeying God."

Besides, I was lazy! And it was dark! And how awfully unpleasant it would be to see it at night. But what if it had suddenly changed? Suddenly, just today. Just how did it intend to transform itself? And if it intended to change—perhaps it would be a sin to kill it. Perhaps before it devoured the frog, it would change and then never again devour anything. What if I kill it? Just at this point, what if I kill it, when it's no longer necessary? . . .

And what's more, how would I kill? There's no sun at night. I'd have to crush it. It would crunch. It's very hard.

I buried my head under the pillow so that everything would be muffled and soft.

Let it happen in its own way! . . . That's how it should be.

I fell asleep.

In the morning there was no little bug-eyed, web-footed frog. *It, it. It* alone remained.

I wasn't sorry. I didn't cry. A certain calm came over me.

Without speaking, and biting my lip with determination, I went downstairs to the sideboard for a spoon. With the spoon I fished out the sleepy, satiated monster. Then I took it out onto the iron balcony.

The sun had not yet heated the sheets of metal. It was still around the corner.

Should I wait? No, I've waited long enough!

I splashed out the water and shook it out onto the floor. I looked.

It writhed, disgustingly slapping the metal with its stiff tail, raising its clawed head with its repulsive beady yellow eyes. I saw it; now I saw all of it. I bent over it closely. It was only half of my pinkie, yet it seemed to me I was staring it in the eyes, straight into its disgusting, yellow, voracious, merciless eyes.

I got the rock, the same one from the jar which my little green frog used to sit on. I squashed that repulsive head, with its claws and eyes, with the rock. I crushed it. It crunched. But the armor-plated body still thrashed, still writhed, and the tail stood straight up like a pole.

It was disgusting to look at.

I threw the rock away. The head was completely crushed.

Never mind. Never mind. Soon it will be all over. Still resolute, I went to my room. I grasped the jar firmly with both hands and threw it out the window.

The jar flew, that dirty jar, sprinkling its brackish, dead water far beyond the window, where the clean sand of the flower bed lay. My heart was suddenly pierced, as if with a cat's sharp claw.

Never mind. That way, "everything ended quicker" in my jar. Let it be.

But out there, in the swamp, does everything continue as God had designed? . . .

Cherubina de Gabriak

✍ d. 1928

In an article entitled "Budushchee russkoy poezii" (The Future of Russian Poetry),[1] Valery Bryusov regrets that the works of the talented young poet Cherubina de Gabriak were not represented in *The Anthology*.[2] It is indeed unfortunate that they were omitted.

Cherubina de Gabriak was the literary pseudonym of a schoolteacher, Elizaveta Ivanovna Dmitrieva, whose poetry appeared in *Apollon* (Apollo), a literary magazine published by a group of young poets, the future Acmeists, which was formed in 1907 in St. Petersburg. *Apollo* was an aesthetically oriented, sophisticated periodical which was fiercely attacked by Vyacheslav Ivanov for its "pure aestheticism." There were also some serious disagreements between *Apollo* and the Moscow journal *Vesy* (The Scales), especially when the editorial office of *Apollo* was invaded by Andrey Bely, a frequent visitor from Moscow. In 1909, amidst these literary arguments, Sergey Makovsky, poet, critic, writer of memoirs, editor of *Apollo* (1909–13), printed the poems of his two "discoveries," Cherubina de Gabriak and Anna Akhmatova.

Initially, Makovsky was not greatly impressed with de Gabriak's poetry when she appeared at one of the *soirées* of *Apollo* in 1909, together with several as yet unknown poets who had been invited to recite their works. According to Marina Tsvetaeva's reminiscences, Makovsky displayed "offensive scorn" toward her poems. Then the poet Maximilian Voloshin urged her to send them to *Apollo* under the exotic name of Cherubina de Gabriak. She

availed herself of this advice and wrote to Makovsky. Her letters to
him were interlayed sometimes with an olive tree leaf, other times
with that of a tamarisk. Not suspecting that these letters actually
came from Dmitrieva, Makovsky invited the poet to present herself to the group of *Apollo*. She refused. He sent her a large basket
of roses. She again refused, stating that she wanted to be known
only as a poet, not as a woman. Marina Tsvetaeva reports that from
then on "the whole *Apollo* fell in love with her and began to live
from one of her letters to the next one."[3] Gabriak's poems were
permeated with a catholic spirit, ecstatic and intoxicating in nature. Their themes, the charming and unusual name of the poet,
and certain obscure allusions in her works—all these delighted
Makovsky.

In their respective reminiscences, Marina Tsvetaeva and the
writer and author of memoirs Evgeniya Gertsyk, both very close
friends of Maximilian Voloshin, devote many pages to the descrip-
tion of Cherubina de Gabriak's appearance on the literary scene of
St. Petersburg. Maximilian Voloshin was a great admirer of de
Gabriak's poetic talent. Since in reality she was a young, homely
woman, he wished to surround her with an air of mystery in order
to enable her to achieve fame for her poetic gifts. Among his
books on the black arts, he came across a small and shabby devil
with the name of Gabriok. Voloshin changed the "o" in the last
syllable to an "a," added a mark of nobility "de" to the name, and
rejoiced: "They will never decipher the name!" He took pride in
his device of mystification and claimed that he had "created"
Cherubina de Gabriak, the poet, the myth of a Spanish beauty.
With the aura of that exotic name and the mysterious intrigue of
her foreign origin, "she rose above Russia like the new moon,"[4]
maintains Anastasiya, Marina Tsvetaeva's sister, in her memoirs.
Nobody suspected that the name of Cherubina de Gabriak concealed a modest, plain woman. When Voloshin's deception was
uncovered, Makovsky harshly criticized him for his trickery. Makovsky's confederates, likewise furious with Voloshin, exposed the
poet and, in Marina Tsvetaeva's words, "rudely threw her off her
own, Cherubina's, castle."[5] They defiled her, destroyed her, and
she stopped writing. "It was a cruel day," recalls Anastasiya
Tsvetaeva, "when a group of poets awaited the arrival of a beautiful
maiden with a fiery name at the railroad station. But from the

CHERUBINA DE GABRIAK (lower right). From *Maximilian Voloshin–khudozhnik: sbornik materialov* (Moscow: Sovetsky khudoz-
nik, 1976), p. 154.

railroad car emerged a small and plain woman—and one of the waiting men, himself a *poet* [Nikolay Gumilyov], behaved spitefully, improperly. Max [Voloshin] challenged him to a duel. However, it was this moment of the collision between reality and fancy which decided Cherubina's fate. She disappeared, became effaced, fell silent. Only the sheets with her poems have remained. . . ."[6] The duel which took place between Voloshin and Gumilyov was a "pure duel in defense of honor," says Marina Tsvetaeva, for "Voloshin had never been a warrior."[7]

Sergey Makovsky behaved himself like a gentleman; he urged Cherubina de Gabriak to continue the publication of her beautiful poetry in his journal. She, however, allowed him to publish only those poems which had already reached *Apollo* through the mail. Her encounter with Gumilyov at the St. Petersburg railroad station meant the end of her literary career. She lost her desire to write, and the reading public ignored her. "Her voice was no longer heard, but there was no end to her friendship with Max Voloshin. She was not an everyday occurrence in Max's life—she was a great event for him. Of his own accord, he remained with her for a long time, forever,"[8] said Marina Tsvetaeva. In her *Reminiscences,* Evgeniya Gertsyk also mentioned de Gabriak's and Voloshin's profound and devoted friendship, which influenced the latter's entire life. De Gabriak stayed with Voloshin at his famous and hospitable Cocktebel in the Crimea for long periods of time; and when she died in 1928 in Turkestan, he felt her absence until the end of his life—both as a devoted friend and an original poet. Anastasiya Tsvetaeva recalls that he was particularly fond of her poem:

> In the sky a red cloak flutters . . .
> I did not glimpse his face!

> В небе вьется красный плащ ...
> Я лица не увидала!

Voloshin saw a special charm in de Gabriak's poetry, in her characteristic, intimate manner of speaking about Christ. It was in the manner of *Sainte Thérèse de Jésus,* as if a woman were speaking of a man who is dear to her. In his analysis of her poetry, Voloshin noted that her speech was self-confident and thus alien to the *Zeitgeist;* he therefore could not help thinking of an ancient soul, which lived a separate and isolated life and which disclosed itself through her verse. This ancient soul within Cherubina de Gabriak strove desperately to express itself, and her poetry reveals her never-ceasing inner struggle with this spiritual stranger; hence the dramatic tension and heightened emotional effect in the poems. Voloshin conceived of them as an artful expression of de Gabriak's awareness of this ancient soul's superfluous dreams and exiled existence.[9]

From Marina Tsvetaeva's reminiscences the present-day reader may conceive of de Gabriak's painful duality:

In this young, modest schoolteacher with a limp, there lived an immodest, not at all schoolmarmish, cruel talent, which not only did not limp but, like Pegasus, never even touched the earth. It lived alone inside Cherubina, devouring and burning everything else . . . It was Maximilian Voloshin who understood that the gods, who had granted her own inner essence, added to this essence something opposite in nature, namely, her exterior appearance—her face and life. He understood that before him there was a tragic and catastrophic union of the soul and the body. No, not union, but rupture. She could not but continually suffer as did George Sand, Charlotte Brontë, Mary Webb, Julie de Lespinasse, and many other uncomely lovers of God. De Gabriak's plain face in life could not but hinder her in her talent—in the spontaneous revelation of her soul. There was a confrontation of two mirrors—that of her manuscript which harbored her soul, and the mirror of external reality which distorted her soul. Hence, the cruel mob logic of her intellect which gazed numbly at the quandary of her existence: "I cannot love myself—in this guise. I cannot live with myself—in this guise. This is—not I."[10]

Marina Tsvetaeva could never forget how Maximilian Voloshin one day presented her with the precious gift—Cherubina de Gabriak, "the living heroine, and the living poet, the heroine of her own poem."[11]

In her versification, Cherubina de Gabriak availed herself of rarely used closed forms of ancient poetry—the rondeau, villanelle, rondel, and various systems of interlacing and repeating lines, as seen in her long poem "Zolotaya vetv'" (The Golden Bough).[12] Without any unnecessary pretentiousness, she used these forms gracefully and naturally, as if they belonged to her everyday language. Her poem may be referred to as a lai, a medieval type of lyric poem composed of asymmetrical couplets each sung to its own melody. This form, revived in the seventeenth century, was skillfully adopted by the poet in the first decade of the twentieth century. In its concise lines "The Golden Bough," moreover, presents a distinct psychological complexity. Cherubina de Gabriak's revival of the lai may also serve as an example of her daring craftsmanship.

There is a remarkable alternation of ironic passages with those expressing "fatigued capriciousness" in de Gabriak's poetry, and her irony is marked by profound sadness. Since she played with both Love and Death, her lyricism, like that of Zinaida Hippius and Poliksena Solovyova, was "daring."[13] The poet Johannes von Guenther, who personally met de Gabriak in the Ivanovs' Tower, gave a perceptive evaluation of her work: "Die Verse, die man mir vorlas, waren von einer seltsamen, feinen Trauer, die ins Blut griff. Eine zurückgedämmte Leidenschaft, eine Sehnsucht, die sich aufbäumte. Russische Verse von grosser, manchmal fast artistischer Vollendung [. . .] Sie las noch mehr, zum Teil schöne Verse in der damaligen Manier der Symbolisten, nur vielleicht noch um eine Nuance aparter. Es war etwas so Besonderes in diesen Versen.[14]

Marina Tsvetaeva, who also analyzed de Gabriak's art, points to its modernistic character, albeit with a reliance upon certain ancient forms. She took two passages from de Gabriak's poems:

> Even the sonnets of Ronsard[15]
> Failed to shake off my grief.
> Everything said by the poets
> I've known a long time by heart!

> Даже Ронсара сонеты
> Не разомкнули мне грусть.
> Всё, что сказали поэты,
> Знаю давно наизусть!

> And I hate the image of brazen orchids
> In the faces of high society!

> И лик бесстыдных орхидей
> Я ненавижу в светских лицах![16]

and stated that she had selected this stanza and distich as illustrations of Tsvetaeva's own rhythm and Anna Akhmatova's imagery and diction. Though Cherubina de Gabriak's poems preceded Tsvetaeva and Akhmatova in their unique and innovative use of meters and imagery, Tsvetaeva recognized a kindred spirit. "All poetry, past, present, and future," concluded Marina Tsvetaeva, "is written by one and the same, nameless woman."[17]

Regardless of Cherubina de Gabriak's appearance or the split in her soul, her great poetic gift is evident. It is unfortunate that her fresh, original, and poetic voice was so crudely silenced (if we are to believe in the legend[18] which surrounds her) by the male-dominated literary group of *Apollo,* who, unmindful of her talent, valued physical beauty more than true poetic sensitivity.

NOTES

1. Valery Bryusov, *Dalekie i blizkie* (Moscow: Skorpion, 1912).

2. *Antologiya* (Moscow: Musaget, 1911), p. 206.

3. Marina Tsvetaeva, *Proza* (New York: Chekhov, 1953), p. 152.

4. Anastasiya Tsvetaeva, *Vospominaniya* (Moscow: Sovetsky pisatel', 1971), p. 404.

5. Marina Tsvetaeva, *Proza,* p. 152.

6. Anastasiya Tsvetaeva, *Vospominaniya,* p. 404.

7. Marina Tsvetaeva, *Proza,* p. 163.

8. *Ibid.,* p. 153.

9. For more details, see Maximilian Voloshin, "Goroskop Cherubiny de Gabriak," *Apollon,* No. 2 (1909), 3.

10. Marina Tsvetaeva, *Proza,* p. 148.

11. *Ibid.,* p. 147.

12. *Apollon,* No. 2 (1909), 3–4.

13. In. Annensky, "O sovremennom lirizme," *Apollon,* No. 3 (1909), 29.

14. Johannes von Guenther, *Ein Leben im Ostwind: Zwischen Petersburg und München, Erinnerungen* (München: Biederstein Verlag, 1969), pp. 284–287. "The poems which were read to me contained an unusual and refined sadness which was profoundly gripping. A reserved passion, an anguish, which surged upward like a wave. Russian poems of great, sometimes almost artistic perfection [. . .] She recited more verses to me, some of them beautiful poems in the manner of the Symbolists of those days, but perhaps by a nuance even more attractive. There was something quite special in these poems."

15. Pierre de Ronsard, sixteenth-century French poet.

16. This poem was written by Cherubina de Gabriak in response to a man who had sent her a bouquet of flowers.

17. Marina Tsvetaeva, *Proza,* p. 148.

18. Many other legends circulated in St. Petersburg and in Moscow concerning Cherubina de Gabriak. I. V. Odoevtseva and Yu. K. Terapiano, both Russian *émigré* writers in Paris, informed me in a recent interview, for example, that they

suspect Maximilian Voloshin signed his own poems with the name of Cherubina de Gabriak. They based their judgment on the high level of artistry the verses exhibit. This information, however, could not be verified by evidence. For more details, read Sergey Makovsky, *Portrety sovremennikov* (New York: Chekhov, 1955), pp. 335–358, and Marina Tsvetaeva, "Zhivoe o zhivom," *Sovremennye zapiski,* No. LII (1933), 249–254.

THE RED CLOAK

Someone said to me: "Your beloved
Will be wrapped in a fiery cloak . . ."
Whose sling hurled a stone,
Crashing with frenzied force? . . .

Whose flint arrow
Is buried in the sand by the spring?
Whose fleeting hoof
Left its imprint in the rock?

Whose gleaming visor
Glinted past, there, in the thicket?
In the sky flutters a red cloak . . .
I did not glimpse his face.

Apollo, No. 10 (1910)

КРАСНЫЙ ПЛАЩ

Кто-то мне сказал: « Твой милый
Будет в огненном плаще ...»
Камень, сжатый в чьей праще,
Загремел с безумной силой?..

Чья кремнистая стрела
У ключа в песок зарыта?
Чье летучее копыто
Отчеканила скала?..

Чье блестящее забрало
Промелькнуло там, средь чащ?
В небе вьется красный плащ ...
Я лица не увидала.

THE SPINNING WHEEL

When the Great Bear stands
At its zenith above the white city,
I weave silver threads
And the spinning wheel rattles.

My hour has come, the steps are creaking,
The door squeaks . . . O, who will enter?
Who will kneel beside me,
To prick herself like me?

The door has swung open, and at the threshold
A blind girl stands;
A nine-year-old, with eyelashes severe
And brow wreathed in violets.

Enter, unexpected tsarevna,
Sit by the window at the spinning wheel,
May my spindle sing
Melodiously under your hand!

. . . Why so short a time? Are you tired?
On your pale fingers—a trace of crimson . . .
Ah, it's decreed you shall learn
Of love and death at age thirteen.

Apollo, No. 10 (1910)

THE CRUCIFIXION

A wreath woven of sharp thorns
Encircles your poor brow like a crown,
And from your eyes—dark shadows.
Before you, on my knees
I bow, as if at vesper's sacrifice;
Onto my dress, drops of blood
Like garnets drip from your feet . . .

Still no one has yet guessed
Why my gaze is so troubled,
Why from Sunday mass
I've long since been returning last,
Why my lips tremble,
When the cloud of incense hovers
Like barely bluish lace.

Let the monks mutter curses,
Let hell fire await the sinners—
Before Easter, in spring, at the new moon
From a wizard known to me,
I bought the bitter stone of love—the astarote.[1]
And today you will descend from the cross
At the hour preceding earth's sunset.

Apollo, No. 10 (1910)

РАСПЯТЬЕ

Жалкий лоб твой из острого терния
Как венец заплетенный венок,
И из глаз твоих темные тени.
Пред тобою склоняя колени,
Я стою, словно жертва вечерняя,
И на платье мое с твоих ног
Капли крови стекают гранатами ...

Но никем до сих пор не угадано,
Почему так тревожен мой взгляд,
Почему от воскресной обедни
Я давно возвращаюсь последней,
Почему мои губы дрожат,
Когда стелется облако ладана
Кружевами едва синеватыми.

Пусть монахи бормочут проклятия,
Пусть костер соблазнившихся ждет,—
Я пред Пасхой, весной, в новолунье
У знакомой купила колдуньи
Горький камень любви—астарот.
И сегодня сойдешь ты с распятия
В час, грядущий земными закатами.

---

1. The poet may be referring to some sacred stone used in the worship of Astarte (Ashtoreth, Atargatis), the Phoenician goddess of fertility and sexual love, the West Semitic form of the goddess Ishtar. She was also regarded by the classical nations as a moon goddess (probably through confusion with another goddess), and in accordance with this view, which prevails in literary tradition, was identified with Selene and Artemis. More commonly, and with better reason, she was identified with Aphrodite.

THE GOLDEN BOUGH

To my teacher

Among starry runes, in their signs and symbols
The weary centuries treasure their delirium,
And all the petals of the heavenly crown
Whisper of happiness and torments.
On them burn rubies of crimson blood;
In them, sorrowful, in a sparkling shroud,
My love lies close to your dreams.

My love lies close to your dreams
In all its wanderings, in all its concerns,
Your sadness is no burden to my love,
Your sadness remains in my memories,
The imprint of my love is on your face,
My love has engraved our names
Onto a magical ring in a single inscription.

A shared anguish has engraved our names
On the pattern of Fate as a single inscription;
But I am alone, alone in my searchings,
And Saturn's course runs deep . . .
Yet I myself chose the agate gloom,
Evening's hand leads me across the flames of sunset
Into the Constellation of Dreams.[2]

Into the Constellation of Dreams
Evening's hand has woven a vision of white Jordan,[3]
Of the purity of the heavenly flower,
Of the wedding feast at Cana in Galilee . . .[4]
But there is a blank in the design of my Fate . . .
All of me trembles, all of me seeks supplication . . .
But there are no prayers for the ocean of stars.

---

2. The poet may also be referring to Somnus—in Roman mythology, the god of Sleep, son of Night, and twin brother of Death; identified with the Greek Hypnos.

3. Reference to Jordan River, where Jesus liked to stroll and where He is said to have walked on the water.

4. At this feast Jesus performed His first miracle by turning water into wine. See John 2:1, 11; 4:46, 54; 21:2.

But there are no prayers for the ocean of stars . . .
Before this assembly of suns the voices grow still . . .
The wreath burns on the tearful Constellation Eridanus,[5]
And the Hair of Veronica flutters.[6]
I have passed through the fiery bounds;
Above me is a diamond dew
And the unwound fabrics of our thoughts.

The unwound fabrics of our thoughts
And the wide river of withered days
Flow, like a dream, into the opal mist.
May our power beyond the world be strong,
For the terrestrial symbols of power are alien to us;
Our narrow path, our difficult deed of passion
Anguish has twined with gloom and radiance.

Anguish has twined with gloom and radiance
My love in all its glitter;
How agonizingly fragile is the thread of life,
What sadness there is in its distant outlines!
No matter what dreams we might wish to enfold us,
May that which is bequeathed to us come true
Amidst the starry runes, in their signs and symbols.

Amidst the starry runes, in their signs and symbols,
My love is close to your dream,
Evening's hand has engraved our names
As a single inscription in the Constellation of Dreams.
But there are no prayers for the ocean of stars,
And the unwound fabric of our thoughts
Anguish has twined with gloom and radiance.

Apollo, No. 2 (1909)

---

5. It is also possible that Cherubina de Gabriak refers to Eridu, the ancient Samarian City of southeastern Iraq. The place was a center for the water god Ra.

6. Reference to the Constellation *Coma Berenices*—Berenice's Hair—so named by Ptolemy III, whom Berenice had married. Berenice (273–221 B.C.) was a queen of Egypt.

ЗОЛОТАЯ ВЕТВЬ

Моему учителю

Средь звездных рун, в их знаках и названьях,
Хранят свой бред усталые века,
И шелестят о счастье и страданьях
Все лепестки небесного венка.
На них горят рубины алой крови;
В них, грустная, в мерцающем покрове,
Моя любовь твоей мечте близка.

Моя любовь твоей мечте близка
Во всех путях, во всех ее касаньях,
Твоя печаль моей любви легка,
Твоя печаль в моих воспоминаньях,
Моей любви печать в твоем лице,
Моя любовь в магическом кольце
Вписала нас в единых начертаньях.

Вписала нас в единых начертаньях
В узор Судьбы единая тоска;
Но я одна, одна в моих исканьях,
И линия Сатурна глубока ...
Но я сама избрала мрак агата,
Меня ведет по пламеням заката
В созвездье Сна вечерняя рука.

В созвездье Сна вечерняя рука
Вплела мечту о белом Иордане,
О белизне небесного цветка,
О брачном пире в Галилейской Кане ...
Но есть провал в чертах моей судьбы ...
Я вся дрожу, я вся ищу мольбы ...
Но нет молитв о звездном океане.

Но нет молитв о звездном океане ...
Пред сонмом солнц смолкают голоса ...
Горит венец на слезном Эридане,
И Вероники веют Волоса.
Я перешла чрез огненные грани,
И надо мной алмазная роса
И наших дум развернутые ткани.

И наших дум развернутые ткани,
И блеклых дней широкая река
Текут, как сон, в опаловом тумане.
Пусть наша власть над миром велика,
Ведь нам чужды земные знаки власти;
Наш узкий путь, наш трудный подвиг страсти,
Заткала мглой и заревом тоска.

Заткала мглой и заревом тоска
Мою любовь во всех ее сверканьях;
Как жизни нить мучительно-тонка,
Какая грусть в далеких очертаньях!
Каким бы мы ни предавались снам,
Да сбудется завещанное нам
Средь звездных рун, в их знаках и названьях.

Средь звездных рун, в их знаках и названьях
Моя любовь твоей мечте близка,
Вписала нас в единых начертаньях
В созвездье Сна вечерняя рука.
Но нет молитв о звездном океане.
И наших дум развернутые ткани
Заткала мглой и заревом тоска.

"Sang de Jésus-Christ, enivrez moi."
—St. Ignace de Loyola

In my dreams I am close to arrogance,
Within me—are the temptations of sin,
I do not know chaste blessedness . . .
    The flesh of Christ, sanctify me!

Like the maiden who extinguished the icon lamp,
Rejecting the Bridegroom's summoning,
I stand at the heavenly fence . . .
    The pain of Christ, heal me!

And the mute door will arouse
A daring thought in the fallen ones:
What if beyond it there is insanity? . . .
    The passion of Christ, strengthen me!

Overcome with an anxious tremor—
I now do not wish to accept
That I considered wisdom a lie . . .
The blood of Christ, intoxicate me!

Apollo, No. 2 (1909)

Мечтою близка я гордыни,
Во мне есть соблазны греха,
Не ведаю чистой святыни ...
　　Плоть Христова, освяти меня!

Как дева угасшей лампады,
Отвергшая зов Жениха,
Стою у небесной ограды ...
　　Боль Христова, исцели меня!

И дерзкое будит раздумье
Для павших безгласная дверь:
Что, если за нею безумье?..
　　Страсть Христова, укрепи меня!

Объятая трепетной дрожью—
Принять не хочу я теперь,
Что мудрость считала я ложью ...
　　Кровь Христова, опьяни меня!

I seek refuge at the threshold of the temple
Before the Virgin of All Treasures,
　　May your oriflamme
Shelter me from wicked beasts . . .

I have run here from the noisy streets,
Where blind wings beat in the darkness,
　　Where the world's temptations and the whole of Seville
Await their madmen.

But I lay before your pedestal
My dagger and fan, flowers and cameos—
　　To the glory of God . . .
O Mater Dei, memento mei!

Apollo, No. 2 (1909)

Bitter and wild—the smell of the earth:
The fields are o'ergrown with dark carnations!
Having flung my garments onto the grass,
I burn, like a candle, in the evening field.
Running into the distance, my steps are moist,
Tenderly naked, I blossom by the water.
Like white coral in an overgrowth of vines,
I am scarlet in the scarlet of my scarlet hair.

Apollo, No. 2 (1909)

They've locked the door of my abode
With a key lost forever;
The Black Angel, my guardian,
Stands with a flaming sword,
　　But my anguish won't see
　　The luster of the wreath and the purple of the throne,
And on my maidenly hand—
The useless ring of Solomon.
The rubies of deep pride
Won't illumine my dark gloom . . .
I have accepted our ancient sign—
The holy name of Cherubina.

Apollo, No. 2 (1909)

SONNET

"Nuestra pasión fué un trágico soneto."
—G. A. Becquer

My love is a tragic sonnet.
In it, there is the imperious structure of the sonnet's repetitions,
Of separations and meetings, and new returns—
The surf of Fate from the darkness of former years.

The unconsummated delirium of two maidens,
The transport of two souls, the torment of two doubts,
The double temptation of heavenly seductions,
   But each of them said proudly, "No."

Following the even lines, the uneven tercets
Came to me in a returning sequence,
The sonnet's vault closed above me.

The questions and answers have been repeated:
"Do you accept life? Will you follow me?
Will you accept the Sacrament from my hands?"
                  "No!"

Apollo, No. 2 (1909)

СОНЕТ

Моя любовь—трагический сонет.
В ней властный строй сонетных повторений,
Разлук и встреч и новых возвращений—
Прибой судьбы из мрака прошлых лет.

Двух девушек незавершенный бред,
Порыв двух душ, мученье двух сомнений,
Двойной соблазн небесных искушений,
   Но каждая—сказала гордо, « нет. »

Вслед четных строк нечетные терцеты
Пришли ко мне возвратной чередой,
Сонетный свод сомкнулся надо мной.

Повторены вопросы и ответы:
« Приемлешь жизнь? Пойдешь за мной вослед?
Из рук моих причастье примешь? »
            « Нет! »

Ego vox ejus!

In the blind nights of the new moon,
Filled with a mute anxiety,
Bewitched by a sorceress,
I am standing by a dark window.

The candles, doubled by the glass,
Shine both before and behind me,
And the strange appearance of the room
Threatens with the chance of a meeting.

In the dark-green mirrors
Of the ice-covered, ramshackle windows,
Not mine, but someone's pale curl
Is barely reflected, and a vague fear

Constricts my heart with a crimson thread —
What if a distant thunderstorm
Should show me a familiar face in the window
And reflect her eyes?

What if I shall presently see
The lowered corners of the mouth,
And before me will stand that woman
Whom I hate so sweetly?

But the dark water of my windows
Has frozen in its silence,
And that one who has exhausted my soul,
I shall never meet.

Apollo, No. 2 (1909)

Nadezhda Teffi

née Lokhvitskaya, 1876–1952

Born in St. Petersburg, and a younger sister of the poet
Mirra Lokhvitskaya, Nadezha Aleksandrovna Teffi distinguished
herself as a writer of belles-lettres and journalism, poetry and
prose, the comic and the serious. In her autobiographical sketch,
she remarked that Tolstoy's *Childhood* (1852) and *Adolescence*
(1854) and Pushkin's prose were the first works she read. She then
became interested in Russian poetry and even attempted to write
satirical poems and draw caricatures. The first examples of her
poetry appeared in August, 1901, under her maiden name in the
journal *Sever* (The North). She was dissatisfied with these poems,
however, and in 1901 the journal *Niva* (The Fields) published her
first story, "Den' proshol" (The Day Has Passed), also under her
maiden name. Several of her feuilletons in verse appeared in the
journal *Zvezda* (The Star) and in the Sunday issues of the newspaper *Birzhevye vedomosti* (The Stock Gazette). She also submit-
ted poems and short stories to Russian periodicals such as *Novosti*
(The News), *Rus'* (Russia), *Teatr i iskusstvo* (Theatre and Art),
Beseda (Discussions), *Rodnaya niva* (The Native Fields), *Bayan*
(The Bard), and many others.

Many of her poems were translated into German. Teffi's poetry is modernistic in its emotionally heightened style and its
colorful imagery. In her volume of verse *Sem' ogney* (Seven Fires,
1910), which includes a play written in orientalized prose, there
appear modernistic images, epithets, and poetic devices which
she artfully wove into her stanzas[1] and which she borrowed

from Heine, the French poet Leconte de Lisle, Blok, and Bal'-mont.

While she was writing her poetry, Teffi continued to publish short stories, both comic and serious, until the abortive Revolution of 1905. In the years surrounding this uprising, Teffi's stories evinced marked political overtones against the tsarist government. She contributed to the first legal Bolshevik journal, *Novaya zhizn'* (The New Life), the editorial board of which consisted of Social Democrats and liberal members of the literary avant-garde, including such colorful figures as Zinaida Hippius and Maxim Gor'ky. In November, 1905, Lenin took control of the journal, converting it into a party organ. At this time Hippius, Teffi, and other representatives of Russian belles-lettres withdrew from its editorial staff.

Teffi's most significant work was done for the comic-satirical St. Petersburg journal, *The Satyricon* (later *Novy Satirikon* [The New Satyricon]), and for the popular Moscow newspaper *Russkoye slovo* (The Russian Word), to which she regularly contributed feuilletons. Teffi's second volume of works, entitled *Yumoristicheskie rasskazy* (Humorous Stories), appeared in 1910. It reveals the author's keen sense of observation, her wit, and her gentle, almost elegiac humor. Its target is not the human personality, but the humdrum of everyday life, gray, dull, uneventful, and therefore all the more dramatic in its static nature. Against this background human beings appear not as evil, wicked, or stupid; rather, they are pitiful, intimidated, weak, often ridiculous, and always unhappy. They are presented with artistic detachment and tact—Teffi does not mock or satirize them. The critic Anastasiya Chebotarevskaya compared Teffi's stories, "highly benevolent in their elegiac tone, and profoundly humanitarian in their attitudes,"[2] with the best stories written by Chekhov. Their plots are diverse, taken from various manifestations of life—everyday human existence, psychology, political situations, the social milieu, and so forth. There are no fantastic elements; the language is lucid and correct; the portraits are drawn in distinct relief. And Teffi's skill in characterizing man's inner world and his exterior situation is obvious. Her early volumes stood out in the overcrowded Russian book market and impressed the reader with their "organic unity."[3]

Nadezhda Teffi

Between 1911 and 1918 Teffi published six more collections of humorous stories and numerous small, inexpensive editions. Among her many publications was a volume of primarily serious stories entitled *Nezhivoy zver'* (The Lifeless Beast; Petrograd, 1917), which was later reprinted in emigration under the title *Tikhaya zavod'* (The Peaceful Backwater; Paris, 1921). These volumes, with their exquisite wit and lively, lucid style, were well received in Russia. The many reviews written in St. Petersburg and Moscow granted Teffi an inimitable position in the history of Russian belles-lettres. Almost unanimously, Russian critics lauded her natural plots, her fluent, refined, and elegant style, her understanding and knowledge of the psychological depth of life's ordinary events. They further praised her lively, witty dialogue, swiftly unfolding action, economy of artistic details, and, finally, her graceful "infection" of the reader with a sincere gaiety which is at the same time profoundly tragic. Vasily Nemirovich-Danchenko once exclaimed: "Who doesn't know Teffi and that graceful humor which places her much higher than even such world-renowned writers as Jerome Jerome and Mark Twain?"[4] He also held Teffi in high esteem as an outstanding and original lyrical poet: "Teffi is the author of charming, delicately painted poems, which she, however, regards with indifference."[5] Her treatment of erotic themes, especially her distinctly Eastern eroticism, was not offensive to Nemirovich-Danchenko. He, too, compared her subtlely humorous and delicate stories to those of Chekhov.

The October Revolution ended Teffi's creative work in Russia. Although greeting the February Revolution with enthusiasm in the manner of other liberally minded Russian intellectuals, Teffi turned away in horror from the Bolshevik *coup d'état* in 1917. She left St. Petersburg in 1919 via Istanbul, and in 1920 she settled in Paris and began to contribute short stories to the Russian newspapers there, *Poslednie novosti* (The Latest News) and *Vozrozhdenie* (La Renaissance). These stories portray the Russian *émigrés* in France and their pathetic, frequently ridiculous, attempts at readjustment in a foreign country. With irony combined with bitterness, and with criticism combined with pity, Teffi depicts the vulgar, quotidian existence of the Russians in France and their little tragedies. Among her frequent themes is the memory of a happy childhood and the longing for love which is unattainable, together with a desire for death as a release from the void incomprehensibility and cruelty of life.

Teffi's pre- and post-*émigré* comic stories present the emptiness of man's earthly existence and his attempt to escape it through beautiful dreams and illusions. With irony, the writer tears the veil from these ideals and strivings for a higher, more beautiful world, leaving the reader with a "comic equivalent of the dead world, portrayed in the early Symbolist poetry," as is aptly stated by Edythe Haber in her essay "Nadezhda Teffi."[6] Love as a sincere emotion is also missing in Teffi's comic sketches. As in her earlier stories, Teffi's *émigré* characters conceal their shallow and unresponsive nature from themselves and from others by pretending to be something more than they actually are. This portrayal of the Russian *émigrés* intensifies and enhances a vision of life which emerged from her earlier writings; for example, in the previously mentioned *Seven Fires,* which is serious in mood and themes.

Many of her short stories and feuilletons written in exile deal with the profound questions of human interrelationships and the meaning of life, as had her poetry and plays written in Russia. Although often funny, her works of the later period display a mood dominated by pathos, and even by hopelessness and despair. The weary tone gains the upper hand over the former biting wit. Thematically, however, her comic stories of the pre- and post-*émigré* periods reveal a persistent pattern, and the same vision of the world characterizes her early sketches and her late *émigré* works, including the more solemn poetry of *Seven Fires.* Both in style and content the latter may be linked with Symbolist poetry. Imagery, poetic devices, and flamboyant style all point to the similarities between Teffi's serious poetry and the works of the Russian Symbolists. Her dualistic vision of the universe may also be identified with theirs. Earthly existence is void, meaningless, and dead; "true reality" lies elsewhere. Distant and unattainable, it exists only as a dim reflection on earth. The soul longs for this higher spiritual reality, yet it can never detach itself completely from the dead and mechanical world of finite experience. This perception of the world lies at the heart of Teffi's entire artistic work. Paradoxically, however, in her comic stories she maintains that this ideal, beautiful, spiritual world does not exist at all. It is merely a mirage; it can be meaningful, joyous, and beautiful, yet underneath there is nothing but the boring reality of the empirical world. Only into a world of treacherous but sweet illusions can the soul escape; but this world of illusions is nevertheless superior to a dead and banal existence on earth.

This thematic pattern emerges from all the works which Teffi wrote in France. There she published seven volumes of short stories, as well as a major collection of poetry, *Passiflora* (1923); a novel, *Avantyurny roman* (An Adventure Novel, 1932); a volume of memoirs, *Vospominaniya* (Reminiscences, 1932); and many other works. Some contain pieces published earlier in Russia. She also republished many of her complete volumes written in St. Petersburg. The following collections appeared in emigration: *The Peaceful Backwater; Chorny Iris* (The Black Iris; Stockholm, 1921); *Vecherny den'* (The Nocturnal Day; Prague, 1924); *Gorodok* (The Small Town; Paris, 1927); *Vsyo o lyubvi* (All about Love; Paris, n.d.); *Kniga—Iyun'* (The Book—June; Belgrade, 1931); *Ved'ma* (The Witch; Paris, 1936); *O nezhnosti* (About Tenderness; Paris, 1938); and *Zigzag* (Paris, 1939). The first two volumes are especially funny, even though they express the suffering and bewilderment of a recent exile. *The Nocturnal Day, The Small Town*, and *All about Love* also deal with the absurdities of *émigré* life. In exposing the oddities of this life, Teffi shows an affinity with Mikhail Zoshchenko's artistic method. In many ways they are the *émigré* equivalent of the latter's short stories concerning the Soviet citizen's everyday life and his bewilderment and inability to live in harmony with new and alien surroundings.

Teffi's *Reminiscences* and *An Adventure Novel* differ from her collections of short stories. In *Reminiscences*, Teffi relates her escape from the Soviets in 1919 through the use of the hyperbolic grotesque. *An Adventure Novel* is "an un-Russian novel according to its exterior appearance,"[7] in that it has many short chapters with unexpected, frequently very intriguing epigraphs from Heine, Goethe, Anatole France, Dostoevsky, Theocritus, etc. Its action unfolds rapidly, and the whole novel is written in short and energetic sentences. Furthermore, Teffi was very successful with stories about animals, of which, like Chekhov, she spoke with profound warmth. Remarkable also are her stories about an everyday empirical reality which is occasionally ruffled by the intrusion of fantastic elements, as in *The Witch*.

Despite the limited Russian-language publishing facilities available abroad, and though the circle of her readers became considerably smaller, Teffi remained one of the most popular writers in Russian. Her books received favorable reviews in all influential Russian journals and newspapers abroad, just as they had in Russia prior to the October Revolution. Her works in prose were translated into French, German, Polish, Czech, and other languages, and she was often invited to various countries in Europe to recite her short stories at literary *soirées*.

Soviet criticism, on the other hand, gave a negative evaluation of Teffi's work in emigration. Victor Yakerin, for example, objected to her protagonists, whom he saw only as disreputable characters and stereotypes—"princes, generals' wives, shallow and frivolous actresses, and health-resort guests."[8] Since Teffi's "philistines of yesterday, dead and with their souls decayed ages ago," no longer existed in the Soviet Union, the critic dismissed her works as being unnecessary for the Soviet reader. Her stories, said Yakerin, "could tickle slightly only a similar, decayed soul, dying somewhere in a remote, god-forsaken hole of our revolutionary country."[9] Still another Soviet critic claimed that her satire was ineffective and fruitless. He disapproved of her humor, her artistic method, the allegedly repetitive nature of the events described, and the prevailing mood of boredom and anguish. Her major fault was her indifference to a conscious, political platform and a "vital pathos of struggle,"[10] which he mistakenly believed hindered her development as a powerful satirist. He, too, failed to see the artistic originality of the writer, and thus was unable to fathom the essence of her metaphysical universe.

NOTES

1. For more details, see Valery Bryusov, *Dalekie i blizkie* (Moscow: Skorpion, 1912).

2. Anastasiya Chebotarevskaya, "Teffi. *I stalo tak . . . Yumoristicheskie rasskazy*, St. Petersburg: Izd. Kornfel'd, 1912," *Novaya zhizn'*, No. 7 (1912), 255.

3. Vlad. Kr., [Vladimir Kranikhfel'd] "Teffi. *Yumoristicheskie rasskazy*. Izd. Shipovnik, St. Petersburg, 1910," *Sovremenny mir*, No. 9 (1910), 171.

4. Vas. Iv. Nemirovich-Danchenko, *Na kladbishchakh: vospominaniya* (Revel: Bibliofil, 1921), p. 140.

5. *Ibid.*

6. *Russian Literature Triquarterly*, No. 9 (Spring, 1974), 454–472.

7. Gleb Struve, *Russkaya literatura v izgnanii* (New York: Chekhov, 1956), pp. 113–114.

8. Victor Yakerin, "Teffi. *Nichego podobnogo i vechera.* Izd. Kosmos, 1927," *Krasnaya nov'*, No. 4 (1927), 231.

9. *Ibid.*

10. "Teffi. *Tango smerti: sbornik rasskazov,*" *Na literaturnom postu*, No. 4 (1928), 87.

HUMOROUS TALES

BOOK I

". . . For laughter is joy, and in itself—is good."
— Spinoza, *Ethics*, Part IV,
Statute XLV, Remark II

BEYOND THE WALL

The Easter cake most decidedly did not turn out well. Crooked, with the crust oozing down from the top, pasted over with almonds, it resembled an old, rotten toadstool, swollen from the autumn rains. Even the magnificent paper rose stuck into it couldn't impart the desired shapeliness. Its little scarlet head drooped as if examining the big patch decorating the gray tea cloth, and thus emphasized even more the lopsidedness of its pedestal.

Yes, the Easter cake did not turn out well. But everyone, without uttering a word, agreed to ascribe no importance to this detail. Indeed, this was completely understandable: Madame Shrank ["Cupboard" in German], as mistress of the house, would gain nothing by pointing out the inadequacies of her own food; Madame Lazenskaya was a guest invited to end the Lenten fast and, as is customary, was required to find everything excellent. As far as the cook Annyushka was concerned, it would certainly not be to her advantage to call attention to her own negligence.

The other dishes could not be better: A ham sliced into small pieces, alternating with slices of smoked sausage, formed a two-colored star on the plate. A roasted chicken, sprawled in the most defenseless position, revealed that it was stuffed with rice. The small cheese *paskha*[1] wasn't much to look at but, to make up for that, was so fragrant with vanilla that Madame Lazenskaya's nose involuntarily turned in its direction. Eggs dyed bright colors enlivened the entire scene.

Madame Lazenskaya had been ready to begin eating for quite some time. She tried, out of politeness, not to look at the table, but the whole of her small, sharp face with its frizzy, sparse hair and the dirty lilac ribbon on her wrinkled neck conveyed a tense ex-

---

1. A Russian Easter delicacy.

pectancy. Raising her hairless eyebrows (she darkened them in with a burnt match), for a while she would examine with interest the little bookstand covered with a crocheted cloth, the same one she had seen daily over a period of nine years; then, lowering her eyes and gathering her toothless mouth into a tiny lump, she would shyly pick at her handkerchief trimmed with torn lace.

The hostess, a buxom brunette with pendulous cheeks like those of an angry bulldog, walked around the table with an air of importance, smoothing the gray embroidered apron on her rounded stomach. She was perfectly aware of Madame Lazenskaya's condition—the woman had been feeding herself throughout Lent on baked potatoes without butter—but this affected indifference angered her all the same, so she purposely tormented her guest.

"It's shtill early," her mighty bass voice droned. "They shtill haven't rung the church bell."

She spoke with a thick German accent, puckering her full upper lip, which was decorated with a thin black moustache.

The guest continued to pick at her handkerchief silently, then began making small talk.

"Tomorrow I'll probably get a letter from Miten'ka. He always sends me money on Easter."

"That's shtupid of him. You'll fritter avay the money on perfumes, just like always. Coquette!"

Madame Lazenskaya laughed ingratiatingly, pursing her mouth into a little trumpet so as to hide the absence of her front teeth.

"Hiu-hiu-hiu! Ah, what a tease you are!"

"I'm telling you the truth," croaked the encouraged hostess. "To valk into your room—it's like getting it vit a shtick over the nose. Jars and vials, boddles and eau de cologne—a real observatory."

"Hiu-hiu-hiu!" whistled the guest, throwing a coquettish look at the little bookstand. "A woman should smell sweet. Subtle perfumes have an effect upon the heart . . . I love subtle perfumes. One must have a feeling for such things. *Vervaine*—is a light and sweet fragrance; *Ambergris royale*—is musky. Take two drops of the *Ambergris*, one drop of *Vervaine* and you get a real fragrance . . . Really," she bit her lips, searching for the words, "earthy and heavenly. Or take the basic perfume *Tréfle incarnat*, it's spicy as if touched with cinnamon, and add to three drops of it one drop of

White Iris . . . You'll go out of your mind! You'll simply go out of your mind!"

"Vhy shoold I vant to go out of my mind?" Madame Shrank said sarcastically. "I voold rather go to *Ralle* and buy some eau de cologne made from flowers."

"Or take the delicate *Isaurie*," not listening, Madame Lazenskaya continued to fantasize, "take only one drop of it to every five of the heavy *Fenouil* . . ."

"Nevertheless, I love Lily of the Valley most of all," interrupted the heavy bass of the hostess, who had decided it was finally time to show she too knew something about perfumes.

"Lily of the Valley?" the guest repeated with astonishment. "You like Lily of the Valley? Hiu-hiu-hiu! Dear God, don't tell anyone that you like Lily of the Valley! Oh, my God! Everybody will laugh at you. Hiu-hiu-hiu! Lily of the Valley! What vulgarity!"

"Oh, oh! Vhat refinement!" Madame Shrank said, now offended, "How important all this is! I don't see any great intelligence in shtarving oneself—just to hoard money for perfume! How horribly fascinating—enough perfumes for three rooms, but she has a face like a fist."

Madame Lazenskaya, her head now bent quite low, flicked a speck of something off her blouse with her fingernail. Only her large crimson-colored ears were visible.

"It's time," the hostess announced at last, sitting down at the table. "Annyushka! Bring the coffee!"

Madame Shrank did not use table bells in her home. Her voice boomed like a Chinese gong and was heard with equal clarity in every nook and cranny of the small apartment. Often while tidying up the entrance hall she would grumble, and the cook would answer from the kitchen at the top of her lungs. In order to speak with Madame Shrank, it was not at all necessary to be in the same room with her.

"Hurry up and get it out here!"

Far off, the crash of a falling poker resounded, a little dog yelped, and in the doorway appeared the overpowering figure of Annyushka, attired in a bright red blouse sashed with an old military officer's belt. Her round cheeks, rubbed with beets for the holiday, rivaled the coloring of the Easter eggs lying on the dish. Her hair, a dirty gray color, was heavily pomaded and teased into a high coiffure, crowned with a rosette of crimped green paper from a medicine vial. Modestly lowering her eyes as though embarrassed by her own beauty, Annyushka set down the tray with the coffee pot and cups.

"Put on an apron, you shcarecrow!" Madame Shrank droned gloomily. "Who gave you permission to curl a crow's nest on your head? Madame Lazenskaya, take a look at how much she's pinched her cheeks! Ga-ga-ga!"

"Hiu-hiu-hiu!" Madame Lazenskaya whistled like a bird.

"It's not true, I didn't even think to pinch 'em," Annyushka said in self-defense, gingerly passing the sleeve of her frock over her face. "I swear! By the icon on the wall . . . I swear, it's from the heat. I baked the Easter cake, roasted the chicken . . . There's such an inflammation in the kitchen!"

She left, angrily slamming the door.

"How do you like that!" the hostess said indignantly. "You can't even say one vord! And she calls herself a servant! She makes herself up, makes her hair look like a used shcrub brush, and you don't dare even tell her anything. Every Sunday it's like that. As soon as everyone leaves—right avay she paints her cheeks, takes the military belt, puts it on, and then shtarts singing the liturgy. But I come back on purpose, open the door vit my own keys, and hear everything in the entrance hall. For about two hours she sings in full voice: 'Lord, have mercy! Lord, have mercy!' She bellows like a bull. All my nerves simply crackle. All I need is for some foolish tenant in the apartment to think that I'm the one who's singing like that . . ."

"It's a pity about Dasha," added Madame Lazenskaya, "she was much more modest."

"Vell! Every day a new admirer. That's all they have on their minds!"

Madame Lazenskaya felt a twinge of guilt and fell silent.

"It's a remarkable thing," the hostess continued, while carving the chicken. "All they have on their minds is admirers. Vell, as far as Annyushka is concerned, she at least doesn't go outside . . ."

"Tomorrow I'll go," a wail resounded from the kitchen. "Even if you cut my throat, I'll go . . . you should be ashamed in front of people. Even the chief janitor pesters me. 'When,' he said, 'are ya goin' to go outside, you witch?' 'This is the first time,' he says, 'I seen a devil the likes of you—never leave the house.'"

"How do you like that!" the hostess said, bewildered. "Vhere vill you go, you have nobody here?"

"There are lots of places to go . . . I'll go to any cemetery. In our village everyone goes to the cemetery when there's a holiday. You think you've found a fool; me—not know where to go! I know better than you or anybody else!"

"Shtop howling, my nerves are crackling because of you!"

Madame Shrank went up to the buffet and, turning her back to Madame Lazenskaya, shuffled something around, quietly tinkling the shot glasses. Then she threw her head back slightly and, locking up the buffet, returned to her seat, coughing in embarrassment. The entire time her guest carefully examined the little bookstand.

Madame Lazenskaya had long been acquainted with this small maneuver and knew that, having pulled off her little trick, Madame Shrank would become unusually patriotic and would love to talk about Germany, though she'd never once laid her eyes on that country, since she was born and raised in Petersburg. At such times Madame Lazenskaya's own patriotic feelings would be somewhat offended and she would attempt to change the topic of conversation. She didn't dare contradict her hostess, always feeling a little guilty before her whiskered companion. The problem was that, as the tenant of a tiny room at Madame Shrank's, she was often unable to pay for it on time, and Madame Shrank would condescendingly allow her to pay in installments.

"There are no servants like that in Berlin," the hostess said reproachfully, while dispatching a large piece of ham into her mouth.

The guest was silent, gathering the rice with her fork.

Madame Shrank for a long time contemplated what sort of unpleasantry she might hurl at her.

"Vhy are you so qviet? Probably you're dreaming vhat kinds of perfumes you'll be buying vit Miten'ka's money? Vhat makes him send it? There shtill are shtoopid sons on this earth! You know, after you're gone, there'll be nothing left for him. And vhatever vas left by the father, in three years you've managed to throw it to the vind . . ."

Madame Lazenskaya's face became covered with splotches.

"You know, Madame Shrank," she quickly interrupted, "today I saw some red broadcloth exactly the same color as the riding habit I used to have. Remember? I was telling you about it. Well, exactly, exactly . . ."

"I shoold think you voold recognize that riding habit, since you've trotted through tventy thousand rubles in three years vit the officers."

"Hiu-hiu-hiu!" howled the guest, hoping to mollify her accuser.

"Vhat are you laughing for?"

"I just remembered something funny," said Madame Lazenskaya, becoming suddenly serious. "Yesterday you were talking about that old man . . ."

Madame Shrank's face slowly broadened into a smile; her eyes squinted, the corners of her mouth flowed deeply into her squishy cheeks.

"Ga-ga-ga! 'Allow me, madame, to eshcort you' . . . I turned around—My lord! Such thin little legs, barely shtanding, holding on to the cane vit both hands . . . A blue nose—brows completely gray . . . 'You? Eshcort me? You shoold qvickly run along home.' His eyes bulged out at me, he didn't undershtand anything . . . 'Run along home,' I said—'it's time for you to die, run along qvickly!' Ga-ga-ga! And how he shtarted to shpit, ga-ga-ga!—how terribly angry he got!"

"Oh, stop it! Hiu-hiu-hiu! I'll die laughing! Hiu-hiu-hiu! Ah, that Madame Shrank is always saying something funny! . . ."

"'Faster,' I said, 'hurry. It'll be very unpleasant for us all, if on the shtreet . . .'"

"Oh! Hiu-hiu-hiu! . . ."

"Oh, shtop, Madame Lazenskaya! You've shaken all the powder off your face . . ."

Both ladies, regardless of the ten years they had spent together, never called each other by their first names. Once a relative of Madame Shrank asked her what her tenant's first name was and she, to her own amazement, admitted that she had never been curious to find this out.

"Ah, these men!" Madame Lazenskaya sighed languidly. "Lizaveta Ivanovna was telling me . . ."

"Your Lizaveta Ivanovna is always lying," the hostess suddenly burst out like gunpowder. "She can't tell you anything in that Finnish babble[2] of hers. Today she tagged after me into the meat shop, waving her arms, shcreaming; I vas embarrassed in front of the passers-by. As ve crossed the shtreet, I said, 'Valk faster,' and then how she began to shcreech, 'I can't valk faster, some horses have advanced on me!' Simply a disgrace! She could have said, 'Excuse me, Madame Shrank, I find myself surrounded by a huge crowd of horses.' How many years has she been living in Petersburg and she shtill can't shpeak properly. Shtupid old Finnish hag!"

Madame Lazenskaya wanted to try the sausages very badly, but she was afraid to express her desire while the hostess was so upset, and so she again changed the topic of conversation.

"Yes, these men, they're simply such . . . such . . ."

Madame Shrank pricked up her ears like a thrush to whom someone had whistled a familiar tune.

"Have some sausage! Vhy so little? All the same, men are thoroughly amusing people. I once had a boarder—young, handsome, the son of an admiral. He vas from Kharkov and came to Petersburg to take the exam for the rank of general in the civil service . . . 'Madame Shrank,' he said, 'you have roses' petal on your cheeks . . .'"

"I don't recall ever meeting him."

"No, he vas here about two years before you! Ga-ga! . . . Roses' petal!"

"A lovely remedy for wrinkles, *Crème-Simone* pomades," Madame Lazenskaya added rather inappropriately. "Try it, Madame Shrank. It's simply amazing how it works on the skin! All my life, I've never used anything except *Crème-Simone*. Every morning and every evening, put a little on some cotton and then rub it in so . . . You absolutely ought to . . ."

"Ga-ga-ga!" the hostess rocked good naturedly. "I might have tried that cream if you hadn't told me that you use it. But since you've varned me, no, thank you! Dear God, Madame Lazenskaya, don't be offended—but never in my life!"

---

2. Using a disrespectful term for the Finnish language which was popular in St. Petersburg.

The guest blushed and grinned crookedly.

"And vhat a shpendthrift yet!" the hostess continued. "You shooldn't throw your money avay on all sorts of simmons and likar-pops! You should save money. Vhen my husband vas alive, I had diamonds the size of fists dangling from my ears; believe me, people behaved completely differently toward me then. No matter vhat I said—everything vas sensible. Now, alas, no one praises my intelligence; yet as I recall, even then I babbled only nonsense. Money—it's a great power. If you vere to have money, you too voold be viser than everyone and colonels voold come to pay their respects to you, and you voold receive a prize for your beauty."

Madame Lazenskaya, her lips blossoming into a strained coquettish smile, adjusted the lilac ribbon on her neck, while Madame Shrank once again went to the buffet and tinkled the shot glasses . . .

"Ve in Berlin know the value of money. In our Berlin everyone knows that. From whom did the electric shtreet lamps on the Nevsky Prospect come?—From the Germans! From whom the large buildings? The Germans built them. And fabrics, and silk, and the various sciences—history, geography—everything is from the Germans, they invented all of this!"

Madame Lazenskaya blushed and then grew pale. She wanted to argue, but she didn't know what to say; besides, she still hadn't tried the *paskha,* and after political arguments decorum demands that one leave the room.

"How intricately this rose has been placed in your Easter cake—it simply makes one want to smell it," she said with quivering lips.

After an ominous silence, Madame Shrank suddenly said: "Lizaveta Ivanovna's tenant read in the newspapers that there vas a shtrong earthqvake in Berlin. Very shtrong. There are never any earthqvakes in Russia."

This was a little too much even for Madame Lazenskaya. Suddenly her whole body began to tremble and she became covered with red blotches.

"That's not true! That's not true!" she screamed in a thin, cracked speech. "Several times there was an earthquake in Russia. There was one in Vernoy . . ."

"That doesn't count," the hostess said in a forcedly calm, bass voice, "that vas beyond the Balkan Sea, that's no longer vithin the natural borders of Russia . . ."

"That's not true!" Madame Lazenskaya said, convulsively shaking her little fist. "You've intentionally invented it. You think that I'm poor, that I have no fatherland! . . . You should be ashamed! Everyone knows that there was an earthquake in Russia! You're being dishonest! You're lying! Lying! You've been talking about that old man for five years already, and you're always saying that it happened a day or two ago. You should be ashamed!"

She jumped up and, having quickly stamped her small heels, she stumbled past the chairs, ran to her room, and latched the door.

It was quiet in the tiny room. Through the small casement window, together with the strong and damp scent of spring, there slowly drifted the quiet ringing of the Easter service bells. It tormented and troubled the soul like the echo of a distant, unfamiliar happiness, and the air gently swayed with deep, heavy gusts.

Beyond the window a wall, beginning somewhere far below, rose high into the dim sky—an endless wall, smooth, gray . . .

It was quiet in the tiny room, and no one stopped Madame Lazenskaya from having a good cry. With her head bent low and her elbows propped up on the window sill, she cried for a long time. Later, when the tears had dried, her bitter resentment subsided, and she calmed down. She got up, went to the chest of drawers, and, opening the top drawer, pulled out a bottle wrapped in a little silk rag. Cautiously, she took out the cork and slowly extended her nose forward, inhaling the contents with quivering nostrils. Then she carefully wrapped the bottle again and, as though it were a swaddled child, quietly and tenderly laid it in its former place.

Slowly, her hand still trembling after the excitement, she pulled out a little box of powder and, having powdered her face, hung her wet handkerchief across the back of the chair, painstakingly smoothing out the creases in the lace.

"Annyushka," Madame Shrank's voice boomed in the distance, "tell Madame Lazenskaya she can have some coffee vhen she shtops all that nonsense. I can't vait all night. Here's a piece of the Easter cake. The rest I'll take down to the pantry. I'm going to sleep. My nerves, too, are crackling."

Madame Lazenskaya's heart began to pound loudly. She knew that Annyushka had been asleep for a long time, and that the hostess was saying this specifically so that she, Lazenskaya, would hear it. Softly she crept up to the door and listened, waiting for Madame Shrank to leave so that she could go out to the dining room.

Little by little the wall beyond the window turned pink under the first scarlet rays of the rising sun. A lively little dawn breeze brazenly tapped the small casement window and, passing through in a gentle stream, fluttered the handkerchief drying on the chair.

A FASHIONABLE LAWYER

On this day there were few people in the court. No interesting cases were anticipated.

On the benches behind the ballustrade three young fellows in Russian shirts languished and sighed. In the area set aside for the public there were several students and young women and, in the corner, two reporters.

On the agenda was the case of Semyon Rubashkin. As it was stated in the record of proceedings, he was accused of "spreading false rumors about the dissolution of the First Duma" in a newspaper article.

The accused was already in the courtroom, sauntering before the public with his wife and three friends. They were all exhilarated, somewhat excited by the unaccustomed surroundings, and they chattered and joked.

"I wish they would start already," said Rubashkin, "I'm as hungry as a dog."

"From here we'll go straight to The Vienna for breakfast," his wife said, daydreaming.

"Ha! ha! ha! When they lock him up in prison, then you'll have a breakfast," the friends quipped.

"It would be even better if he were deported to Siberia for life," she said coquettishly. "Then I'd get married again."

His friends laughed heartily and slapped Rubashkin on the shoulder.

A stocky gentleman in a dress coat entered the courtroom and, haughtily nodding to the accused, settled down at the lectern and began pulling papers from his briefcase.

"Who is that?" the wife asked.

"That is my lawyer."

"A lawyer?" his friends were astonished. "You've lost your mind! Hiring a lawyer for such a trifling case! Yes indeed, old fellow, that's enough to make a hen laugh. What's he going to do? There's nothing for him even to say! The court will directly move to dismiss the case."

"Well, as a matter of fact, I had no intention of hiring him. He himself offered his services. He's not even taking any payment. He said, 'We take such cases out of principle. Fees only insult us.' Of course, I didn't insist. Why should I insult him?"

"It's not nice to insult someone," his wife agreed.

"Yet on the other hand, what harm can he do? He'll chatter for five minutes. Perhaps he'll even be useful. Who knows what the court may do to me? They might even consider imposing a fine on me, and he could settle the case in my favor."

"Hmm . . . yes, it is possible," his friends agreed.

The lawyer stood up, smoothed his whiskers, knitted his brow, and walked up to Rubashkin.

"I've looked over your case," he said, adding gloomily, "take heart."

He then returned to his seat.

"A crank!" his friends burst out laughing.

"D-devil," said Rubashkin, shaking his head anxiously. "He smells of a fine."

"Please rise! The court is in session!" announced the bailiff.

The accused sat behind the ballustrade and from there waved to his wife and companions, smiling both perplexedly and proudly, as if he had just received a vulgar compliment.

"A hero!" one of his friends whispered to the wife.

"Russian Orthodox!" The accused briskly answered the judge's question.

"Do you admit to being the author of the article signed with the initials 'S. R.'"

"I admit it."

"What else can you add, concerning this matter?"

"Nothing," said Rubashkin in amazement.

At this point the lawyer jumped in.

His face turned purple, his eyes bulged, the veins on his neck throbbed. It seemed as if he were choking on a lamb bone.

"Your Honor!" he cried out. "Yes, here before you is Semyon Rubashkin. He is the author of this article and the purveyor of rumors concerning the dissolution of the First Duma. He is the author of the article signed only with two letters, but these two letters are 'S. R.' You ask, why two? And I ask, why not three? Why did he, a loving and devoted son, not use the name of his father, as is customary among Russians? Is it not because only the two letters 'S' and 'R' were necessary for his purposes? Is he not a representative of that terrible and powerful party?

"Your Honor! Is it possible that you entertain the thought that my client is simply a modest hack newspaper writer, who has casually uttered an unfortunate phrase in an unfortunate article? No, Your Honor! You don't have the right to insult him, a man who, it is possible, symbolizes the secret power, so to speak, the nucleus, I would say, of the emotional essence of our great revolutionary movement.

"'His guilt is insignificant,' you would say. 'No!' I would exclaim. 'No!' I would protest.

The judge called to the bailiff and asked him to clear the public out of the courtroom.

The lawyer took a sip of water and continued: "You're looking for heroes in tall white Caucasian hats! You don't recognize the modest toilers—the ones who don't poke their way ahead with the shout 'Hands up!' but who secretly and anonymously direct a powerful movement. Was there a tall white Caucasian hat on the leader of the robbery of that Moscow bank? Was there a tall white Caucasian hat on the one who sobbed for joy on the day of the murder of von der . . . However, I represent my client only in the matters before us. But even within these limitations I can accomplish much."

The judge asked to have the doors closed and the witnesses sent away.

"Do you think that a year in prison will make a bunny out of this lion?" He turned and for a moment pointed to the perplexed, perspiring face of Rubashkin. Then, pretending to tear himself away from that sublime spectacle only with great difficulty, he continued: "No! Never! He will enter the prison as a lion, but will leave as a hundred-headed hydra! He will coil around his stunned enemy like a boa constrictor, pitifully crushing the bones of the administrative tyranny in his mighty teeth.

"Is it Siberia that you have in mind for him? Well, Your Honor! I will say nothing to you . . . I ask you only this: Where can Gershuni be found? Gershuni, whom you sent to Siberia?

"And why bother? Is it possible that prison, exile, hard labor, torture (which, I might add, for some reason or other was not used on my client)—is it possible that all these horrors might tear from his proud lips at least one word of admission or at least one of the thousands of names of his accomplices?

"No, Semyon Rubashkin is not that sort of fellow! He will proudly mount the scaffold, he will proudly push aside his hangman and, having said to the priest, 'I have no need for consolation!' will himself put the noose around his proud neck.

"Your Honor! I can already see that noble image on the pages of *The Past*, together with my article about the final minutes of this great champion, whom the hundred-mouthed Fame will make into a legendary hero of the Russian revolution.

"Indeed, I will proclaim his very last words, delivered with the shroud already over his head: 'May wickedness disappear' . . ."

The judge did not allow the defense counsel to continue.

The defense counsel obeyed, asking only that the judge accept his statement that his client, Semyon Rubashkin, absolutely refuses to sign a plea for mercy.

The judge, not bothering to leave the courtroom for the deliberation, changed the article on the spot. He deprived the petty bourgeois Semyon Rubashkin of all civil rights and sentenced him to be put to death by hanging.

They carried the defendant unconscious from the courtroom.

A group of young people at the courtroom cafeteria gave the lawyer a tumultuous ovation.

He was affably smiling, bowing, and shaking hands.

Afterward, having snacked on some little sausages and drunk a tankard of beer, he asked the courtroom reporter to send him a proofsheet of the speech for the defense.

"I don't like typographical errors," he said.

In the corridor, he was stopped by a gentleman with a contorted face and pale lips. It was one of Rubashkin's friends.

"Can it be that this is the end! No hope whatsoever?"

The lawyer smiled drearily.

"What can be done! That's the nightmare of Russian reality!"

A NANNY'S TALE ABOUT A MARE'S HEAD

"Well, and what is your opinion about coeducation?" I asked my neighbor at five o'clock tea.

"How can I explain it to you! . . . If it were a question of my own education, then, of course, I would be entirely on the side of the new trends. Ah, it would have been such fun! Small romances . . . Scenes of jealousy over penmanship lessons, trifling instances of selfless cheating . . . Yes, it's very enticing! But for my own daughters I would have preferred education according to the old method. It's somehow more peaceful! And you know, it seems to me that it would be somewhat unpleasant to meet, in public, a gentleman who once conjugated with you: *'Nous avons, vous avons, ils avons'* . . . or something even worse than that! Such memories quite dampen one's ardor."

"This is all nonsense!" the mistress of the house interrupted. "That's not the point! The main point which parents and educators should focus their attention upon is the development of fantasy in children."

"Really?" the host said in amazement and formed his lips, apparently intending to make a quip.

"*Finissez!* We don't need any foreign nurses and governesses! None at all. Our children need the Russian nanny. The simple Russian nanny — the inspiration of poets. That is, above all else, what all Russian mothers must see to."

"*Pardon!*" my neighbor interjected. "You said something about poets . . . I didn't quite understand."

"I said that Russian literature is greatly indebted to the nanny. Yes! The simple Russian nanny! Our best poet, Pushkin, according to his own admission, was in his best works inspired by his nanny. Remember how Pushkin spoke of her: 'Decrepit old dove of mine . . . decrepit old dove of mine . . . my treasures are hidden in your depths . . .'"

"*Pardon,*" a young man interrupted, having raised his head slightly from the sugar bowl, "it's as if he were referring to an inkwell . . ."

"What nonsense! Can an inkwell nurse? And all these marvelous works! *Ruslan and Ludmila, Evgeny Onegin*—just think that his nanny taught him all of that!"

"Is it possible, even *Evgeny Onegin?*" my neighbor expressed her doubts.

"Remarkable!" the master of the house said in reverie, "such marvelous music . . . And it was all done by the nanny!"

"*Finissez!* Only now, since I've engaged a dear old lady for my children, do I feel at peace with myself. Every evening she tells the children her charming fairy tales."

"Yes, but on the other hand overindulging in fantasy is also harmful!" my neighbor noted. "I knew a dentist . . . He imagined so frightfully much about himself . . . That is, that's not what I wanted to say . . ."

She blushed slightly and fell silent.

"And how much trouble we had with those foreign governesses! At first there was a Swiss one. My God, how she tortured us! To this day Ivan Andreich can't think of her without shuddering. Imagine, do you know what she harassed us with? Tidiness! Every morning she cleaned all the windows with a toothbrush. The procedures she instituted were absolutely extraordinary! She insisted on dinner at three o'clock, and she expressly forbade supper. Ivan Andreich began to go to the club, while I would run on the sly to the Fillipov pastry shop to eat their little tarts. Looking back on it now, I positively cannot understand how she held such power over us. We simply didn't dare make a peep!"

"They say there are certain fluids . . ." interjected the master, having assumed an intelligent expression.

"*Finissez!* Finally we managed to free ourselves of her. I took on a German woman. Everything was going quite well, although she strongly resembled a horse. You'd send her to take a walk with the children, and from a distance it seemed as if the children were riding in a cab. I don't know; it could be that it didn't seem so to others, but at least to me it seemed that way. Everyone's entitled to his own opinion; all the more, I—their mother."

We didn't argue, and she continued.

"Once, when I came into the nursery, I noticed—Nadya and Lesya were rocking their dolls to sleep and singing some kind of little German tune. At first I was actually happy—a success in the German language! But then, as I listened—Lord, what was that! I couldn't believe my own ears: '*Wilhelm schlief bei seiner neuen*

Liebe!'—they drawled with their thin little voices. I almost went right out of my mind."

The housemaid walked into the room and reported something to the mistress of the house.

"A-a! How excellent! It's now six o'clock, and nanny will begin telling the children her tale. If you wish, ladies and gentlemen, to admire this little scene in the genre of . . . in the genre of . . . what's it called? They were two brothers . . ."

"Karl and Franz Moor," whispered the young man.

"Yes," the mistress was about to agree, but just then she recalled. "Oh, no, the family name began with D . . ."

"Was it Reshke, perhaps?" the husband suggested.

"*Finissez!* In the genre . . . in the genre of Makovsky."

"Exactly—a little scene in the genre of Makovsky. I always surround it with such fantasy. We light the little icon lamp, nanny sits down on the carpet, the children sit around her. *C'est poétique.* What do you say, shall we go?"

We agreed. The mistress led us to her husband's study and, quietly opening the door into the neighboring room, signaled us to be silent and attentive.

In the nursery it was almost totally dark. Only a green icon lamp burned. It was quiet. A rasping, old woman's voice broke through mumbling lips and in a drawling manner began:

"In a certain kingdom, but not in our state, there once lived an old man with an old woman. The old couple was very old and had no children.

"The old man grieved, he did, and then went to the forest to chop firewood.

"He chopped and chopped. Suddenly from out of nowhere there rolled out of the forest a mare's head.

"'Hello, daddy!' it says.

"The peasant got frightened, but then saw there was nothin' he could do.

"'You, mare's head, how can I be a daddy to you?' he says.

"'Why by takin' me to live in your hut.'

"The peasant grieved, he did, but then saw there was nothin' he could do. He took the mare's head home with him.

"The mare's head rolled under a bench; for three years it lived, drank, ate, and called the peasant 'daddy.'

"The third year, the mare's head rolled out from under the bench and says to the peasant:

"'Daddy, hey daddy, I want to get married!'

"The peasant got frightened, but there was nothin' he could do.

"'Well mare's head, who do you want to marry?' he asks.

"So the head answers, 'Go to the palace and propose to the tsar's daughter for me.'

"The peasant grieved, he did, but there was nothin' he could do. He went to the palace.

"And in the palace lived the tsar's daughter. A beauty among beauties. She's got a sharp little nose, but her eyes is tiny, like they was cut with a sickle.

"She lives richer than the richest.

"She's got everything her little heart could wish for. She drinks champagne, she eats olive oil, and nibbles on honey cakes. Her dress is trimmed with three flounces and velveteen.

"In the palace, the rooms is so huge not even a pen could describe 'em. The tsar himself has to ride from chair to chair in a troika.

"There's heaps of servants in the palace. In every corner five hundred people pass the night.

"The old man started to propose to the tsar's daughter for the mare's head.

"The tsar grieved, he did, but he saw there was nothin' he could do. He gave away his daughter to the mare's head.

"The wedding began; there was a devil of a feast. The tsar served up pickled food, and soaked food, and roasted food, and boiled food, and from off his own royal back he gave the old man spankin' new bast shoes and the crust of a pie.

"The old man went back to his old woman. They began to live happily and even had children. Honey dripped down his whiskers, but none got into his mouth!"

"*C'est fantastique!*" the young man grunted, covering his mouth with his hand.

"Sh-sh-sh! *Revenons* back into the living room!"

HUMOROUS TALES

BOOK II

DOG DAYS

The earth turns slowly, yet however much you linger and however much you procrastinate, you still won't escape fate, and every
year, at the designated hour, the time comes for our unlucky planet
to enter the constellation of Canis Major.

In my opinion, even Canis Minor would be entirely enough for
us to cope with; but, I repeat, you won't escape fate.

Thus begin for poor humanity the most ludicrous days of the
entire year, the so-called *kanikuly* [Russian word for holidays],
from the Latin expression *dies caniculares*, or, simply translated,
Dog Days.

The influence of the Great Dog is evident in literally everything:
in repertoires, in restaurant menus, in pictures, in trains, in hous-
ing repairs, in cabbies, in freckles, in salesmen, in one's health,
and in hats.

The Dog leaves his mark on everything.

If you see a lady wearing, in place of a hat, a spacious accom-
modation for poultry and garden produce—don't judge her too
harshly. She isn't to blame. This rooster with its entire household
and fourteen turnips, among which there are two tomatoes sea-
soned with carrot tops—the Dog stuck this together for her. She
isn't guilty—believe me!

And take the Dog Day salesman, for instance!

Ask him to give you a spool of black thread, the simplest black
thread, and he'll assume a pensive expression, crawl up somewhere way on top, stand *à la* the Colossus of Rhodes with one leg
on the shelf of goods, the other on the counter, at which point he
steps on your finger (take your hands away!) and, only after he's hit
you on the head with a hatbox which fell off the shelf, will he
present you—in a very dignified manner—with a bolt of blue
velvet.

"I don't need blue velvet," you'll say meekly. "I asked for a spool
of black thread. Plain No. 60."

"Excuse me, Ma'am. It certainly is blue, isn't it?" And the apologetic salesman will then crawl somewhere below, under the counter—so deep that for a few moments only the lower edge of his jacket is visible. When, prompted by a natural curiosity, you lean down to see what he's doing there, he'll suddenly stand up and shove a box right into your cheek.

In the box there'll be ribbons and lace, which he'll magnanimously present to you for your selection, promising to give a discount.

Finding out that you still persist in your desire to purchase a spool of black thread, he'll become very upset and, after diving under the counter, he'll vanish into a nearby closet. That'll be the last of him! However long you might wait, he won't return.

You'll go to another store and ask for pink veil. It's possible that the Dog has so confused things by now that you might inadvertently succeed in purchasing your spool of thread, too. There's no other way to get it.

On the trains, the Dog's power is felt in the scheduling of certain local and express trains—scheduling in which there's neither rhyme nor reason; they amble along haphazardly, without definite rates of speed or direction.

You board such a train and think: "Where are you carrying me, my dear fellow?"

To ask would indeed be frightening. And to what purpose?

You'll only put the conductor in an uncomfortable position.

But what is most amazing of all about the trains is the fervor of their whimsicality. The train might suddenly stop at some small station and not budge an inch one way or the other! It'll just stand there for two hours.

The passengers will become nervous. Imaginations will begin to work.

"Why are we standing still? Probably ran over a peasant woman."

"Not a peasant woman—a heifer. It was yesterday that they ran over a peasant woman here—they don't run over peasant women every day. It's probably a heifer today."

"Oh, they wouldn't stop because of a heifer!"

"Of course they'd stop. They'd have to pull the wheels out of her."

"The conductor simply went to have tea and that's why we're standing still," some skeptic will interject.

"Went to drink tea, indeed! Someone wants to rob us, that's it. Most likely they're cleaning out the first car right now, and they'll eventually get to us, too. The situation is clear—we're being robbed."

But the train will begin to move just as unexpectedly as it had stopped, and for a while everyone will be annoyed that no sort of abomination had occurred.

Yet why had they stopped?

Of course the conductor, a not-quite-literate man who has nothing in common with the Pulkovsky Observatory, couldn't explain to you that all this had been the trick of the Great and nasty Dog.

Under the influence of this same Dog, a restlessness overtakes people. They travel, not knowing themselves where or why. They're not looking for a cooler place, since many, for example, like to visit Berlin in the summer. And it's generally known that they have such heat waves there that even a horse wouldn't show his nose on the street without a hat for any amount of money, and every respectable cow there has a parasol.

Everyone escapes from his long-occupied abode, leaving the apartment to be watched over by some good-natured grandmother of the aunt of the cook twice-removed. During the day these old women air out the rooms and hang their pockmarked noses out the little windows. Booming across the emptied courtyard, reverberating from the high walls, their lively, thrilling conversations echo and re-echo.

"Marfa-a!" a nose croaks from the casement window of the second floor. "Marfa-a!"

"A-a-a!" booms and reverberates against all the walls.

"Who-o-o-o?" a nose, stuck out a window on the second floor, squeaks.

"O-o-o!" the courtyard answers.

"The tub got cracked at Potapovna's!"

"A-a-a!"

"Got smacked?" the nose from the second floor squeaks.

"Got cracked! The tub got cracked at Potapovna's!"

"A-a-a!"

"A pup?"

"Tub! Tu-ub-b!"

"U-u-u-b-b!"

"At the Protasovs'?"

"At Potapovna's! The tub at Pota . . ."

Close the window, die like flies in the oppressive air, just don't listen to how the little old women talk.

They're under the special protection of the Great Dog.

At night, by the way, they kill these little old women and plunder the apartments.

The burglars firmly believe that these old folks are left specifically for their convenience. If not, there wouldn't be anyone to open the doors for them. To have to break the entrance latches, locks, and bolts all by themselves would be very troublesome, awkward; especially since it would be difficult not to make noise. But a dear godly old woman like one of these—she's not just a person, she's gold—she'd open up and let you in.

The Great Dog only rejoices. What's it to him!

But of all the Dog's scourges, worst of all, naturally, is the sun.

I won't argue that several years ago the sun was very much in vogue. Its name was written in capital letters; poets dedicated verses to it, in which they glorified its various winsome qualities and good deeds.

I, I must confess, never followed this trend.

"Let us be like the sun!"

No, thank you! That means—get up at five o'clock in the morning!

That's not for me!

The sun, if one discusses it calmly and dispassionately, is the most intolerable creature in all the universe. Of course, it is good that it helps cucumbers grow and so forth. Yet it would be better if humanity could find the means to get along with its own measures, warming and lighting its earth and growing on it what is needed, without any outside help.

The sun is intolerable!

Imagine a being with a round red mug, daily rising even before the break of day, and scoffing at you all day long.

It creates such a steamy heat that you can't breathe. It plops brownish blotches onto your cheeks; it peels the skin off your nose.

All around, wherever you look, it breeds flies and mosquitoes. What else could be worse! Yet people dote on it.

"Ah, sunrise, sunset!"

"Ah, dusk, dawn!"

You'd think it was an amazing trick—that the sun set! Any other person could get up and sit down over two hundred times a day, yet no one would ever be moved by it.

People grovel because of their gains and profits. They lickspittle to the sun because it grows their cucumbers.

It's a shame!

You live and don't notice anything around you. Then, when the Dog Days suddenly begin, the sun cooks you, fries you, it even burns you on your sides—and then you start to think more seriously about the entire situation.

Oh, believe me, I'm not making a fuss or rebelling against the sun because of any sort of freckles! No, I'm above that; besides, there are veils to prevent freckles. I simply do not want, merely on account of material profit (from the cucumber), to cringe before that banal, red physiognomy which looms up there, high above us!

Come to your senses, ladies and gentlemen! Look at yourselves! It's shameful! Huh?

ALL ABOUT LOVE

A PSYCHOLOGICAL FACT

It seems to me that I am a ruined man.

I'm convinced that nothing will help me, no sort of medicinal drops, not even a short leave of absence and a trip to the south.

I've gotten off the track. I have been drinking for four days, and yet I'm not a drunkard. I would venture to say I behave myself as a gentleman, and certainly cause no scandal, though things are not far from that stage now.

But how did all of this happen, and why? It's as though I've lost my identity.

What sort of person am I?

Here I shall take an objective look at myself.

Am I normal? Of course I'm normal. Even more than normal. I've always conducted myself exceedingly well. Whenever I have been insulted, I've not only not brawled, but, like a thorough gentleman, I've only smiled in response.

I am kind. For example, I gave Penin fifteen francs, knowing that this would not be repaid, and I don't even reproach him.

I am not envious. If someone is lucky—the devil with him, let him be lucky; I don't care.

I love reading. I am intelligent. I had a subscription to *The Field* in 1892 and read it with enthusiasm.

My physical appearance is pleasant. I have a full, calm face.

I am employed.

In a word, I—am a dignified human being.

What has happened to me? Why do I want to crow like a rooster and guzzle vodka? Of course, this will pass. But what, exactly, has happened? I can't even tell anyone about it. It's a sort of psychological state that's had me shaking for four days. Yet when you think about it, especially if you begin to talk about it, there isn't any real tragedy involved. Why, then, have I lapsed into such a condition? What is the cause of this psychological fact?

Now we will calmly discuss her. I mean, very calmly. And we will observe her as would an outsider, just as we have looked at me.

A stranger would notice, first of all, that she is terribly tall. As we used to say in Russian, "She's so tall you could hang a cow on her." It's an expression of folk wisdom; although where would such a situation occur that it would be necessary to hang cows? Under what circumstances are they hung? Well, enough. I don't want to waste time on difficult and confusing considerations.

And so—she is tall and clumsy. Her arms dangle. She walks like a duck. Remarkable legs—the higher you go, the thinner they are.

She never laughs. It's a strange thing but, only now, at the finale of our relationship, have I become aware of this fact. It wasn't that I didn't notice before (how can you not notice?), but it was as if I didn't understand.

Next, it is necessary to note that she is not beautiful. This is not just according to a particular taste. According to any and all tastes. Her face has an offended, dissatisfied expression.

But the main thing is—she is a fool. You simply can't argue with this. This point is obvious and definite.

Just imagine—even this wasn't clear to me immediately. Now it seems to hit you right in the eye—yet for some reason it evaded my instantaneous identification, and that's all there was to it. Perhaps it's because, not foreseeing the subsequent events, I did not dwell on her personality.

Now we shall commence with the main narrative.

I met her at the Efimovs' (they've always played all sorts of dirty tricks on me). She arrived and at once asked what time it was. They answered that it was ten. Then she said: "Well, in that case I can spend exactly half an hour with you, because at exactly nine-thirty I have to be in a certain place."

To this Efimov, laughing, replied that there was no use in hurrying, since nine-thirty had already passed half an hour ago.

She then stated, in an offended tone, that there would be a big difference in whether she was late two hours or three.

Efimov again laughed.

"Well, then," he said, "according to you, for example, to be late five minutes for the train, is much better than half an hour."

She was quite amazed.

"Well, of course."

At that time I still didn't realize that she was a fool; I thought she was joking.

It then turned out that I had to walk her home.

On the way, it came out that her name was Raisa Konstantinovna, that her husband was a chauffeur, and that she was a waitress in a restaurant.

"My family life is ideal," she said. "My husband is a night chauffeur. I come home—he's already gone, and when he returns, I'm already gone. Never any quarrels. Everything's perfect bliss."

I thought she was being sarcastic. No; her face was serious. She meant what she had said.

In order to say something, I asked if she liked the cinema.

She answered: "Very well. Why don't you come to get me, say, on Thursday?"

Well, what was I to do? I couldn't tell her that I hadn't invited her. It would have been impolite.

So I went.

And that's how it began.

See for yourself what strange things happen in this world!

I was walking her home, arm in arm.

"You're so charming," I said.

Well, you know, one has to say something.

And she answered: "I guessed it long ago."

"What?" I asked in amazement.

"That you love me." [Using the familiar form of "you."]

She blurted it out. I actually stopped dead in my tracks.

"Who?" I said. "That is, whom?" I said. "In a word, what?"

And she, in the same haughty manner, continued: "It's not necessary to get so excited. You're not the first, you're not the last, and love, in general, is a quite natural phenomenon."

My eyes bulged out. I was silent. And note, even at that point I still didn't understand that she was a fool.

She, in the meantime, developed her thought even further, and in the most unexpected direction, but with extraordinary seriousness.

"We," she said, "won't tell my husband anything. That can be done later, when your fateful emotion takes on a more definite form. This is important. Do you agree?"

I gripped my head with both hands: "Indeed, indeed. Under no circumstances in the world should we tell him."

"Meanwhile, I will be an inaccessible vision for you. I will mend your underwear, read verses with you. Do you like cottage cheese pancakes? Sometime I'll make cottage cheese pancakes for you. Our affair must be like a golden dream."

And I kept saying: "Exactly, exactly."

Frankly speaking, this idea of hers concerning darning flashed me its smile, so to speak. I'm a disorderly bachelor and a damsel who is immediately willing to display her feminine solicitude is an extreme rarity in our age. Of course, in her state of exaltation, she somewhat misinterpreted my compliment; but once it had produced such wonderful results, such as putting my wardrobe in order, then one could only rejoice and be grateful to fate. Of course, she was not attractive to me, but (again—what folk wisdom!) one neither drinks water from the face nor, all the more, from the figure.

When saying good-bye, I kissed both her hands. And then, at night, reviewing the entire adventure, I even smiled to myself. In my lonely life I could only welcome the appearance of such a wonderful woman. I even remembered her cottage cheese pancakes. Not too bad. Not too bad at all.

So I decided that everything was pretty good and I calmed down.

The following day I came home from work, opened the door, and saw her sitting in my room. She had brought some dried biscuits.

She said, "I thought about us and decided to use the familiar form of 'you' between us."

"For goodness sake, I'm not worthy."

"I permit you."

What the devil! I didn't want to at all!

I persisted. "I'm not worthy. Period."

But she kept on talking about the most unrelated topics. And they were all such strange things.

She said, "I know that you are suffering. But suffering ennobles. So look upon me as a higher creation, as your unreachable ideal. We do not need crude passions, we are not cannibals. A poet once said, 'Only the morning of love is beautiful.' Look, I brought some dried biscuits. Of course, the French don't have dried biscuits like we used to—Chuyev dried biscuits. They have rubbish, and don't even know it. You know, above everything else I value the fact that you are a Russian. The French are simply not meant for lofty feelings. A Frenchman, if he marries at all, does so only for two years, and later, 'betrayal and divorce.'"

"What's the matter with you? Where did you get such an idea? I myself know many honorable husbands among the French."

"Well, they're exceptions. If they haven't separated from their wives, it simply means that they like to have company when they hoard their money. Have they really any higher needs at all? Everything is unnatural with them. Flowers aren't natural, cucumbers are the size of logs, and they have simply no concept of dill. And wine! No amount of money will get you a natural wine from them. All their wines are fake."

"What are you saying!" I yelled. "France is praised all over the world for its wine. France has the best wine in the world."

"Ah, how naïve you are! That's all fake."

"Where did you get these strange notions?"

"A certain person explained all of this to me."

"A Frenchman?"

"No, in no way a Frenchman. A Russian."

"Where does he know this from?"

"Oh, he knows all right."

"What does he do, work at a winery or something?"

"No, not at a winery. He lives with us at Beaurieres."

"Then how can he judge?"

"And why can't he judge? He has been in Paris for four years. He is very observant. It isn't as easy to deceive everyone as it is, for example, you."

At that moment I began to tremble all over. However, controlling myself, I said in the most polite tone: "He is simply a blockhead, that Russian of yours."

"Well, if it pleases you to degrade one of your own kind . . ."

"I don't have to degrade him. He's a blockhead."

"Well, go on kissing your Frenchmen. I'll bet you even like their beef. But where among them can you find filet mignon? Where is the rump? Do they really have beef like ours? Their bulls don't even have the same parts as ours do. We had Circassian bulls. But they haven't the slightest notion about Circassian meat."

I didn't know exactly what her point was, but for some reason this made me terribly angry. I'm not a Frenchman and there was no reason for me to be offended, all the more because of beef, but somehow this upset me extremely.

"Excuse me, Raisa Konstantinovna, but I will not allow such statements about the country sheltering us. I consider this to be unkind of you and even ungrateful."

Yet she continued: "Go ahead and plead, plead their case! Can it be that you even like the fact that they don't have sour cream? Don't be ashamed, please, speak out. Does it please you? Are you ready to kneel before them? Are you happy to trample Russia?"

How loathesome she became, how drawn; her mouth so distorted, her face so pale!

"Trample, trample Russia!"

What happened to me at this point, I myself don't know. I just grabbed her by the shoulders and screamed with a bleating voice:

"Get out of here, du-u-mmy!"

I kept on yelling so loudly that the neighbors began to knock on the wall. I was completely shaken.

She was still on the stairs, screeching something about Russia. I didn't listen. I was trampling her dried biscuits. And I did the right thing, because if I had gone after her I would have finished her off. Because in me, at that moment, there lurked a murderer.

I was a hair's breadth away from the guillotine, for how can you explain a Russian dummy to a French jury?

They wouldn't be able to understand this. Indeed, they couldn't. Such knowledge has not been granted them.

TWO DIARIES

How interesting human documents are at times! Naturally I am not speaking about identity cards or passports and visas. I have in mind those documents which testify to the inner life of a person, known to no one—the diary which one keeps for oneself alone and carefully conceals from others.

Letters never reveal the human personality very precisely, for every letter is written with a very definite aim. It might be necessary, let us say, to move a benefactor to tears, or to put a supplicant in his place, or to express condolences which, like good wishes, are always couched in exaggerated tones. There are refined literary letters, there are even coquettish ones, and how many other kinds there are! They are all designed specifically to produce this or that impression.

The secret diary is quite a different matter. Almost everything in it is true and sincere. This is the unique characteristic of the secret diary, the sort not intended for publication, but quite the contrary, the kind which fears all types of public revelation. Come now, is it possible to consider the diary of Tolstoy a very trustworthy document when we know that Sofya Andreevna asked him to tone down and even delete certain entries?

A secret diary seldom falls into someone else's hands. But I was fortunate. I was so lucky that it is difficult to believe: I have in my hands not one diary, but two. They belong to the married couple Kashenev, Pyotr Evdokimych and Marya Nikolaevna. These diaries cover one and the same period of time, apparently the most vivid in their married life. Comparing the entries of these two diaries according to their dates, you get such a phenomenal picture that at times you simply want to shout, "The devil take you, you unhappy idiot, where are your eyes?" You'd like to shout many other things, too, but of course there wouldn't be much sense in these retrospective exclamations.

And so I offer for the reader's attention both diaries, arranged according to dates.

Of course, I have not presented all of the materials unedited— I took the liberty of omitting certain entries.

"5th of September. Bought on sale at Maison de Blanche a white collar for thirty francs. It turned out to be trash; good only for a cow to wear."

This was from the diary of Marya Nikolaevna. From the diary of Pyotr Evdokimych:

"2nd of October. Again I rubbed my foot where I have the crooked toe."

Many entries of this nature, since they do not form links in the general chain, were deliberately omitted by me.

Here are the diaries:

From the diary of Marya Nikolaevna Kashenev:

1st of November:

"I think that I will never forget yesterday evening. Those who saw me yesterday will never forget it either. Never was I ever so beautiful and so lively. My eyes sparkled like diamonds. I wore a green dress, which quite effectively brought out the whiteness of my shoulders and alabaster back. That nincompoop of mine, of course, was angry. He was envious that he couldn't display his shoulders. Now, that would have been a sight!

"Sergey did not once take his impassioned eyes off me. So as not to make that nincompoop of mine suspicious, I flirted with that idiot Gozhkin. I was marvelously beautiful. I was like a Bacchante. I ran up to the piano and sang 'I love you and crave your caresses.' I sang splendidly. My best proof was that Petrova and Kuzhina left immediately, while my nincompoop cast his raging eyes at me. Sergey Zapakin was as white as a sheet.

"I can imagine why Petrova and Kuzhina were angry. Yes, dears, it's difficult to compete with me. Especially since Kuzhina had struggled into a tight-fitting turquoise cossack dress. What a fool!

"Naturally, my nincompoop threw a fit. Did I howl with laughter!"

From the diary of Pyotr Evdokimych Kashenev:

1st of November:

"A terrible scandal took place. That big ninny of mine suddenly began to sing! It was so shameful that I will remember it until the last day of my life. I've been married to her for seventeen years and never imagined that she had such a horrible voice. And what's worse, she accompanied herself on the piano so disgustingly and out of tune. In my embarrassment, I didn't know where to look. The dear boy Sergey Zapakin was plainly suffering on my behalf. Gozhkin, on the other hand (obviously all of this was done precisely for him!), thanked her in the most impudent manner for 'the afforded pleasure.'

"How terrible!

"Petrova and Kuzhina, only God knows the quality of these dubious women, even they couldn't stand it, and jumped up and left.

"We have lived together for seventeen years. I've had to endure all sorts of disgraceful things; but that she would burst out singing in the eighteenth year of our marriage—this I could never have foreseen. No way. At this point, my imagination failed me.

"After the guests had left, naturally, an ugly scene broke out. She laughed brazenly, while I screamed like a martyr and even broke a milk jug."

From the diary of Marya Nikolaevna:

6th of November:

"Tomorrow is my birthday. I told this to Sergey. On this joyous day I should be with him.

"For some reason he became pensive. So the nincompoop won't suspect anything, I've also invited Gozhkin for tomorrow."

From the diary of Pyotr Evdokimych:

6th of November:

"What charming people still exist on this earth! Yesterday Sergey Zapakin appeared to be very worried for some reason. I pointed this out to him. The poor fellow, with tears in his eyes, admitted that he has an old mother in Belgium whom he is supporting as much as he is able. Now it is absolutely essential that he send her two hundred francs, though at present he doesn't have such an amount available, and this is tormenting him horribly. Of course, I immediately offered him this trifling amount. It was touching to see his gratitude."

From the diary of Marya Nikolaevna:

8th of November:

"Yesterday morning Sergey called. 'I would like to be the first to congratulate you. Excuse my modest gift—I sent you several chrysanthemums.'

"Within an hour they brought me an enormous basket of glorious, golden chrysanthemums. Such a basket must have cost no less than two hundred francs.

"My nincompoop fidgeted and fumbled through all of them, trying to find a card. Then he said, 'Nevertheless, I know that this is from Gozhkin. Your cunning won't save him. Today, I'm going to throw him down the stairs.'"

From the diary of Pyotr Evdokimych:

8th of November:

"Composure, composure, composure. I'll track Gozhkin down and finish him off."

From the diary of Marya Nikolaevna:

20th of November:

"I told Sergey, 'This deception has exhausted me. I want to be with you [using the familiar form], in your embrace, inseparable for the rest of our lives, for eternity.' 'Eternity?' he repeated. 'Why be so dismal? We could go for two days to St. Germain. Think up a good reason for your husband.'

"I told the nincompoop that Liza Khryabina has invited me to visit them in St. Cloud for about two days. She doesn't have a telephone, so it will be impossible to check up on me, and he himself won't appear unexpectedly, since he simply cannot stand the sight of Liza."

From the diary of Pyotr Evdokimych:

20th of November:

"Sergey Zapakin was here today. He came into the study to sit with me for a moment. Again he appeared very worried. I immediately sensed the problem. 'Well,' I said, 'has your dear old mother caused you a lot of trouble again?' He blushed a little. 'Why,' he said, 'do you say that . . .' But I reasoned with him. 'Why should you hide this from me?' I said. He became even more confused, but by then I said frankly, 'You probably need more money for your mother?' At this point he even chuckled, he was so touched by my perceptiveness. I gave him four hundred francs. In our times such a person is a rarity."

21st of November:

"My ninny expressed an unshakeable desire to go to another dummy in St. Cloud. Her nerves, can't you see, are all on edge. We know these nerves. I replied to her in my most naïve voice, 'Go, my beloved. I'll ask Andrey Gozhkin to come and have breakfast and dinner with me every day—it's so boring by oneself.' In response, she burst out in a most affected laugh. And it was exactly this laugh which gave her away. She wanted to hide her irritation, but instead her unnatural behavior only emphasized it. Now let her linger in St. Cloud. I purposely won't hurry her; I'll suggest that she stay there even longer. Ha-ha!"

From the diary of Marya Nikolaevna:

2nd of February:

"How strangely this nincompoop of mine is acting. He has some sort of unhealthy love for Gozhkin. He literally can't part with him. He barely catches sight of him and he's already dragging him along to the study, to smoke, or to play chess. On the other hand, he tries in every way possible to get Sergey to be around me. He asks him to take me to the theatre, to the movies, even to visit our friends. This is all very strange. Is he thinking of catching us by surprise? Not long ago he went to Rouen for two days and took Gozhkin with him. 'You,' he said, 'have never been there, you're a young man, you need to develop.' And he took him. It is becoming simply indecent. Of course, Gozhkin is very happy to travel at my nincompoop's expense."

From the diary of Pyotr Evdokimych:

2nd of February:

"Sergey Zapakin is a pleasant little fellow, but I find that his old hag is a little crazy. I'm beginning to have enough of his little old mother. Now she needs money for a holiday. Then for a doctor, then for a winter coat. Somehow it's become a habit that I help him . . . Nevertheless, on his part, this is touching. That dried-up Gozhkin doesn't think at all about old folks. Yet Zapakin has thoughts only of his old mother. A rare young man."

From the diary of Marya Nikolaevna:

20th of June. Vichy:

"I simply don't know how to explain this. Sergey doesn't answer my letters. He promised to come—he still hasn't. My nincompoop's lost his marbles completely. This spring he went with his Gozhkin to Corsica, and now he's sitting with him in Paris and doesn't answer my letters either. I'll simply go mad. But what's with Sergey?"

From the diary of Pyotr Evdokimych:

25th of June:

"How repulsed I am by the ugly mug of that idiot Gozhkin! Every day he eats dinner and then sits here the entire evening. But

I can't let him go—he'd make a run for Vichy. He's gorged himself on expensive foods like a hog, and is snoring in the armchair. He's drowning in his own fat. What indeed did she ever see in him?"

26th of June:

"An unusual event. Zapakin came, terribly disturbed. It turns out that the old woman needs an operation, and at once. As he spoke, he had tears in his eyes and his lips quivered. 'This,' he says, 'is the last time that I will run to you for help. In two weeks I am marrying a woman who is quite wealthy, but for now it's a secret.' Well, I congratulated him and gave him money for the operation. I said, 'Write me how well she recovers from the operation and whether she has suffered much.' He promised."

From the diary of Marya Nikolaevna:

28th of June:

"Oh my God, what I've lived through! Sergey came yesterday. It's all over. He's getting married."

From the diary of Pyotr Evdokimych:

1st of July:

"I received a telegram from my dear Sergey Zapakin. 'She went through it fine, didn't suffer much, died forever.' A strange telegram. I hope it won't be necessary to send him money for the burial."

2nd of July:

"Aha! A telegram from my better half: 'I'm in a terrible state, if you can't come yourself, send Gozhkin.'

"Aha! I've finally succeeded! She's screaming, the witch. So, I should give her Gozhkin! Well, now I'll deal with you. I'll be leaving this evening."

TWO ROMANCES WITH FOREIGNERS

It was a quiet evening.

Across the wall sped the lights of automobiles. Their horns blared, the streetcars clanged. Like a screeching owl, the bell of the neighboring movie theatre pierced the ear, announcing the next showing.

Nevertheless, for these two women, sitting with their feet propped on a small, wobbly ottoman, this evening was quiet. The day with all its anxieties and troubles had ended, and in these two or three hours before sleep one could allow oneself not to think about anything or worry.

On such a quiet evening the conversation usually revolves around intimate subjects. Walking around a half-dark room can be rather unpleasant; it's better just to sit quietly. In a relaxed position even one's thoughts become more settled, not jumping from one topic to another. The most habitual liars lose their inspiration, become more straightforward and sincere.

The young in such moments readily talk about death. Older people—about love. The very old—about various pleasant hopes.

Those two ladies who had their feet up on the wobbly little ottoman were no longer in their first blush of youth and, therefore, talked about love.

"No, everything is finished for me now," one said.

Had it been lighter in the apartment, we would have seen that she had a very tired face, dull eyes, and that she was wrapped in a fluffy shawl, which was always the tiniest bit torn at the shoulder yet was comfortable and smelled of perfume and cigarettes; in short, the traditional shawl of a doleful Russian woman!

"Don't exaggerate, Natasha," answered the other one. "You're still young. Who knows?"

"Young?" Natasha said with a slight, bitter laugh. "No, my dear, after what I've lived through, I feel seventy. It's my own fault. I didn't have to betray the memory of Grisha."

"And how many years had you been married to Grisha?"

"Years? Years! Five weeks. We met right before the evacuation. And got married right away. Within five weeks he went to the front. We never met again. He was very nice."

"Well, for only five weeks anyone would fill the bill."

"I d-don't know. I d-don't think . . ." Natasha said in an offended tone.

"Speaking of that, what finally happened between you and your fiancé? I simply don't know a thing about it. When he was courting you, we didn't see much of each other. And then I heard—the engagement was broken. What, did he stop loving you?"

"No, no. He said that he hadn't stopped loving me. His parents didn't allow it. However, it's a very complicated story," sighed Natasha.

"My story was also very complicated, but I'm not sighing, I'm laughing. Did you try to shoot yourself? Poison yourself?"

"No, what are you saying! What a sin!"

"There, you see! And yet you're the one who's sighing. As for me, I actually tried to poison myself, and whenever I remember that, I can't help laughing. How marvelous, how absolutely marvelous!"

"What's so marvelous about trying to poison yourself?"

"Of course, there's not much that's marvelous about that! It made me terribly nauseated. But it was precisely because I tried to poison myself that everything turned out so ridiculous. But I'll tell you all about it later. You tell your story first."

"Fine. Only, where to begin . . . Well, as you already know, I was working at a millinery shop and became acquainted with Madame Rougeaud, with Marie. She was very sweet. We became good friends and decided to open a store together. Her husband was very pleasant, an engineer. Our business went rather well. Marie and I were simply inseparable. During the day we were at the workshop and our small store, in the evening at the cinema or playing cards. I even dined with them so I wouldn't have to prepare my own meals. Frequently a fellow employee of Mr. Rougeaud's would visit their place—a Mr. Emile. To make a long story short, Emile fell head over heels in love with me. At first he didn't appear very attractive to me; he seemed such an empty, banal type. But then, little by little, he began to interest me. We saw each other almost every day, and so persistently, so ardently, and so rapturously did he express his love in every way possible, that I unwittingly began to pay much more attention to him."

"That's it, that's it, that's it! Exactly! Exactly!" interrupted the listener.

"What 'exactly'?" the narrator asked with amazement.

"Nothing, it wasn't anything important. I was just commenting."

"Well, that's how I became more attentive toward him. At this point Marie began to pour oil on the flame: '*Pauvre* Emile! He's dying, they say; *pauvre* Emile! Such a wonderful man and well to do, and you're lonely, who will take care of you? Marry *pauvre* Emile.' Every evening after dinner Emile persisted in demanding marriage. His persistence began to touch me. I began to like him."

"That's it, that's it!" interrupted the listener.

"What is this 'that's it'? Why do you keep screeching?"

"Nothing, it's not important . . . I was just commenting."

"Marie's husband was also trying to talk me into marriage. And, imagine, I began to notice that this same Emile was becoming quite pleasing to me. But, anyway, I still couldn't decide whether to marry him or not. I wanted to test myself and him. Or rather, only myself, because doubting him would have been simply ridiculous. He was suffering and yet blissfully happy at the same time, and the devil knows what else—some sort of concoction of Romeo and Juliet. I tormented him for a long time, but finally I said: 'I think there's a possibility I could take a liking to you!' He—you cannot imagine—actually cried. In his ecstasy he flung himself to kiss Marie. Since he didn't dare kiss me, he kissed her. It was comical and touching at the same time. And right there he decided to invite his parents to Paris, so that they could meet me. Marie's husband explained to me that his parents were wealthy and he wanted to marry expressly with their consent."

"They always drag their parents in!" interrupted the listener, immediately adding, "It's not important, I was just commenting."

"Emile's parents proved to be so very charming, somehow so old-fashioned, so touching, especially the mother. She adored me immediately. We spent entire days together. Either she was with us in our small store or I was at her place. She was so sincere, so sensitive, she understood everything. She was pleased that I hadn't immediately said yes to Emile, that I wanted first to test myself and him. In a word, she was such a dear that I simply fell in love with her and even wept with emotion when she was leaving. We weren't parting for long, though—she promised to come in one month for the wedding. My Emile was jubilant; he beamed, and simply exuded ecstasy. My dear friends, the Rougeauds, were extremely happy for us. Marie was helping me with wedding plans, making gifts, and was happy because of my happiness.

"Suddenly one day, on one accursed, beautiful day, I was sitting with Mr. Rougeaud, awaiting Marie for breakfast. I stepped into her bedroom to powder my face and there I saw, on the table, a little box. The box was partially open and a letter was sticking out of it. The paper was blue, like the kind that Emile used. The handwriting was also like Emile's. I involuntarily glanced at it and saw—it definitely was his handwriting. Of course, this didn't surprise me because they were old acquaintances; why shouldn't he write to her? But as luck would have it, on the part which was distinctly visible to me, was my name: 'Poor little Natasha . . .' I read; and my interest was piqued. Why am I suddenly 'poor'? Curiosity destroyed Eve. I pulled up the letter by its corner, took it out, and read it. At first, just that one phrase 'poor little Natasha,' then the whole letter. The content of the letter was such that no doubts whatsoever could have remained. This same *pauvre* Emile, my happy and madly enamored fiancé, had just developed with my dearest friend Marie a small but unmistakable romance under my very nose. The romance was still in its first bloom; it had only existed for about ten days.

"'Take care,' begged my affectionate fiancé, 'so that poor little Natasha, whom I love so, won't be hurt by our affair.'

"This was all so unexpected, so wild, that I . . . I don't know what happened to me. I fainted. How long I was unconscious—I don't know, but when I opened my eyes, there I saw Mr. Rougeaud standing next to me and reading that same cursed letter with great interest. I wanted to get up—but I couldn't. My legs simply wouldn't obey me.

"He read it, then shook his head.

"'My dear,' he said, 'how you've frightened me. Do you often faint?'

"I screamed, 'Give it back, give me back the letter! Don't you dare read it!'

"He raised his eyebrows in surprise:

"'Is this the reason, this trifle, for your fainting?'

"He embraced me, helped me up, sat me on the sofa, stroked my hair, and kissed me. I was crying my heart out. How could I go on living? Everything had been destroyed.

"He just laughed.

"'This is nonsense,' he said, 'Fume a little, it's healthy, and then forget it.'

"Indignantly, I replied: 'You've got some nerve to say that! He deceived me with your . . . your own wife!'

"But he just waved his hand.

"'Well, so all the better. He deceived you with my wife, so you deceive him with me. Then everyone will be happy.'

"At this point I began to scream—in complete hysterics! And I ran.

"I locked myself in at home and didn't go out for a whole week. I wrote letters to them all. I called off the wedding with Emile, wrote a reproach to Marie, and curses to Rougeaud. But the main letter went to the old woman, Emile's mother. I explained everything to her and sincerely and touchingly said good-bye to her. I never received an answer from her.

"Nonetheless, after a week I had to go to our store. I couldn't stay away any longer. It was, after all, my business, too. My meeting with Marie was awkward. She sneered at me slightly, as if I had made a fool of myself. Gradually she started talking to me. She mentioned in passing that Emile wanted to shoot himself, that in general sensible women do not behave that way, that one shouldn't faint with a compromising letter in one's hands, that such a thing was even indecent; but that she continued to love me and had, therefore, forgiven me all the annoyances which I had caused her. She added however, that after my (my!) horrible behavior, our former friendship could not continue. Then Emile appeared. He sobbed, beat his head against the wall—at first, the back of his head, then his forehead. I was implacable. But, alas, not for long. He somehow managed to convince me. I forgave him. Everything seemed as if it was beginning to return to normal, but then a letter arrived from his mother. The letter was addressed to him, because she had nothing to discuss with a woman like me.

"In the letter to her son she categorically forbade him to marry me, because if I was capable of making such a fuss over mere trifles then what would happen later? What sort of life would it be? 'She would always be fainting and compromising her friends—women respected by society.'

"Emile was very sad. He said that he would be counting on the mollifying influences of time. Mother would reconsider. But while mother was reconsidering, he married someone else."

"Is that all?" asked the listener. "Well, my romance was much more amusing. I'll tell it to you. I'll tell it, only at this point it all seems so stupid. If it were light in the room, I'd actually be embarrassed to face you."

"Don't be silly. We're old friends. I won't turn the light on. Let's sit in the dark a little longer. Well? Who was your romance with? Also a Frenchman?"

"No. You'll never guess. With a Rumanian!"

"Well, how did you manage that one? Did you really fall in love with him?"

"And how! Simply a tragedy. Ha-ha-ha!"

"A tragedy, yet you're laughing," her friend remarked in amazement. "Or are you hysterical?"

"Ah, my dear, if you only knew how funny it was! I tried to poison myself."

"What's so funny about that?"

If there were light in the room, we would have seen that the one who tried to poison herself was a chubby brunette with lively, black, prominent eyes, and tidy curls, in an inexpensive but fashionable little dress, her face made up, her eyebrows plucked, her hair arranged nicely; she looked calm and content. You'd look at her and think: She's lying. Such people don't poison themselves.

"What's so funny about that?" her friend continued, still amazed. "If you poisoned yourself, obviously you must have suffered."

"And how! Ha-ha-ha! What makes it even funnier is that I did suffer."

"Well, tell me about it. We'll have a laugh together," the friend said ironically.

"Well, my dear. I was working at that time at the beauty parlor of Madame Ferflukh [intentionally misspelled "Accursed" in German]. We were fairly successful. You know that this is a very psychological business. You think you just apply some cream, rub it in, and there it is—finished. No, my dear, it is much more than that. Especially if a customer is advanced in age and has had various disappointments in love. In such cases an intimate conversation is a must. While you're plucking her eyebrows, you may remain silent because it's painful for her, and she's probably groaning. When you clean her pores, this moment is also not suitable for such a conversation. It is, so to speak, almost a medical operation in itself. But when you reach the make-up stage—the creams, colors, rouges, powders; here every woman's soul opens itself. Why this is so—frankly speaking—I can't explain, but it is a fact—and you can verify this with any facial masseuse. Sometimes I'm absolutely amazed at what they, these customers, say! You'd think that even under torture one wouldn't reveal such things. If I were to jot everything down, there easily would be enough romances for several volumes. And what romances!

"So, I had this customer, a rather silent one. I regret to say that I thought she was quiet simply because of her age.

"The old woman was small, slender, with a sharp little nose, cheeks pulled up and sewed to her temples, and the skin from under her chin pinned behind her ears. She was a good customer, not stingy with tips. When the sitting was finished, her servant would come and wrap her up in her fur coat and carry her in his arms to the car. Exactly, in his arms. She was usually so tired. Several times it happened that she would be lying before me, while I was attaching her eyelashes, and she'd open her mouth—a black, ghastly mouth, with the skin stretched tightly across her cheeks—and start to snore. She would fall asleep from fatigue. She led a very exhausting life. Visits, fittings, *premières*, teas, dinners, concerts, sports. Yes, yes—sports. She went to play golf. Just think of it! At her age and to take such torment upon herself!

"Once she appeared to be in quite a special frame of mind. She seemed sort of wound tight like a spring; she smiled and was very coquettish. She ordered all sorts of creams and rouges—she was going to America.

"Then suddenly, completely unexpectedly, she grabbed me by the hand.

"'Dearest!' she said, 'If only you knew how much I don't want to leave! Especially now. But my husband demands that I come at once. Some business or other. It's probably all nonsense. But right now I'd really like to stay here. Do you understand me?'

"Well, of course, one is always supposed to understand such a client.

"I sighed and said: 'Oh, how I understand!'

"But what there was to understand, for the life of me I didn't know.

"And she actually began to tremble.

"'I,' she said, 'met him two days ago and decided to ask him to handle my local affairs. Ah, if you knew! If you only knew! He isn't some young dance-hall gigolo. He's nobility itself. Such wisdom! Such heart! Such lovely dark hair! I hadn't even managed to settle his duties with him—and now I have to drop everything and rush off. But I'll return, I'll return soon.'

"She didn't get a chance to finish pouring out her heart to me, since they knocked on the door of our booth with the message that a certain Mr. Pierre wanted to see my client.

"She could barely breathe.

"'It's him!' she whispered, 'it's him!'

"A young man entered the room, quite handsome, only somehow too *comme il faut*. Do you understand? Too fair, too rosy, crimson lips, hair so black as to be almost navy, brows rounded—like something right out of a Ukrainian painting. But nevertheless handsome. Terribly polite. He brought the old woman tickets from some other lady. He'd gone to my client's place, found out that she was here, and since the matter was urgent took the liberty of coming, and so on.

"My old woman began to quiver violently.

"He grabbed her by the arm and whirled her away.

"So, let him whirl her away—what's it to me?

"But then, about two days later, this same Pierre reappeared and came straight to me. He very politely excused himself and asked whether Madame Wood happened to forget her gloves here?

"'You mean,' I asked, 'that she hasn't left yet?'

"'No,' he answered, 'she left the next morning, but, you see, she charged me with finding her gloves.' I told the *chasseur* to look around and ask at the cash register.

"But Mr. Pierre kept on looking at me and smiling so strangely.

"'You're probably terribly bored working here, considering your exceptional appearance.'

"I assumed a dignified air. I answered, 'Not a bit. I love to work.'

"But he continued: 'Confronted with the constant fatigue of others, it's absolutely a must that you have some diversion, otherwise you might simply strain your nerves. Perhaps,' he went on, 'you'll allow me to take you to the cinema?'

"I agreed, still, however, with great dignity.

"He became terribly happy and shouted to the *chasseur:* 'Don't look for the gloves, I've already found them.'

"At this point I realized that he had invented all of this in order to see me.

"I confess—this really intrigued me. Here, I thought, is a person who frequents fine American circles, and suddenly he reacts to my appearance so strongly.

"Well, things followed their usual course.

"He came to my place often. And the usual, 'Do you love me, do you really love me?' was heard over and over.

"I remained, in our Russian manner, full of ambiguities: neither yes, nor no, even if you drop dead.

"He was completely exhausted.

"'Elena,' he said, 'you're a saint. You're St. Elena, and I shall perish like Bonaparte.'

"For about two months I led him on. Finally I said: 'Rather yes than no.'

"Of course, he was beside himself.

"'In that case,' he said, 'let me bring some pastries.'

"He did bring some, but, in his absentmindedness, ate them all himself.

"By the way, I found out that his name—it's hard to believe!—was Cock-a-doodle-doo. Perhaps in Rumanian it sounds very chic. Perhaps it's the Rumanian equivalent of Musin-Pushkin, Shakhovskoy, and Gagarin. How do we know? Certainly, it sounds terrible, but I was so in love that I even swallowed Cock-a-doodle-doo.

"He began to press for the marriage. The thought of having a name like Cock-a-doodle-doo seemed unpleasant, but it was no longer really an issue.

"He was a salesman who worked on commission. His earnings, it seemed, were not bad. However, I didn't know anything definite about this.

"So he began to court me as my real fiancé, and even presented me with a rather domestic little gift. He gave me a small electric iron. It was very nice of him. We always hid it together in a small cupboard in the hall.

"Everything was approaching its blissful consummation. Once, recalling our first meeting, I said to him: 'In my opinion, dear Pierre, that old witch was in love with you and she had special intentions for you.'

"He turned red with indignation. 'Where did you get that idea from? You made everything up.'

"I told him how she had alluded to someone with whom she had just become acquainted.

"He questioned me in great detail; apparently he was very outraged by my suggestion. I tried to smoothe over the unpleasant effect with a joke, but he became rather inattentive, lost in thought. Apparently I had greatly offended him. And imagine: After that very incident, something seemed to have snapped. He came less often, was silent about the wedding. Whereas I, as so often happens in such cases, really clung to him from then on. It was as if he had tied a wire to my tooth—the farther he pulled back, the more it hurt. No matter what I did—affecting indifference, crying, singing gypsy romances—nothing helped. My Cock-a-doodle-doo was leaving me. I was tormented to the breaking point.

"My American client returned—she came to have herself glamorized. She was very happy and gave me one hundred francs.

"I said to the others at work: 'Our old woman is kicking up her heels for some reason.'

"The manager laughed and said: 'She has a gigolo. That rosy-cheeked guy who came to see her here before her departure. I constantly come across them riding in the car and saw them twice in a restaurant.'

"I was barely able to sit through my work, and barely made it home. I wrote him: 'When you read these lines, come, and I myself "in silence" will bid you farewell.'

"I sent this message and got a small jar of rat poison, dumped out the pills, and swallowed them. I kept sobbing and swallowing. I had no desire to live. He would come—I thought—and then realize what I had meant by bidding him farewell 'in silence.'

"The rat poison was awful. For an entire twenty-four hours I was turned inside out. But the scoundrel came only after a few days.

He sat sideways, never looking at me, rattling some stupidity, something about his parents disapproving of married children. I cried in torrents during the whole speech.

"Then he stood up, said that my image would forever remain before his spiritual eyes, and that he was too noble to make me unhappy and subject me to his family's vengeance.

"He made a spectacular exit with his hand over his eyes.

"I threw open the window and waited for him.

"As soon as he walked out through the entrance, I would throw myself onto the pavement. There. Let it be done.

"But for some reason he lingered in my hall. I heard the closet door squeak. What could that have meant? The entrance door clicked. He's left! But what did he do there? Why did he open the closet?

"I ran into the hall and opened the closet. My lord! Well this . . . well this really beats all! He took away his electric iron! The i---r-on!

"Believe it or not, I simply sat right down on the floor and laughed. I laughed so hard that I began to feel better, and actually felt quite good.

"'Oh my God!' I said, 'What a wonderful thing it is to live in Your world!' And now that I've remembered all of it, ha-ha-ha, now that I've remembered, I'll probably keep on laughing until morning. The iron! The i---r-on! I would have thrown myself onto the pavement, my skull would have been smashed to pieces, and there he'd be, with an iron in his hands! What a sight!

"Yes my dear! Such things happen in life that you couldn't possibly imagine, even in your wildest dreams."

Adelaida Gertsyk

🖋 d. 1925

Adelaida Kazimirovna Gertsyk's childhood was spent at Aleksandrovo, a large settlement in the south of Russia which had often been visited by Ivan the Terrible and his bodyguards. Her childhood memories were also linked with the environs of the Troitsko-Sergieva Lavra, where her father, a prominent railroad engineer of Polish descent, owned an estate. Her mother was German. Adelaida Gertsyk's younger sister, Evgeniya, a close friend of Vyacheslav Ivanov— his *sorellina*, as he used to call her —was a gifted and sensitive translator of authors such as Selma Lagerlöf, William James, Alfred de Musset, J. K. Huysmans, and Nietzsche. Evgeniya devoted many pages in *Vospominaniya* (Reminiscences)[1] to her memories of her sister.

Intimate friends and frequent collaborators in their literary endeavors, the sisters lived in Moscow and St. Petersburg. There they met and became friends with Vyacheslav Ivanov, Maximilian Voloshin, Lev Shestov, Nikolay Berdyaev. S. N. Bulgakov, Marina and Anastasiya Tsvetaeva, Aleksey Remizov and his wife Serafima (née Dovgello), Gerzhenson, the philosophers Nikolay Ilyin and Vladimir Ern, the composer-innovator Shimanovsky, and many other distinguished representatives of the Russian intelligentsia. Particularly warm relationships developed between Adelaida Gertsyk and Maximilian Voloshin, Lev Shestov, S. N. Bulgakov, and Vyacheslav Ivanov. The latter dedicated to her a sonnet:

> Thus you glide, alien to the merriment of maidens,
> Like a deaf-mute and secretive shadow . . .

314

Так ты скользишь чужда веселью дев
Глухонемой и потаенной тенью ...

In 1908 Adelaida Gertsyk married Dmitry Evgenyevich Zhukov-sky, publisher of the Merezhkovskys' journal *Novy Put'* (The New Direction, 1903–4) and translator. When she spent the entire winter with him in Paris, Vyacheslav Ivanov viewed her as a criminal: In his eyes, she had betrayed his image of her as the woman of solitude.

In the memoirs of Marina Tsvetaeva's sister Anastasiya, Adelaida Gertsyk emerges as an extremely charming woman, but homely and almost completely deaf. Marina Tsvetaeva developed an intimate friendship with Adelaida. They used to recite their poetry to one another and together read various books, among them *The Story of Gösta Berling* (1891) by Selma Lagerlöf, *Conversations with the Devils* (1852) and *Goethe's Correspondence with a Child* (1835) by Bettina Brentano, the works of Marceline Desbordes-Valmore, of the French poet Anne de Noailles, and so forth. For Marina Tsvetaeva, Adelaida Gertsyk's friendship was as cherished as her deep affection for Maximilian Voloshin. "It is thoroughly possible," Tsvetaeva stated, "that in her life I was even a greater event than I had been in the life of Max."[2] Elsewhere she added: "They—Maximilian Voloshin and Adelaida Gertsyk—have remained throughout my entire life the two people who are bound in one and the same book of my youth. Now and forever, they are interlaced in the unity of my gratitude and love."[3] In *Marina Cvetaeva: Her Art and Life*, Simon Karlinsky states that this close friendship exercised a noticeable influence: Gertsyk's "style was later to have a marked impact on Cvetaeva's own prose writings."[4] Adelaida Gertsyk, in turn, was a great admirer of Tsvetaeva's poetry.

Anastasiya Tsvetaeva, also a lifelong friend of Gertsyk, vividly describes her first meeting with the poet. Gertsyk was accompanied by Maximilian Voloshin, who had prepared the Tsvetaeva sisters for this meeting. He had told Marina earlier: "Her volume of poetry[5] appeared this year, as did yours, too. You need one another very much. She is considerably older than you, her fate is tragic—please speak louder to her—she is deaf."[6] He then recited by heart some of her poems to Tsvetaeva, and she was greatly impressed. There was a distinct echo of Russian folklore in them:

> Before, it used to be, nights
> Hovered dark, darkling dark.
> There were beastly beasts around,
> There roved wood-goblin thoughts . . .
> You would drive them away with songs,
> You would brighten the darkness with songs.

> ... Прежде, бывало, ночи
> Реют темны-темнисты.
> Звери вокруг зверисты,
> Лешия бродят думы ...
> Песнями их разгоняешь,
> Песнями тьму просветляешь.

"This is some kind of incantation," said Marina Tsvetaeva. "It is some sorcery . . . 'Hovered dark, darkling dark' . . ." Voloshin replied: "But what do you say about 'wood-goblin thoughts' roving?" He likened Gertsyk's poems to Russian laments which originated from the ritual grieving at funerals. Marina Tsvetaeva felt a mystical significance in the fact that within one and the same year all three volumes of poetry had appeared—Voloshin's, Gertsyk's, and her own.

Soon after this introduction Adelaida Gertsyk "entered Marina's and my own life for a long time,"[7] recorded Anastasiya Tsvetaeva in her memoirs. She noted that Gertsyk—because of her deafness, estrangement, and unusual tactfulness—appeared somewhat confused and helpless in her daily life.

Her deafness surrounded her like a wall, separating her from people, their voices and views [. . .] She tried not to reveal her sadness. She was endowed with a refined sense of humor and was quick to grasp the gist of a witty remark, easily joining in the general merriment. Her gifted nature manifested itself in everything about her. She had an ability to experience delight and an inability to censure people. Her arms, light and giving, were always outstretched—to everybody. Her primary emotion was always gratitude—for peace [. . .] Endowed with will power, kindness, and a remarkable courage unique to her, she lived bravely and simply, ready to endure any blow that life might deal her [. . .] How

EVGENIYA (left) and ADELAIDA GERTSYK. From Evgeniya Gertsyk, *Reminiscences* (Paris: YMCA Press, 1973), p. 13.

many years of durable and intimate friendship with both of the Gertsyk sisters was begun at this, the first visit of Adelaida to us![8]

Adelaida Gertsyk's friendship with Maximilian Voloshin was very intense. He was absorbed in reading her poetry, eagerly trying to grasp each line. He read the reminiscences of her childhood with interest, and he helped her to deepen and to generalize her own initial poetic impulses. She often visited him in Cocktebel, and he frequently came to see the Gertsyk sisters at their estate, Sudak, in the Crimea. There, after the October Revolution, the sisters Gertsyk were joined by Anastasiya Tsvetaeva, and together they endured the aftermath of the Bolshevik *coup d'état*. Voloshin, moreover, had been Dmitry Zhukovsky's best man at Adelaida's wedding in Paris, and he had stayed with them in France for a long time. It was a long and fruitful relationship, enriching for both of them. When the poet died in 1925 in Simferopol, Voloshin dedicated a long poem to her memory.[9]

Adelaida and Evgeniya Gertsyk also enjoyed a genuine friendship with Vyacheslav Ivanov and his wife Lidiya Zinovyeva-Annibal. They frequented the Ivanovs' Tower salons, and Adelaida Gertsyk often delighted their literary friends with the poems she recited at those gatherings. Nikolay Berdyaev and Lev Shestov attracted the Gertsyk sisters because of their religious preoccupations. Like the Russian Symbolist writers, the Gertsyk sisters experienced a religious yearning, as it were; they tried to fathom Russian Orthodoxy, accepting and rejecting it almost at the same time, and searched for its "pure origin," its initial concepts and attitudes. Adelaida appeared to be particularly absorbed in spiritual and religious matters, as can be seen in her verse:

> But only the candles before the icons,
> Flickering, know the most absolute essence,
> And their undulating radiance,
> Their meek burning,
> Brings us closer to the ultimate truth.

> И только свечи перед иконами,
> Мерцая, знают самое важное,
> И их колеблющееся сияние,
> Их безответное сгорание
> Приводит ближе к последней истине.

The question of the future of Russia and its true destiny troubled the mind of the poet. She and Berdyaev had held long discussions about Russia and the Russian Orthodox Church, both when they lived in France and Germany after Adelaida Gertsyk's marriage in 1908, and in 1915, when Berdyaev and his wife stayed in Adelaida's Moscow apartment. At this time Gertsyk's salon was frequented by Gerzhenson, Lev Shestov, Vyacheslav Ivanov, Nikolay Ilyin, Vladimir Ern, and the composer Shimanovsky, all of whom joined the spirited discussions concerning their homeland, its immediate future, and the possibility of a religious revolution. The years 1915–17 were the happiest in the lives of the Gertsyk sisters—they felt themselves to be one organic whole with their friends in their search for truth, for a new Russia, and for new forms in art.

After the Bolshevik *coup*, Adelaida Gertsyk wished to live in Paris with her family. She wanted to be close to her former associates who had gone abroad—to Berlin, Prague, and Paris. She felt abandoned and helpless because she could not even communicate with her friends through their new books—their works were proscribed in Soviet Russia. Adelaida Gertsyk and her family returned to Sudak, where they lived without work, in great poverty. They awaited an opportunity to escape to France. Since this proved to be impossible, the Gertsyk sisters decided "to create a new life amidst the crumbling Russian sands . . ."[10] They experienced deep spiritual suffering because "of the crude materialism which had penetrated all spheres of life in Russia, and which overpowered everything,"[11] as Evgeniya Gertsyk recorded in her reminiscences. "They [the Bolsheviks] have not yet done away with philosophy—but they will do so. In the meantime, they have done away with all the humanities in Russia."[12] The Gertsyks could no longer dream about a new exterior life, for they felt that such a new beginning "could not, and should not, be allowed to take place by human volition."[13] But they could hope for an inner, personal, religious renaissance.

Living sometimes in Simferopol, where her husband was given a temporary position in the department of histology at the local university, and sometimes in Sudak, Adelaida Gertsyk developed a severe cold en route to Sudak on May 20, 1925, and died the following month from an inflammation of the kidneys. She was buried in Sudak. These were among the last poems she wrote:

1921

Help me, Lord, Holy Father,
Light the star before me—
Thou seest, I need a guide,
One more step—and I shall fall.
    I know—I am a worthless, lazy slave,
    I could not protect my shelter;
    From Thy Divine ripening field
    I did not gather the harvest.
And now, amidst the bare outskirts,
I am a reed shaken by the wind . . .
Lord! Thou art here the master,
Whereas I am—only a guest . . .
    Let me, then, go tonight,
    I cannot wait till daybreak,
    Let me go to my Father's house,
    Open Thy doors!

Поддержи меня, Господи святый!
Засвети предо мной звезду—
Видишь, нужен мне провожатый,
Еще миг, и я упаду ...
    Знаю, раб я негодный, ленивый,
    Не сумела сберечь свой кров,
    С трудовой Твоей Божьей нивы
    Не собрала плодов.
И теперь, среди голых окраин,
Я—колеблемая вихрем трость ...
Господи! Ты здесь хозяин,
Я—только гость ...
    Отпусти меня этой ночью,
    Я не дождусь зари,
    Отпусти меня в дом мой отчий,
    Двери свои отвори!

1925

They give us books, cold and wise,
And each one speaks of Him differently.
They talk of Him in prophetic words,
And everyone interprets Him uniquely.
Every word about Him—is an offense to me,
Each new book about Him—a new wound.
The more prophetic oracles about Him,
The less I know where the real truth lies.
When His strict words are not heard,
My heart aches from the boredom of life . . .
Like a bird with its wings severed,
Or a home left without a master.
But only the candles before the icons,
Flickering, know the absolute essence,
And their undulating radiance,
Their meek burning,
Brings us closer to the ultimate truth.

Дают нам книги холодные, мудрые,
И в каждой сказано о Нем по-разному.
Толкуют Его словами пророческими,
И всякий толкует о Нем по-своему.
И каждое слово о Нем—обида мне,
И каждая книга—как рана новая.
Чем больше вещих о Нем пророчеств,
Тем меньше знаю, где правда истинная.
А смолкнут речи Его взыскующие,
И ноет сердце от скуки жизненной ...
Как будто крылья у птицы срезаны,
А дом остался без хозяина.
Но только свечи перед иконами,
Мерцая, знают самое важное,
И их колеблющееся сияние,
Их безответное сгорание
Приводит ближе к последней истине.

Known primarily as a poet, Adelaida Gertsyk also left some perceptive pieces of criticism. On November 28, 1924, for example, she informed Lev Shestov: "In our contemporary fiction, there appeared two or three very talented, colorful, and original writers—Babel', Zamyatin, and Seyfulina. Their language is rich and fresh. Of course, theirs is still the same hopeless and crude realism—but this is because of their talent, which creates for one moment an illusion that life is indeed as they portray it. And only later, impelled by your own sensation of humiliation and protest, you realize that their portrayals remain 'on the surface.' As Vyacheslav Ivanov used to say, they lack the 'vertical depth.'"[14]

In harmony with the period, Adelaida Gertsyk had been fascinated with new artistic forms, paying tribute to various poetical schools and literary movements. Her own poetic universe, however, is very original, even paradoxical. Her persona, abandoned by her youthful beloved, neither reproaches him nor complains about his treachery; instead, she pities him because he does not know how to love a woman. Not wishing to assuage her guilt, she urges her soul to trouble her at night—because she has selected the wrong path in life. When life and suffering are in discord in Gertsyk's poetry, she invariably sides with suffering. She censures those who, unwilling to submit to the agonies of their existence, do not allow suffering to acquire any magnitude in their personal lives. One of her *leitmotifs* is her strong desire to tempt—and tame—suffering, even to play with it. Her attitude toward death is no less paradoxical—what is death? What is its poetic image? In her poetry, there is no clear demarcation line between these two realms—of life and death. People do not know how to live; they do not know how to die. Love, too, is as unstable and illusory as death. These poetic dialogues with the "self" are, of course, characteristic of the works of the Russian Symbolists.

Adelaida Gertsyk proceeded from rather tedious anapest in her early verse, through diffused amphibrach and thin iambus, to an ever-increasing experimentation with broken rhythmical patterns in order to express deeper emotions more vividly. She omitted syllables and left lines unended, which gradually resulted in her famous "semi-Sapphic stanza." Gertsyk did not aspire to imitate Parnassian poetry or the refined versification of the early Russian Symbolists, Zinaida Hippius or Konstantin Bal'mont. Her path was different—she was attracted by the elemental force in the Russian folksong, with its typical imagery, repetition, meter, color, and intonation. The early Russian Modernists, Hippius, Bal'mont, and Valery Bryusov, could not lead her along this path, for the Russian folksong was not their forte. Adelaida Gertsyk had to tread this path alone, unaided by the contemporary *maîtres* of poetry. Her verse does not adhere to the artificial canons of versification. It contains funeral (or mourning) songs and lamentations, chants of exorcism and calumny, love spells and lullaby songs. All of these elements reflect the traditional magic symbolism of ancient Russia. According to Vyacheslav Ivanov, Adelaida Gertsyk clothed the elemental force of myth in a poetic garment. Her poetry is a new artistic experience of the ancient folk heritage of the Russian past, couched in contemporary lyrics. Vyacheslav Ivanov highly praised the "pure and strong spirit of the elemental, passionate, generic Slavic speech" which is a salient feature of Gertsyk's poetry. "This speech itself," said Ivanov, "while creating myths and charms, brings [. . .] to the soul the echoes of Yaroslavna's lamentation in Putivl'. The powerful language of these songs [. . .] is accompanied by Gertsyk's forceful, capricious, expressive and melodically flexible rhythm, characteristic of folk poetry."[15] Adelaida Gertsyk's vocabulary abounds in neologisms, old Russian idioms and invocations, dialecticisms, archaisms, and rarely used words. She avoided poetic clichés in epithets and comparisons, but she often used allegory. Her rhythm, language, imagery, and the emotional force of her verse are ingenious and novel in Russian poetry. Valery Bryusov particularly praised Gertsyk's poems "Osen'" (Autumn), "Zakat" (The Sunset), "Na beregu" (On the Shore), "Ne smert' li zdes' proshla" (Was It Not Death That Passed by Here?), "S dal'nego berega" (From a Distant Shore).[16] He lauded her artistic accomplishments and prophesied that she would develop into an outstanding poet.

NOTES

1. Evgeniya Gertsyk, *Vospominaniya* (Paris: YMCA Press, 1973).
2. Marina Tsvetaeva, *Proza* (New York: Chekhov, 1953), p. 157.
3. *Ibid.*, p. 161.
4. Simon Karlinsky, *Marina Cvetaeva: Her Art and Life* (Berkeley and Los Angeles: University of California Press, 1966), p. 32.
5. Apparently *Stikhotvoreniya* (St. Petersburg: Suvorin, 1910).
6. Anastasiya Tsvetaeva, *Vospominaniya* (Moscow: Sovetsky pisatel', 1971), p. 404.

7. *Ibid.*, p. 408.

8. *Ibid.*

9. She was unable to lie, but the truth
Was never heard from her lips:
That soiled, public, lusterless truth
By which a man is struck dumb.
In her speech the severe principle
Of the rough substance of life was transfigured
Into a holy shimmering fabric—
The mantle of Izida. Under her feet
There has flowered, like a meadow of sprouting mysteries,
The parquetry of halls and the stones of roadways.
Reality without trace has turned to dust
Under the fingers of her distracted hand,
And from childhood her learning hindered her in understanding books,
Impoverishing the generous sense of letters;
And the vain laws of physics
Deprived the mystery of Play of its wonder.
The broken lines of her verses, whistling
Like the rustle of ancient grasses,
She whispered with a numenous expression,
Like a village exorcism of evil.
Blind to the days, physically deaf,
God's fool, old woman, child—
She humbly walked through all the ritual of life:
Through toil and marriage, childbirth and want.
The events of life's liturgy
(The cycle of births, illnesses, and deaths)
Are imprinted on her soul like dreams,
Like signs of another existence.
When her life bared its teeth in the years
Of shootings, hunger, civil strife, and hatred,
She, in faith stretching forth her hand,
Followed it to marketplace and prison,
And, begging abjectly, she heard the liturgy
From on high and understood
That bread is truly the Flesh of Christ,
That blood and sorrow are in truth the Wine.
Death came—she did not recognize it;
Suddenly she vanished in the darkness of the valleys,
In the silence of the plains of wormwood,
In the gray stones of Sogdian antiquity.

Sogdiana was a province of the Persian Empire, 525 B.C. Maracanda (modern Samarkand) was its capital. Sogdian art, created in Sogdiana in the early Middle Ages, incorporated many cultural streams: the remains of Sasanian culture, that of post-Guptan India, and of China from the Sui and T'ang periods. Wall painting and carved wood were favored types of decoration for dwellings. Their sources for themes were Iranian (Zoroastrian), Near Eastern (Manichaen, Nestorian), and Indian (Hindu, Buddhist) arts. Sogdian art, which helped to preserve much of the tradition and knowledge of Sasanian Persia, died out in the tenth century by the sword of Islam.

10. Evgeniya Gertsyk, *Vospominaniya*, p. 184.
11. *Ibid.*, p. 185.
12. *Ibid.*
13. *Ibid.*, p. 186.
14. *Ibid.*, p. 185.
15. Vyacheslav Ivanov, "Zametki o poezii," *Apollon*, No. 7 (1910), 41–42.
16. Valery Bryusov, *Dalekie i blizkie* (Moscow: Skorpion, 1912), p. 151.

My fields! My sheaves!
Unmown—unbound—
I walk through them, I look at them,
But their story has not been told.

Thunderless, dreamless
Days hover o'er them,
The night miserly, motionless and blind,
Withholds its charms.

No one sows there, nothing ripens
Amidst the forgotten stubble;
Whether it's pity I feel, or grief—
You will never force me to tell.

Some kind of visions
Sleep-filled—chilled—
Rise like shifting
Mists, or burial mounds.

Poems (St. Petersburg: Suvorin, 1910)

Поля мои! Снопы мои!
Некошены—невязаны—
Хожу по ним, гляжу на них,
А быль их не рассказана.

Безгрозные, безгрёзные
Над ними дни маячатся,
Не деет чар скупая ночь,
Стоячая, незрячая.

Не сеется, не зреется
Среди жнивья забытого;
Жалею ли, горюю ли—
Про то нельзя выпытывать.

Какие-то видения
Небужены—застужены
Вздымаются зыбучими
Туманами, курганами.

IN THE WIND

What is it, heard
In the steppe so faintly?
What does it say, swaying
With the silent grass?
In the wind floats
A distant languor.
A wandering soul
Whispers with the winds:
    —"I have no name,
    I'm nothing, save a quest.
    Banished into the night
    From the dreamy lair—
    Am I not a dark seed
    Thrown into the wind?
    Not fully baptized
    In the fiery font,
    Held forever captive
    By my own immortality.
His Visage darkened,
The distance increased,
Oh how short is an instant!
How long—sorrow!
I am a toy of the winds,
A whisper of streaming dreams,
An incessant heat,
The weeping of a nocturnal soul.
I shall break the chain,
And rise as a wave—
The steppe is flooded
By feathergrass–anguish.
    All that is not forgotten,
    All that is not gotten
    Is rushing after me
    Like a homeless retinue . . .
    And there is no hand
    Which might bless me—
    Oh stop for a moment!

Heed, heed me longer!
In vain I whirl
Amidst impassable roads . . ."
And again it began to surge forth,
A slave to the winds.
The laments grow faint
And are heard yet farther away —
Like amber silk
The steppe sways.

Poems

ПО ВЕТРУ

Какая быль в степи
Невнятно слышится?
С немыми травами
О чем колышется?
По ветру стелется
Истома дальняя,
С ветрами шепчется
Душа скитальная.
   — «Мне нет названия,
   Я вся — искание.
   В ночи изринута
   Из лона дремного —
   Не семя-ль темное
   На ветер кинуто?
   В купели огненной
   Не докрещеная,
   Своим безгибельем
   Навек плененная.
Затемнился Лик,
Протянулась даль,
О как краток миг!
Как долга печаль!
Я игра ветров,
Шопот струйных снов,
Неуёмный зной,
Плач души ночной.

Разорву я цепь,
Захожу волной—
Замывает степь
Ковылем-тоской.
　Все незабытое,
　Все недобытое
　За мною носится
　Бездомной свитою ...
　И нет руки меня
　Благословляющей—
　О погоди на миг!
　Внимай, внимай еще!
　По бездорожию
　Кручу напрасно я ...»
И вновь зазыблелась
Ветрам подвластная.
Стихают жалобы,
Все дале слышатся—
Шелками русыми
Вся степь колышется.

The keys have drowned in the sea—
Of life, of former years . . .
　In this sea—the water is dark,
　In this sea—depths can't be fathomed,
And no longer for us—a return.

We emerged past the border for an instant,
The air seemed torrid to us—
　At this evening hour
　Someone's forgotten us,
And locked the door with the key.

We awaited something, it seems,
Loved someone there—
　Days streamed by melodiously,
　The color of the soul was ardent . . .
　—Wasn't it merely a dream?

Words and names were forgotten,
And the shadows of shadows glide past . . .
   How long must we stand at the walls?
   Was captivity here or there?
It's impossible to recall or to know.

Our garments were left there,
Our soul and gaze are clear.
   Shouldn't we regret it? . . .
   Somewhere in the sea's depths
Lie the keys of life.

Poems

Ключи утонули в море—
От жизни, от прежних лет …
   В море—вода темна,
   В море—не сыщешь дна,
И нам уж возврата нет.

Мы вышли за грань на мгновенье,
Нам воздух казался жгуч—
   В этот вечерний час
   Кто-то забыл про нас,
И двери замкнул на ключ.

Мы, кажется, что-то ждали,
Кого-то любили там—
   Звонко струились дни,
   Жарок был цвет души …
—Не снилось ли это нам?

Забылись слова, названья,
И тени теней скользят …
   Долго-ль стоять у стен?
   Здесь или там был плен?
Ни вспомнить, ни знать нельзя.

Там забыли одежды наши,
Прозрачны душа и взгляд.
   Не надо-ль жалеть о том?..
   Где-то на дне морском
От жизни ключи лежат.

Somewhere in an azure field,
Beyond the white days in their shrouds,
Beyond the deep nocturnal dreams,
Freedom soars and splashes.

There is no anguish of desires there,
There, talk dies away into oblivion,
The holy lotus blossoms . . .
—Would that I could but reach the border!

Everything's being consumed on my path,
What doesn't burn—will freeze with the cold . . .
But there, only there, only in the blue
Desert beyond the lakes,
Beyond the mountains,
The heart is silent, the heart understands.

Poems

If I am always dressed in white,
And innocently look others straight in the eye—
It is not so that they should talk to me—
Not so that they should love me:
I hold sacred the passage of time,
    That everything proceeds as it must.

If I sit a long time by the window,
And my face glows like the dawn,
This does not mean I am waiting or calling,
And the blue window does not lure me;
But the cause of my soul's burning passion—
    I do not know myself.

When I am gay—
My gaiety's quite different:
I'm gladdened not by people, or for them . . .
I leave them, unsociable as always—
Harboring no offense in me,
    My love is not for life.

Flowers glowed in a dark forest,
Something's been revealed today in the silence,
Fate secretly contacted someone—
And still one more border is laid
    Between other people and me.

          A Bed of Golden Flowers: The First
          Basket (St. Petersburg: Ory, 1907)

I have known for a long time that I am autumnal,
That my heart is brighter when the garden is fiery,
And the amber leaf, burning out, floats down
Ever more selflessly, ever more oblivious.

The autumn, with its red-gold play,
Gilded my sadness long ago.
Flowers please me—scorched flowers—
And mountains melting in their blue captivity.

Blessed is that land destined to die—
The willing heart trembles like a thread . . .
Unfathomable height and misty distance:
How sweet not to know! . . . how easy not to be! . . .

          A Bed of Golden Flowers:
          The First Basket

THE FOREST

Along the branches, above the resinous shadows, a dark-winged
    god
Alit upon the slippery firs and reclined comfortably on a pine,
Turning his pale and beast-like face toward the sunset . . .
The cry in the thicket grew lonely, fused, bronzelike.

In that lingering howl is the rustle of needles, a murmur, and
    the surf;
The multi-voiced forest, sensate yet deaf, moans.

The faceted crown burns amongst its glowing stones;
There is fire both in the anguished gaze and in the rings.

Does not the tsar in the groaning needles have my face?
Is not the ring on my finger the tsar's?
A spark flashed in the fiery crown; do you hear me?
Is it I who slumbers, slumbers—and hears the bronze moan in
    the fire?

Do you wish the Word from me, my forest double?
Your soul has nestled close to mine, as to its source!
Your burning gaze stings with a call—my voice is fettered . . .
Who is blind here? Who can see? Who is prophetic—and mute?

A Bed of Golden Flowers:
The First Basket

I live in a desert, far from the world.
Only the free wind carouses around me.
But I've no need for this freedom,
My soul has no use for it.
I no longer seek earthly treasures,
I travel on, ignoring others' eyes,
And greet with coolness equally
The young and the old, both days and nights.
The small lights of alien wishes flash by . . .
Here comes the morning in its dove-colored array;
I escort the night to its last border
And kiss the edge of its gilded vestment.

Poems

The miracle is ripe like a magic treasure,
Like a clear shout, like an unfriendly gaze,
It urges me wrathfully, it sheds its rays,
And summons my soul to its dark destruction.
    Do not call—do not shine!
    I cannot bear the gifts!

I am the soul—I am dark,
Living amidst the gloom.
Do not pierce my darkness
With golden light.
Within my dream—I—a vessel,
Will reel—capsize—
Having forgotten, having shed all,
How can I sail in response to your call!
   I soar, I fly
   Wherever I wish—
   Now I whisper,
   Now fall silent . . .
I do not know the captivity of His Visage and words,
I do not know His speech—I fear the call,
And the blind rocking
Knows no order . . .
   Do not call—do not shine!
   I shall sink all the gifts!
   Amidst the darkness—without any fate
   I am alone—I am mute.
Silence, you menacing call from thence!
I do not, I do not need the miracle.

Poems

Созрело чудо, как клад волшебный,
Как яркий оклик, как взор враждебный,
Торопит гневно, лучи роняет,
И в темный омут к душе взывает.
   Не зови—не свети!
   Мне даров не снести!
   Я душа—я темна,
   Среди мрака жива.
   Не вноси в мою тьму
   Золотого огня.
   Среди сна—я—ладья,
   Покачнусь—подогнусь—
   Все забыв, уронив,
   Где мне плыть на призыв!

Рею, лечу,
Куда хочу—
То шепчу,
То молчу ...
Я не знаю неволи Лика и слов,
Я не знаю речи—мне страшен зов,
И не ведает строя
Качанье слепое ...
Не зови—не свети!
Затоплю все дары!
Среди тьмы—без судьбы
Я одна—я нема.
Стихни, грозный призыз оттуда!
Мне не нужно, не нужно чуда!

Index